Some White Guy's Book

Some White Guy's Book

Unexpected Memoirs, Thoughts, and Facts about Race and Ethnicity in America

Ken JP Stuczynski

AmorphousPublishingGuild

www.Amorphous.Press

Buffalo, NY USA
©2020

Published by Amorphous Publishing Guild, Buffalo, NY USA
http://Amorphous.Press

To all people
who strive to understand
and be good to one another

Contents

Part III. Black and Blue

Part IV. Where Do We Go From Here?

Introduction

At the moment I am writing this, we live in a world where everyone is shouting and no one is listening. There's a gulf between people who deny there is a problem and those who experience it every day. We don't accept the legitimacy of how other people feel. We won't own up to our own feelings. We fear being judged as badly as we judge others. Around people who we consider different, or not part of our in-group, it's like walking on glass. Some want to reach out to find or be an ally but don't know how. And there are both racists and anti-racists who are downright fanatical. Why can't we just get over it? Won't it just stop if we don't keep *making* it an issue?

Over half of Americans believe racism is a real problem. Even if we insist we can just not participate, race and ethnicity is a minefield we ignore at our own peril. Elizabeth Warren once said, "If you don't have a seat at the table, then you're probably on the menu." Many of us feel left out because of our identity. Or maybe the world is changing into something we don't recognize anymore, and want people to cut us some slack. We shouldn't have to take a college course to learn enough racial literacy just to be part of society. But we tiptoe around these issues every day. It continues to break apart not just communities, but families and friendships. We are pitching battles over what "America" is and isn't, and what we should or shouldn't do about it.

Maybe this book is a gift and you're wondering why it's in your hands. Maybe this doesn't interest you, but it interests someone else who wants you to know some things important to your relationship with them. If you don't care about what others think or how they feel, I can't help you. I'm not sure what can. But we are each responsible to inform our conscience and live according to it. That's my only charge to you.

Not scared away yet? People who insist on engaging us on such topics are invading our space, forcing us to question ourselves, and threatening our very identity. Guess what – I'm going to invade your space. Some of what you read here isn't going to be comfortable. It may make you angry. You might not even know *why*. I will represent points of view that I may find offensive, too. But you need to hear them anyway. And if you have heard them already, have you really listened?

We are coming from so many different places, but ultimately the fear, anger, and even hate, are things we share in common more than we can know. Well, we *can* know, but that requires toning down our judgment and having what I call "Compassion of Mind" – we need to try and experience their position, not by putting ourselves in their shoes, but by being them as *they* are and where they are coming from.

This works both ways, We will admit our own human prejudices and circumstances only as much as we can let go of shame or defensiveness. We all have to deal with that, playing different roles in different situations. Looking within to inventory our feelings and beliefs, only then can we decide what to do with it all.

But who do I think I am? Why is a "White guy" writing about race? Should I be concerned about crowding the podium while other voices aren't being heard? Absolutely. Will my conscience allow me to be silent? Absolutely not. Will my message be easier to accept by people like me? Maybe. Can I at least speak for White people in general to help People of Color understand where "we" are coming from? Not really – I'm still learning what that would even mean. But we all play a role and can share that, even if just a little. So why say I'm White at all? Because I have to admit I'm going to bring in my personal socialization whether I am aware of it or not. It can't help but be part of the message.

Only in writing this did I realize how unexpected a life I have. I'm Polish by adoption, reintroducing some of that heritage into my family. In college, I was a member of the Black Student Union and Latin American Student Organization. I'm an Interfaith minister who was a chaplain for a Confederate soldier descendants group. My step-family is Snipe Clan Seneca Tribe. Touches of Asian culture have graced my life, from philosophy and martial arts to my wedding attire. My family's faith tradition is Roman Catholic, but the Tao Te Ching sits with a Bible on my scripture stand. My doorpost has a mezuzah. I listen to music from all times and lands, and have friends and connections around the world. As Terence says, "nothing human is alien to me."

I know people who've traveled the world but their horizons were never broadened. Many people have "a Black friend" but know nothing of their personal life. People think fortune cookies are a Chinese tradition. And we assume over a billion Muslims across dozens of cultures have the same customs based on what someone may have experienced while deployed in Saudi Arabia. We don't know what we don't know, and in so many ways Americans are insulated not only from the world, but from each other.

Personally – and I didn't realize this until later in life – I experience things a bit differently from others. There really wasn't a label for it when I was a child, but I probably would have been diagnosed on the autism spectrum if it were today. I never had a sense of boundaries or identity as separate from others. I don't fear talking to anyone, and have little sense of privacy. I am attracted to and naturally trust people who are different. I find any excuse I can to connect with people. It's awkward at times, but I'm grateful for it.

Empathy is mostly directed at people we can see with our own eyes and we think of as our "in-group" – other boundaries I don't have. I mourn for people who suffered centuries ago. I don't need individual names to see broad injustices as tangible things that make my blood boil. It always feels personal when people are in need. And when people hate and oppress and harm each other on any scale, regardless of color or uniforms, it breaks my heart.

America, you're breaking my heart. Not just for things in the past, but what we are doing to ourselves right now. And I just can't accept it must be that way.

Forgive me if I get too abstract at times. My degree is in Philosophy and I've spent a lot of my life studying and writing about the social psychology of prejudice and fanaticism. But this isn't meant to be a textbook or scholarly work. You can fact check anything here and I will be grateful for any corrections. But let me be clear – I'm not trying to prove anything or convince anyone. However, you will probably find out things you never knew, heard points of view for the first time (even if you do not agree), and find out what other voices are really saying.

Bell Hooks once quoted David Whyte, who says "The conversation is the work." Once you consider the what and why of those things that cause deep divisions, socially and psychologically, you can realize and appreciate common ground. What you do at the end of sharing this part of my journey with me is on you. But if you find yourself a more understanding person, and show more Love for those around you, together we will make our world, and our country, a better place.

PART I

LIVING COLOR

1. Okay, I Guess I'm White

Okay, I'm White. I admit it. My wife says no matter how I talk, or what I wear, or what I listen (and dance) to, I can't escape it. And I'm not just sunburn-prone White, but socks-with-sandals White. Weird Al's *White and Nerdy* should be my theme song. But I don't *feel* White. And maybe that's part of what being White means – like a fish not thinking about water.

But for me, it's more than that. When I talk about "White folks", I sometimes forget I'm one of them. You may think it's silly or I'm just saying this, but I really do think of myself first as a human being, a citizen of the world. When I talk about people of other cultures and ethnic backgrounds, I don't think of them as "other" but part of a wider variety of human experience I honestly feel a part of. I don't think of myself as "not-Black" or "not-Asian" or "not-Greek" just because I may be easily considered "White" or "Polish" or "American". And I'd rather err on the side of appropriation than xenophobia.

Regardless, you'd think I'd understand what it is to be White just because the world says I am. Not so. It even took painful deliberation for me to decide if the word "White" should be capitalized. And if you don't know already, that is a longstanding controversy. Let me walk you through that. Black and white are colors, obviously, but also identify specific people or groups, and therefore are proper nouns. Maybe that's oversimplifying, given the baggage capacity of racial language. You wouldn't believe the diverse opinions on this! Various journalistic and educational institutions have weighed in on both sides with every possible position.

Some argue while being Black is a distinct social experience, "whiteness" is just a skin tone, not an identity. Furthermore, it smacks of ideologies we shouldn't emulate. Columbia Journalism Review says capitalizing White "risks following the lead of white supremacists." After all, terms such as "White Power" and "White Pride" conjure up vivid images of militant racism, even if that need not always be the case.

Earlier this year (2020), The Associated Press started to capitalize the word Black. It's interesting that this hadn't been broadly done until now, and many news publishers still do not, even though they capitalize Asian, Latinx, etc.. But there is a push to downplay White as not distinct enough, in contrast to Polish-American or Italian-American. It may also be a political reaction against "Whiteness", a sort of reversed prejudice.

However, the Center for the Study of Social Policy (CSSP) makes an interesting argument that not capitalizing White is wrong for social reasons, rather than grammatical consistency or fairness. To use lowercase for White is "an anti-Black act which frames Whiteness as both neutral and the standard. ... [White] is a specific social category that confers identifiable and measurable social benefits." The argument continues that not giving credence to White as an identity makes it invisible and difficult to talk about.

As an author and publisher, my choice is purely grammatical-logical and agrees with the American Psychological Association Style Guide. I capitalize all such terms (unless quoting someone else) whenever it refers to a specific group identity. Inclusive to this, I capitalize Liberal and Conservative in the context of group identity, but not as a general adjective. Please don't read into it. As for choices of Black versus African-American (and other similar terms), we'll figure that out later, but I will try to be true to the language of the historical context and meaning.

Now that we got the letter 'W' out of the way, where do I fit in? It seems that race is about being one thing versus another. You can't be White unless there are people who are not-White. And the relationship between those two has some impact on our identity, even if we never examine it. My relationship was defensive, but not in the way you may think.

To be honest, I'm not sure why, but I've been sensitive to prejudice and oppression in all its forms as far back as I can remember. As a young child, I recall offering to punch one of my peers in the face when he spit out the "N-word" in reference to our waitress as soon as she left our table. I have no idea why it infuriated me, but it did. I never heard him use it after that.

It wasn't like I knew People of Color, at least not personally, and things like ethnicity or race were always background noise, if I noticed it at all. I was raised in Depew, New York − what I call a "lily-white suburb", which means I had no reason to give it a second thought. But when I ventured out into a larger world, meeting vastly different people was a welcomed experience.

Maybe it was also because of television. I grew up with *Fat Albert and the Cosby Kids*, but to me, they were just kids in a different neighborhood. I watched *The Jeffersons* and *Different Strokes*, and there were plenty of themes involving race issues. Strangely, I identified myself with those main characters at least as much or more than those sharing my own paleness. They were just human beings, not 'racial others'. There were shows where race wasn't central but made occasional forays, such as *Barney Miller*, *WKRP*, and others, but I never thought of Venus Flytrap as a supporting character or Ron Glass as a token actor.

Race wasn't forbidden to discuss, but not something brought up at the dinner table, at least as best I can remember. Only once was I counseled by my father, talking about an imagined rainbow-patterned creature I named a "Color Dolphin" while splashing about in a hotel pool. Apparently, the name of my mythical beast might be taken the wrong way by other guests.

Otherwise, race issues were on television, or in the past (seemingly), and opinions were rarely expressed by anyone in my life. I just didn't see color as more than another life circumstance. At least not consciously, or so I am told. I can't dig down into my psyche deep enough to know for sure if I was immune to such socialization or to what extent that even existed. If you are White and reading this, be assured I don't feel any right to impose an answer on you either way. I would just ask you to leave it as an open question.

The point is that I was openly offended by people speaking of others as less than themselves, though it was rare to see it firsthand. I was even called a N*lover as early as 6th grade for calling someone out. I still remember that one "racist" kid, and wonder how they turned out. But I had never thought of myself in terms of race until the moment in college I jokingly refer to as "that time I found out I was White".

Mind you, I never met people of color except for two high school classmates – a brother and sister of Japanese descent who were adopted. Yes, my childhood was that homogenous. When I got to D'youville College, most of the friends I made who had dark skin weren't American, but from countries like Guyana and Kenya. Other friends were from Puerto Rico and Latin America, and when I joined LASO (the Latin American Student Organization), they often would slip into Spanish until someone would see my puzzled face and yell "Ken is here!" and then continue in English. I was trying not to impose, and they were very gracious about it.

In a sense, I was the ultimate minority – not only was D'Youville 96% women my Freshman year, but almost everyone seemed to be either from some faraway place or non-traditional (over 26 years old). I was also part of a small honors program and one of the few Liberal Arts majors in the whole school. In fact, I was the first person to have declared Philosophy as a major in many years. But I thrived on the diversity of it all. There was much to talk about and learn from other people, *especially* if they were different. At least that was how I saw it.

So here's the story: It was my Sophomore year, and I had a circle of friends from the dorms I spent a lot of time with. At some point, I was in the lounge with one of them and she said, as if bestowing an important revelation, something to the effect of, "The bunch of us were talking and decided you are pretty cool for a White guy."

I had no idea what she was talking about. And then my brain ticked off the list: African-American; Chinese; Korean; Hispanic; Black-Hispanic. Holy crap, I WAS the White guy!

To this day, I can't adequately describe how I felt. I don't even remember how I reacted, just that it was … discomforting, maybe even disappointing. I didn't want to be their WHITE friend, just their friend. It felt like a demotion. I wasn't blind to their cultural differences, and even appreciated them, but never thought of them as something distinctly apart from whatever I might be. And this experience gave me a suspicion of what it must be for them when they are surrounded by White people.

By the way, this isn't a pat on the back for my color-blindness. I just never thought of myself as something in particular. Sure I was "Polish" in what felt more incidental than definitive, but I did sometimes see other people in some way as *more* culturally distinct than I was. And maybe this is what is meant by White people seeing themselves as the "default." If you're not something in particular, you're just White.

I didn't want to be anything in particular, but I didn't want to be seen as something-else either. And yet there I was, forced to accept there was a lot of something-else around me, including me. I realized, in a small way, that my friends were somehow apart from the world I was socialized into. Being around racial Others meant, for better or worse, I wasn't in Depew anymore.

2. The Invention of Race

Like I said, I had quite the vanilla childhood. Realities of race were limited to television and things we'd read in books. (This was well before the World Wide Web existed.) I was taught the "official" taxonomy of race in grade school in the 1970s. It was really simple – there were Caucasians, Negroids, and Mongoloids. The last one included "Indians" that weren't from India. Not sure where people from India fit in. But now, thanks to science, we know it was all bullshit.

As late as 1962, an anthropologist actually suggested (without evidence) that different "races" evolved at different times to become modern humans. This reinforces previous notions of inherent moral and cultural characteristics. That's not how any of this works, of course. Ten years later, Harvard evolutionary biologist Richard Lewontin complied genetic data globally and concluded that about six percent of genetic variation could be tied to such race categories. And that's six percent of the total differences in DNA code, which itself is less than a hundredth of a percent among *homo sapiens*. Basically, humans are identical. To Martians, we probably all look the same.

If you think all {insert race here} people look the same, you must know very few people. (In college we used to joke with our friend Steve, who is Korean-American, that all Koreans don't look the same, just him.) The fact is people within a "race" can be more diverse from each other than some people from other races. My first martial arts teacher was of Chinese and German descent and people often thought he was from India; my cousin Susan who is of straight-up Polish descent has been mistaken as Hispanic. You probably know people with such seemingly crisscrossed features.

My wife says that from appearance I am probably Northern European and likely part Irish. I will never know. I am adopted and do not know anything about my biological family. And I will never get a DNA test. Nothing to do with privacy – I *like* not knowing. It makes me feel like I could be related to anyone, and therefore I feel I am related to everyone.

When people do get their DNA evaluated, they are usually dumbfounded or at least a little surprised. It is phenomenally rare to be, like Conan O'Brien, 100% anything (Irish in his case). Yes, we can trace back bits and pieces of that tiny difference to bioethnic groups in specific parts of the world. For example, a group of descended-by-blood Jews will have a much greater incidence of certain genetic markers. This was used to substantiate dark-skinned diaspora down the East coast of Africa, a "lost tribe" if you will. And we are discovering that broad intermarriage has been the norm throughout human history. In fact, there is half a percent chance any person reading this book is a direct descendant of Genghis Khan. That man was clearly a player.

The point is that our physical traits (phenotypes) are a mix of mixed-up genetic lines and our environment. Skin color has as much to do with climate as blood, which is why there are people in India and Australia who are darker than many people in Africa. South Americans are much lighter because of so much lineage from Iberia. I'd say give it a few thousand years, but populations may shift again. I know, I'm simplifying a complex subject, but the bottom line is that race – as a biological thing – really doesn't exist.

But don't feel bad if you didn't get the memo. The medical profession still uses race classification to assess risk, even though there is no basis for it. It's even crept into algorithms. Such digital bias affects the quality of people's care in serious ways, from birthing attention to organ transplant assessments, and even insurance compensation for injuries. Sure, some populations may tend to be more lactose intolerant (two-thirds of humanity) but any one person could be outside that statistic. And you don't have to be African-American to get Sickle Cell Anemia. Risks may be genetic, and you may have your father's nose, but we are all individuals in the end, right down to drugs not working the exact same on any two people. Science recognizes this. Maybe we should be like science.

So who came up with race? By the way, the word "race" comes from the words of earlier languages for "breed." The first use of the term with people was in the 1400s, not coincidentally the beginning of the European slave trade. We classify animals and subspecies in zoology and botany; why not in humans? That's innocuous enough. But there really are much darker motivations. Before the Age of Discovery (read "European Colonialization"), there were always stereotypes of cultural ethnic groups. The term Canaanites meant "traders" and the words for "Syrian" and "banker" were synonymous in Gaul. Even without solidly defined nations and boundaries, there were still recognized countrymen and foreigners, and people of different tribes and clans. Some may have been more or less advanced in technology, or "civilized", which in its literal sense means living in cities rather than entirely rural or nomadic. But outside of philosophical notions, there were no broadly used categorical labels. And in many times and places, there was only one's own group and everyone else.

Even slavery wasn't originally about race. It existed in many forms, some of which lingered on into modern times. Most commonly, people were taken by force through conquest as workers, either for some empire or rich men. Greek slaves were often educated and well-sought after as teachers. Immortal Aesop with his fables is an example. And even those type of slaves, like indentured servants and criminals, could buy their way out of their situation. Most forms were not set up to be lifelong, or endlessly generational. They were not necessarily considered inferior as human beings, except in the standing of the law and purposes of debts.

But the tallships of Europe reaching the far corners of the Earth changed that. There were already self-soothing beliefs on the part of Europeans that they were superior, even to more advanced civilizations like China. The grounds were often religious ("saved" versus "heathen"), but it was also the notion that the organized institutions of Western Europe (formal education, complex legal system, etc.) were somehow "civilized" in an elevated sense and those peoples who "lacked" them were "savage". But it still wasn't along racial lines. A Moor was feared because they were estimated to be Saracens with scimitars, not because they were "black" in skin color.

It was Prince Henry the Navigator who first circumvented the Italian and Islamic slave traders and brought Africans to Portugal in large numbers. We are taught about mercantilism in history class, but usually in the context of gold, when it was more accurately the selling of enslaved people that turned Portugal and other countries into empires. And I must mention here that African tribes did not sell their own people into slavery – they sold the people of other tribes. There wasn't any sense of pan-Africanism or common identity in terms of race. It was European powers that expanded limited local or regional slave-trading into the massive global enterprise that is the primary basis for modern demographics in the Western Hemisphere.

Something else happened when natural philosophy (modern Western science) was applied to the human condition. Historical concepts or race that linger today were fully formed by the time of the American Colonies, but the study of living things really exploded after 1800. Borrowing from racial taxonomies of natural philosophers like Linnaeus, hierarchical theories of peoples of different colors and parts of the world had assigned to them inherent physical, intellectual, and social characteristics. The "science" of race proposed a biological basis for mental and cultural superiority.

Shortly after the American Revolution, the British Empire was still expanding its domination, not with slavery, but subjugation *in situ*. One place – America – was the last big holdout on the trading of human beings. As monarchs fell and liberal democracies rose, what justification could be made for conquest? How could the average American justify decimating and displacing First Nations in its westward expansion?

It's interesting to note that some Native cultures were given special consideration. The "Five Civilized Tribes" – Cherokee, Chickasaw, Choctaw, Creek (Muscogee), and Seminole – were determined worthy in virtue of acceptance of Christianity, intermarriage with Whites, market participation, and literacy (English of course). They were also expected to have or accept the institutions of a central government and plantation slavery practices. That's right – slavery was a requisite for consideration of being "civilized." George Washington held that Native Americans, though biologically equal, had inferior societies. Ironically, the Iroquois Confederacy is said to have been one of the inspirations for the United States Constitution.

Biology-based models weren't the only culprits. Biblical ponderings placed Africans as the sons of Ham, destined to be slaves to the ones of Shem. Some even suggested Africans and Native Americans weren't even descended from a common Adam (polygenesis). Be it science or religion, it was a calculated dehumanization – a rationalization. Yet some still believe the underpinnings of these theories. But even with these excuses, race was ultimately about law. That is perhaps why Ta-Nehisi Coates says in *Between the World and Me*, that "race is the child of racism, not the father."

There was always the issue of justifying the superior legal standing of Europeans in Europe (Britain in particular). As legal systems became more codified, the distinctions as to who had rights and power tended to fall along lines of birthright – social class, which was hereditary, and origin (where you or your ancestors were born). As the Europeans made colonies into empires, people from those other places came in larger numbers to their colonizer's homelands, either by choice or by force. Any significant immigration will usually cause a bit of culture shock, economic shifts, and given human nature, conflict. The psychological need to keep these "others" from taking a share in the power over everything in their culture is not unfamiliar to even a nation of immigrants like America.

The law was used to define who was White ("in" with rights and privileges) or not White ("out" without rights and privileges). Because race was a legal construct, it could be redefined. Southern Europeans were not at first considered White. To this day, those of Iberian heritage are not considered quite White in America, or given special ethnic distinction, even though Spain and Portugal are unquestionably part of Europe.

People even "less White" had it harder. Some Native Americans could not vote until 1948. Chinese immigrants couldn't become American citizens until 1943. In fact, American citizen Wong Kim Ark had to fight to even be let back into the country in 1892, and it took a Supreme Court decision to uphold the 14th Amendment and recognize his birthright. Shortly before this, the Chinese Exclusion Act had prohibited immigration from China. There has never been any other law prohibiting all immigration from any nationality or ethnic group by the United States Government – except an executive order in 2017, most of which was immediately challenged and overturned. An adage oft attributed to Samuel Clemens comes to mind, that "History doesn't repeat itself but it often rhymes."

But let's backtrack to the issue of the civilized and the savage. Once the necessary beliefs and rationalizations were in place, subjugation wasn't just done for profit or power, but an irreconcilable yet real benevolence. From Australia to Canada to the United States, communities thought they were saving aboriginal children by taking them from their parents and teaching them to read, write, and be good Christians. The White man thereby was morally compelled to dictate how entire peoples should (and should not) live for the sake of "civilizing" them for full assimilation into Western culture.

This spin on settler colonialism (or jingoistic imperialism) was most notably rhetoricized by India-born British citizen Joseph Rudyard Kipling. You may know him more popularly for *The Jungle Book*, but it was his 1899 poem, "The White Man"s Burden: The United States and the Philippine Islands", that raised the banner for White men to rule the world. Fortunately, he was met with an abundance of criticism and stirred up anti-imperialist causes. But it was still a testimony to the widespread, tragic actions of Western powers up very recent times.

Now we have a problem to solve. We know that race is not biological, and can be redefined at the whim of changeable law. So is race *real*? Without getting into subjective versus objective reality, the short answer is "It is real because we treat it as real." Consider someone who is Black, meaning unambiguously dark-skinned. They may have near-identical biology, equal rights (in principle), and even be raised by a White family and have no difference in behavior or dialect than me (the author). But he will have a very different experience of the same environment I enjoy. He may not necessarily be treated badly, but he will be treated, at least among the general public, as Black. His color will, without doubt, elicit certain assumptions and expectations – by White people, other people who are Black, and other People of Color. We make conscious and unconscious judgments about who we identify with and who we do not.

However, some of us think strongly in terms of individuals. We want to believe that we treat people as they really are, according to their character, so we don't see how prejudice is a real thing in everyday life. What we neglect to see is that most people do not know each other. They go on first appearances. One man told me that he had trouble crossing the street downtown because he was Black, *unless* he carried a briefcase. Just that slight difference in appearance caused a different judgment to be made about him by motorists. The motorists don't know if he was a panhandler with a borrowed suit or a lawyer. Not that it should matter, of course, and it may not to us, but human beings overall are what they are.

Still don't buy it? John Howard Griffin, author of *Black Like Me*, changed his appearance to experience being an African-American and it was eye-opening. But that was 1961, in the deep South. Today, it's often more subtle – sometimes not so much – but could be as simple as your house being appraised higher simply because you change the family photos to White people and let someone else house sit.

There are endless tests you can use to prove it, but the final exam is this: If you ask the question if the experience of race is real, how far apart are the answers of White people and People of Color? Reality is ultimately that which imposes itself upon you, even if by your belief and the belief of others. And if there is such a thing as race, it is exactly that difference between how and to what extent it imposes itself on you differently than others.

3. Shades of Meaning

One of my martial arts students in the 1990s expressed that they were treated differently because they were "not White". I was confused. They explained they were Hispanic. I jokingly asked (in reference to a concurrent pork industry campaign), "Is that the *other* White meat?" I honestly didn't think of it as "not White", nor did he have any features I would have associated with being Latino. On a side note, I'm still trying to figure out what being "Jewish" is supposed to look like – I couldn't pick the Jewish people I know out of a crowd if I didn't know them personally. And I'm not the only one confused about such things.

A few years ago, I read *Scatter My Ashes Over Havana*, the biography of Dr. Olga Karman, one of my college professors at D'Youville. Never in my life had I met anyone with a stronger command of the English language, and it wasn't even her first language! She escaped the Cuban revolution, eventually settling in Buffalo, New York. She recalls when someone first told her she wasn't White. Her grandfather had sternly told her "Look, you're white. Don't you forget." Her student and friend Raúl Russi, the first Puerto Rican police officer in Buffalo, informed her otherwise.

"You're white, *and* you're not white. Your color is white, but that's only part of it. You're a *latina*, one of us. In that sense, you're not white – not anymore." Addressing her responsive anger, he continued, "You might *think* you're white, but the world out there doesn't think so." In other words, perception is its own reality.

Her further thoughts are important here:

> Cuba had branded me with a singularity that wouldn't go away; It was part of me, a wedge that separated me even from Hispanics. *I'm white but I'm not white. I'm Hispanic but I'm not Hispanic. I am always "something else". Who then am I? What am I?* And then I heard myself answer: *Raúl and the others are your people. He is just giving a name to what you've already become. In Cuba you were white. Here you are Hispanic.*

This hints at profound truths. Color, in the racial sense, can be about your skin, and it can be about your self-identity, but it includes how society sees you. People may change their appearance and try to "pass" as this or that, and you can have a sense of self based on culture – ethnicity – but other's perceptions are inescapable and not under the control of the individual. This also demonstrates that our identity is in part realized by the existence of some "other". You may be one thing versus another where you are from, but in a new place, all of such people are "other" to what is there.

Latinx (a recent gender-inclusive expression for Latina and Latino I only recently figured out was pronounced "Latin-ex") come from a wide variety of places. They can be descended from any combination of Africans, Spanish, Portuguese, and Indigenous Peoples. Heck, let's even sneak French in there given their colonial incursions. Within Hispanic communities in America, what islands people are from can evoke their own prejudices and pecking order. Even on the islands themselves, there is are social class distinctions based strongly on how light or dark-skinned someone is. People marry into whiteness, try to get rid of *pelo malo* ("bad hair", meaning curly), and their media role models tend to be light-skinned. This is likely due to the ruling class originally emanating from European bloodlines, and wealth being transferred along those lines such that the "upper" class tends to be more "White" even today. It's a microcosm version of America, and it's no surprise that descendants from Mexico, or Puerto Rico, or Cuba, have very different voting demographics on a variety of issues.

Colorism plays out in America across the whole racial spectrum. Latinx and African-Americans alike experience more racism if their skin is darker. In the early part of the 20th Century, African-Americans started to take their place in "White society", feeding into a mass market for skin-lightening makeup, hair-straightening products, and later, colored contacts. Perhaps the "kinky" hair of Sicilians was another reason Italians weren't seen as White for a long time, the taming of which created a stereotype of "greasy" hair. This trend of makeup is now international and longstanding, even in Africa.

Are these physical attempts at cultural assimilation reasonable? Or do they internalize racism? At worst we could describe it as wholesale Stockholm syndrome. It is reminiscent of post-war Japan embracing "Americanization" so willingly that some Japanese went so far as to have plastic surgery done to look more "American."

These distinctions are not only external – made by White Society – but internal. Following the Civil War, the battle between assimilating and segregation started in earnest. Groups such as the "Blue Vein Society" were created for upwardly-mobile Negroes, where the qualification was skin light enough to see blue veins. Those with light skin distanced themselves from those with dark skin, and this influence on Black beauty persists today. Conversely, those with darker skin may see those with lighter skin as not "Black enough".

In the 1960s, there was a swinging of the pendulum for African-Americans toward a less assimilated culture. The "Black is Beautiful" movement spearheaded self-defining race and asserting pride. Afros and kente cloth slowly became mainstream. (I love the patterns, but my choices are limited given my wife won't let me wear orange.) Black Nationalism became a force to reckon with. On the other hand, although Blackness may be appreciated as a distinct sub-culture, when mixed into the mainstream, it's downplayed. As recent as the 2000s, some movie promo images digitally whitewash Black actors so they looked less Black. Token diversity may be turning into the new homogeny.

Color is more and more complex for another reason – intermarriage. Since 1967, mixed-raced couples could get legally married in the United States. It took the Supreme Court and a Loving couple to do it. (See what I did there?) For context, the following year we saw Captain Kirk and Lt. Uhura kiss on television. Pew research found in 2010 that about 15% of those surveyed had an objection to intermarriage within their family circle – much higher among those my age and older (50+). In 2013, General Mills closed the comments section on YouTube for their Cheerios commercial portraying a mixed couple and child. In spite of racist comments and hate mail, they stood their ground and kept the commercials. (It's just one more reason I love Cheerios, not that I needed one.) Regardless, about 15% of all newlyweds and over 10% of all marriages in America today are mixed. It should be no surprise then that biracial and multiracial children have become almost commonplace.

I never understood the big deal. I had no idea why my grade-school bus driver had a beef with a mixed couple she would see along her route. She argued that if everyone kept intermarrying, we'd all end up "yellow". My answer was that we'd all still be human beings, and it was never discussed again. In the college dorms, I said out loud a pop star on MTV was hot. A girl in the room thought it was odd I found a certain singer attractive. Mariah Carey was Black or mixed heritage? I guess so. I was more interested in … well … other aspects of her. Okay, it's her hair. And her vocal range. But let's not get sidetracked. Had I been more courageous, there were a few Women of Color I would have gladly asked out or even brought home. I do have to admit though the additional, ulterior motive of seeing how my mother would react. I eventually married a White woman of Polish, German, and Sicilian descent, but adopting a child has been discussed, especially a minority child, as they statistically have much more difficulty being placed.

But being of mixed race poses challenges. Mind you, we're not talking about

Protestants disowning their children for marrying a Catholic (or vice versa), or an Irish lass daring to marry a German mensch. Here I mean where a child looks like a mix of their parents, not clearly taking on the features or skin tone associated with one or the other's race. On the 2010 U.S. Census, 9 million people identified as two or more races, 32 percent more than in 2000 (the first time people were allowed to check more than one box). But this doesn't count those who are of mixed descent who chose to identify as only one designation.

This brings up another issue – being forced to choose. Some forms do not allow multiple answers with regards to race and ethnicity. I know someone that needed to fill out a municipal form in a local suburb and refused to on the grounds the only choices were Black, White, Asian, and Hispanic. There was no Other or Mixed (or better yet, None-of-Your-Damn-Business). But it's more personal than that. Some people who don't look quite like one or another racial expectation get asked all the time, "What are you?" Worse yet, if you identify as Black, someone may say "you're not *really* Black" and if you claim White, the psychological one-drop rule kicks in.

I don't go around asking what people are. They are themselves. But I am interested in them, so I may ask about their accent or appearance in terms of where their ancestors are from. We have to be careful about the wording here, as asking people "what they are" is a sensitive question and can be taken as offensive. In the course of conversation with a woman I worked with on a farm, I learned she was from Connecticut, but grew up and spent most of her life in Hong Kong. When another woman came to work with us, she asked where the first woman was from and I blurted out, "Can't you tell from her accent? She's from Connecticut!" We all got a good laugh, but you may not want to try this at a bus stop.

So what is the upshot of all of this? Things like race, color, language, or ethnicity are complicated. They are both objective and subjective. And there can be diversity within a single person. I will leave you with a final anecdote. The most amazing accent I had ever heard was that of a friend in college. She was African-American and Hispanic, from New York City, and studied French for many years. It was like linguistic honey from bees that gathered from many different fields. You could make out the pieces of her life story from it if you listened close enough. I can't imagine thinking of her identity as a checkbox.

4. Here First

As a child, I never played Cowboys and Indians and I didn't watch Westerns. As far as I knew, Indians – as they were almost exclusively called – cried about landfills (in a television PSA about littering) and lived out West. In my puerile imagination, West was somewhere just outside our neighborhood in the direction the sun set.

In school, we barely heard the story of mass displacement and death. It was framed more simply as skirmishes between frontiersmen and Natives – Cowboys and Indians. There was neither defense nor apology on the part of the expanding new nation, but a definite throwing of shade on the savage practice of scalping. (The fact the practice was borrowed from the French who used it to count bounties on Native lives was omitted.) Even now, many people consider the conquest by Europeans a tit-for-tat at best, with the spoils of a continent being won fair and square. Non-Natives usually care more about retaliatory massacres of settlers and Custer's last stand than the Trail of Tears and smallpox blankets. And yes, they knew what they were doing in spite of limited medical knowledge. It is reasonable to assume this is because our teachers identity with the White man, not the Red. America isn't seen as including Natives so much as the nation that won the war against them.

Conquest isn't the right word. In most wars throughout history, lands were conquered and the previous inhabitants became subjects of a new king or extended empire. The tribal nations of Native America were continuously being relocated or killed, by one-sided treaties or military action. Until more recent times, what was left of Native culture virtually ceased to exist outside of reservations. This systematic process to make way for White settlements and homesteads can only be accurately described as ethnic cleansing bordering on total genocide.

Language reveals much. Explorers described newly found lands as uninhabited, even as they were given the tour by Native guides. This is equally true in the backstory of Australia and other places. One modern national myth described Palestine as "a land without a people for a people without a land" in spite of over a million inhabitants, some families of which trace themselves back over a thousand years. These contexts may not be comparable, but history seems to rhyme. Regarding 19th Century America, Laura Ingalls Wilder writes, with admitted regret, "there were no people [in the West]. Only Indians lived there". She further exposed varying opinions and depictions of her time. Whereas her mother was fearful, and another character cried "the only good Indian is a dead Indian," her Pa's stance was that "Indians would be as peaceable as anybody else if they were let alone."

But they wouldn't be left alone. Manifest Destiny – the nationalism of its time – was the perceived duty to transform all of North America into the image of the fully settled Northeast. Contrary to the grade-school version we have been fed, it wasn't just "sea to shining sea" but the Arctic Circle to Panama. We threatened to annex Canada in 1812 and took over huge parts of Mexico in the 1840s, areas of which we now call things like "California" and "Texas". That's a reason why it's kinda hard to tell Mexicans to go back where they came from. Today, La Raza ("The People") is a political and social movement in the Southwest striving for rights and representation for Mexican Americans, and there is even sometimes talk of secession of previously Mexican territory.

Much of Native identity has been lost. I remember asking my new stepmother if she could tell me anything about the Longhouse religion. She said. "Hell no, we're Baptist!" To be fair, my stepbrothers and stepsister were not technically Native in the sense their father was Seneca, but their mother was German, and the determination for purposes of treaty and law is matrilinear. Even so, my brother Billy competed as a child in pow-wow dance competitions and even my stepmom won a competition for throwing tomahawks.

Much of the culture wasn't lost as much as excised. Boarding schools around the country were filled with Native children taken from their families, not allowed their language, and educated under the pretentious slogan "kill the Indian in him, and save the man". This was not in the distant past, but was ended with the Indian Child Welfare Act in 1978. Research from that time estimated that 25%-35% of all Native children across the country were being removed and placed in this manner.

My step-family lived on "the Rez" much of their early lives. Like other reservations across America, the Seneca Nation (part of the Iroquois Confederacy) is sovereign land. In Western New York, it's made up of a couple of small reservations, the City of Salamanca (where residents pay rent rather than taxes to live there), and the Oil Spring Reservation in Cuba, New York, where petroleum was first discovered in North America. I later discovered there were Iroquois reservations in Canada as well. One thing people note – other than low gas prices, tax-free cigarettes, and casinos – is that almost all housing on such lands is mobile homes. What people do not understand is why, and just assume it's a culturally-ingrained lack of ambition. The simple truth is you cannot get a mortgage or loan to build on property you don't personally own. There are efforts by some banking institutions to crack this paradigm in some parts of the country. The economics and politics of it all is too easy to oversimplify or generalize, but let's just say that economic mobility in the Native American community is complicated and you can't measure it with the same stick as the rest of America.

And there are still battles over treaties. It may be hearsay, but it is my understanding that the words "No taxation as long as the grass is green" were removed from the floor mosaics of Buffalo City Hall. It may just be an anecdotal myth, but there has always been contention over non-Natives being able to buy things tax-free at reservations. Attempts were made to record license plates and go after consumers, but in 1997 state governor Pataki almost started a war. Attempts to collect taxes were met with protests and blocking highways that ran through Seneca territory. In response, State Troopers blockaded the City of Salamanca, resulting in concerns over heating supply shortages and medical professionals not being allowed to cross lines to serve residents. I contacted someone who I thought might have connections in the Nation to see how I could help (offering to be a blockade runner) but it just as quickly ended with the governor backing down. Such squabbles over taxes crop up like weeds again and again.

Even though Native Americans have lands sovereign unto themselves, they are still legal citizens of the United States. This question of whether or not "Indians" could vote or serve in the military actually came up on the Tom Bauerle Show on WBEN. Not everyone heard of the Navaho Wind-Talkers in World War II. Google wasn't born yet so it was harder to find out that Native Americans were given full citizenship in 1924 and the de facto right to vote in various states over the next 50 years. I called in to set him straight based on my personal experience.

I remember sitting in the bleachers as six hawks circled over the football field where a pow-wow was being held – quite auspicious given there are six Iroquois tribes. A single feather spiraled to the ground, dead center of the field. Everything came to a halt. It was explained to the mixed crowd that such feathers must be "reclaimed" by a traditional dance that could only be performed by warriors. And by warriors, that means you must have served in the US Armed Forces. What a historical irony, I thought to myself, but it also seemed right in terms of cultural unity for the future. A few years later, my brother Josh attained that distinction, serving in Afghanistan and Iraq.

My brother Billy (or "Bill" now) stayed with my wife and me just before the pandemic. As he had moved with our parents out West when he was still young, this was his first time back this way as an adult, and connected with a lot of family on his father's side. He and Josh had contact with their Seneca Heritage, but they were, like many of "mixed" heritage, not quite accepted in either world. I did some research to find out more about his heritage to walk with him in his journey. I found that there are only about 10,000 Seneca alive today – less than the population of the village of Depew – and only a hundred or so speakers of the language. If he had stayed longer, we were to visit a Longhouse church service. I look forward to that when he is out this way again.

Before he left, I gifted him a "ribbon shirt" I had for many years. I really liked the attire I had seen at the Erie County Fair's "Indian Village", so I had one made by a member of the Mohawk Tribe (she was Turtle Clan I believe). I wore it a few times here and there, but got a seemingly cold reception when worn at the fair. It may have been like learning French, where in some places it's spoken, people are offended by foreigners always chewing on it the wrong way. I loved the colors, the pattern, the feel of it, but he had a better chance of getting away with it in public.

Let me backtrack a bit. My mother had passed away two or three years before my father married my stepmother, whose own spouse died around the same time. In addition to a daughter and grand-daughter my own daughter's age, she had two teenage boys. So here was my dad, empty-nesting at the age of 60, once again raising two teenage boys. I couldn't think of a better man for the job. And I was gifted with a whole new batch of family, even being blessed with another grandmother I got to know and spend time with – even if only for a few years.

One of my first memories of meeting her young sons was them running around the supermarket. Their mom called them "wild little Indians" in jest. Indians ... I never cared for that term. Columbus was a dolt for thinking he found India, and the appellation carrying over into modern times boggles my mind. It bothers me so much that every time someone says the word, I ask them if they mean someone from India or Native American, even if I already know the answer. The truth is I've been saying Native and Native American before it became PC, but today we have expressions such as Aboriginal (which sometimes refers specifically to Australia Aborigines), Indigenous (which has less of a NatGeo connotation), and First Nations, which I first came across in Canadian circles. As an adjective, I still prefer Native, or Indigenous if in a more anthropological context. But when referring to a group that traces back to the earliest human inhabitants, I really like First Peoples. Sure, tribes displaced each other over the ages, but as a general expression that differentiates it from modern migrations, it works.

The word "Indian" doesn't seem to bother all Native Americans, especially older ones. After my father and stepmother got married, the boys started at Lancaster High School, right near where I had grown up. After much controversy, the school changed its mascot from the "Redskins" to the "Legends". Josh and Billy, possibly the only actual "Redskins" in the school, didn't see the point. Like some politically correct battles, the people most affected may care the least. It's like no one asked those who might be offended if they actually were.

There are professional sports teams all over the place that are changing their names and mascots. Likewise, the people whose cultural identity is being used do not all agree this needs to be fixed. "Official" statements vary not just in regards to individual circumstances, but also over time. Previously against the Chicago Blackhawks keeping their name, the American Indian Center later issued a statement that "there's a huge distinction between a sports team called the Redskins depicting native people as red, screaming, ignorant savages and a group like the Blackhawks honoring Black Hawk, a true Illinois historical figure." Yes, there are those who take pride in their identity or history being used to where some Native Americans are huge fans for exactly that reason.

In a strange side tale, I got flack from a member of the block club for the logo I designed. The main road in our neighborhood is Indian Church Road, and so it made sense to name the club the "Indian Park Neighborhood Association." Around the corner, there is an Indian Park that two hundred years ago was a small Seneca camp and burial ground. Chief Redjacket had a cabin there, and upon death was buried on that land, twice. (Long story.) Anyway, I added to the letters what could be taken as flower petals or headdress feathers around the letter 'i', and a woman claiming to be 1/16 Algonquin thought it was inappropriate. I told her if others agreed and came up with an alternate logo I would gladly change it, but would not go to such trouble over the objection of one person. I will leave it to the reader to judge whether or not I handled it properly, but given the personalities involved, I suspect it was more about attention and control.

On the other hand, we have to compromise sometimes. Old caricatures must end. They just didn't age well as we find greater appreciation for marginalized cultures and groups. Instead, let's follow the serious route of honoring those like Sacagawea, the forgotten guide of Lewis and Clark, with a dollar coin, or supporting the conversion of a mountain into the likeness of Crazy Horse. Will people of Irish descent eventually grow tired of Notre Dame's mascot? Maybe not. Some of us can joke comfortably about cultural imagery; for others, it may harken to a hurtful past, the effects of which still matter.

First Nations or First Peoples are in a contradictory place in the United States as a nation, voting and serving, but not paying taxes. They do not have to live on reservations but are sovereign citizens in those lands. I'd personally like to see our First Peoples represented in Congress. Based on looking at tribal populations (around three million people total), I would suggest one senator and one representative from each side of the Continental Divide representing the tribes the majority of whose populations reside there. Voting would be by residency within state boundaries, not reservations, and it would be fitting as stakeholders to have at least one state legislator from any tribe that has official lands within it. I don't know if this will abate the challenges of losing culture and identity, but isolation or absorption shouldn't be the only choices if we want to have us all live to our fullest potentials as one country.

I said a lot of words at my wedding reception. I raised my glass to those who went before us, meaning parents and grandparents and others who had passed. And then I raised it to the people who lived as stewards of these lands before we took or bartered them away. It was an awkward moment for most, but my stepfamily nodded with approval. I hope we can consider all of America Native lands again, fully shared with us as one nation.

5. How We Are Wired, Games We Play

My high school Freshman English teacher, John Mumm, had a habit of going a bit off-script (okay, way off script). We ended up learning a lot more critical thinking than is usually allowed, and that included the mechanics of prejudice. I say "mechanics" because to most people the word only refers to examples of prejudice, never examining *why* something is prejudice, or how to recognize it.

The literal meaning of prejudice is judging someone (or something) before knowing them (or it). This is in line with the burning question Daryl Davis asks in his movie, *Accidental Courtesy*: "How can you hate me if you don't even know me?"

They say prejudices are learned (or taught), but the capacity for prejudice is natural. Some instincts could be called prejudices, such as common phobias of snakes or heights, but that's not what we're talking about here. Most prejudices are the result of experiences or socialization. And it usually serves us well. It's the way our brain extrapolates or fills in the spaces for unknowns. If a fruit made you sick once, you might have an aversion to fruit that looks like it. Or if you've eaten something a hundred times, you trust it not to make you sick any given time thereafter. If you're taught early on a certain place or act forbidden, you may be conditioned to avoid it, and therefore avoid whatever danger may have caused others to consider it so. It's not a perfect system, but it works most of the time.

With social prejudices, it's a bit more complicated. Individuals can vary wildly in character even if they are very similar in most other ways. Yet we impose identity onto others all the time, even people we know, based on past experiences with other people. It could be how someone dressed in high school. It could be people with a British accent or a lisp. It could be people who wear fanny packs or have a man bun, or people with a Liberal Arts degree, or own guns, or drive a muscle car, or are Yankees fans. You get the idea. I have a curious prejudice against young white people who wear hard-cap baseball hats off to the side. Any given individual wearing one may be a fine gentleman, but to me, they just look like a punk. I'll have to work on that.

Our prejudices don't make us bad people unless we let them. Prejudice is natural; what you do with it is a choice. I can choose to not treat someone a certain way based on stereotypes and assumptions. Sometimes it may mean consciously being extra courteous just to be sure. But it's usually subconscious, like the way we hold our purses tighter around people who look or dress differently than us. Someone African-American told me that if he wants to safely cross the street downtown, carrying a briefcase will find cars giving him space instead of pressing him. I myself know I'm treated differently depending on how I'm dressed, and I'm sure we've all experienced that at some point. One or more things send a signal to our brains. That is why, sadly, someone with a briefcase is more important or worthy of consideration than someone wearing their pants a bit low.

In a positive vein, if a woman wears a hijab at a party, I may warn them my potluck appetizer contains pork. I may start a conversation about sports with someone wearing a team jersey. The odds are in my favor I am right, and it's of little consequence if I'm wrong. These are casual, relatively neutral deductions. If the woman isn't Muslim, or the jersey an underappreciated gift, I'm being courteous or friendly, not overly intrusive or accusatory. Reasonable people won't be offended.

Prejudice is possible because of unfamiliarity with either an individual or a group. On one side, it may be judging a whole group based on one or more individuals. On the other, it is judging someone based on the group we associate them with. The latter is all about stereotypes. And they've been around forever, and are ever-changing, sloppy, even contradictory. Roman emperor Julian asked,

> [W]hy it is that the Celts and the Germans are fierce, while the Hellenes and Romans are, generally speaking, inclined to political life and humane, though at the same time unyielding and warlike? Why the Egyptians are more intelligent and more given to crafts, and the Syrians unwarlike and effeminate, but at the same time intelligent, hot-tempered, vain and quick to learn?

Maybe it's because stereotypes aren't people and people aren't stereotypes. There is a saying that stereotypes may be true, but are never the whole truth. There may be traceable social and historical reasons for a stereotype.

A lot of ethnic stereotypes in America come from the immigrant experience. If most of the people from a certain country don't speak the language and are only given menial jobs, they may be branded as stupid. Polish jokes come to mind. When my sister-in-law lived in the Netherlands, a play on this stereotype was met with confusion. They explained that Poles were considered the smartest people in Europe. In recent times of restricting visas to professionals and students, it is no wonder people from East or South Asia are often assumed to be highly intelligent. For good, bad, or otherwise, we see individuals we are exposed to as representative of their ethnicity, even if the label covers a billion other, different people.

Sometimes it's more selective than just color. There is a strange tendency for people from Africa to be given more employment opportunities than African-Americans. Maybe it is a hint of a Frech or British accent. Or maybe there is just so much more pre-judging of African-Americans. The latter is definitely true, to the point that a White person with a criminal record has the same chance statistically of landing a job as an African-American with no record.

We may also judge African-Americans by comparisons to immigrants in general. What people do not understand is the "migrant advantage", where people who migrate tend to be more resilient and successful than their countrymen (where they came from or where they go to). Immigration and visitor (visa) policies often give precedence to those more educated or skilled as well. It is no wonder that we associate some ethnicities of recent migrations with entrepreneurialism, such as restaurant ownership and corner stores, and professional fields, such as medicine.

Where things get the most dangerous is when global geopolitics enter the equation. In our American melting pot, some ethnicities feel the heat when the nations they came or descended from are in conflict with the United States or its allies. During the Great War, many Germans changed their names, and the names of any business that had the world German in it. This was the first rallying cry against "hyphenated Americans." In World War II, over 100,000 citizens, mostly of Japanese descent, were interred and their properties taken without any due process. Heck, there was a fear that if Kennedy were elected, there would be required national fealty to the Holy See. And with President Obama's middle name being the same as Iraqui dictator Saddam's last name ... let's just say even perceived ethnicity can be weaponized.

Many prejudices are borrowed. They are about groups of people we've never interacted with, but heard about through our families, friends, or the news. That's socialization by proxy, but harder-to-cure prejudices are ones that are from personal experience. For example, we may know of an abusive husband of a particular ethnicity. Now we won't usually associate someone's actions with their ethnicity *unless* it's an ethnicity we don't have any other contact with, in which case they become the representative of that culture in our minds. It's not even conscious until we realized we've done it, and we may never reach that point until it's challenged by others. And it's not rational. The back of our brains will wince from the trauma or empathy of bad experiences.

Second-hand prejudice can be easily overcome by eliminating unfamiliarity. For example, it is impossible for me to think of Mexicans as lazy. The migrant workers from Mexico I worked with on the farm were the hardest-working people I've ever seen. But then another hard-to curb prejudice has formed – I may expect someone else Mexican I may meet to have a similar work ethic. Maybe the odds are in my favor, maybe not, but the point is thinking about it this way is natural when you only know a few people, and it's hard not to make those associations. The best we can do is be aware of them and try not to let it give cause to disrespect.

Prejudice is perhaps most intractable with immersive social exposure. I know a friend who finds it hard not to place particular moral values on African-American culture. He blames music, fatherlessness, and other things, all of which we will get to later in this book. But the fact is he grew up in a bad neighborhood. Like so many others in Buffalo (and other cities), old, stable neighborhoods experienced a demographic shift. African-American populations settled in urban areas and demographics shifted. Property ownership gave way to slum lords, redlining crept in, and quality of life declined to the point of urban blight (more than half of an area's properties being abandoned or razed). Again, we'll talk about the interplay between poverty, prejudice, and race later, but the mental association is what we're talking about. By choice or circumstance, the stereotype forms where we see "those people live like that." It's like Native Americans in their trailers.

White residents in all-White neighborhoods are apprehensive (at the least) when African-Americans move in, remembering those "lost" neighborhoods of the past. Then they are surprised to find their fears unfounded. "What nice neighbors," they may say, criticizing instead the "White trash" a few doors further down to show off their wokeness. But they still don't get a sticker for being "Prejudice-Free" because that new family becomes an example of why other people "of their kind" should, but don't, aspire to be like our Black neighbor. We see the ones we know as individuals, but the rest are still an amorphous generality. The stereotype holds, and we feel justified to maintain our opinions of others in their group, or the group as a whole. Again, it's about unfamiliarity.

Limited familiarity is perhaps even worse. If you spent a few years in Saudi Arabia, where women are treated horribly and can't even legally drive, you may develop strong, guttural opinions about Middle Easterners or Islam with respect to women. Nevermind that Pakistan had a woman prime minister, as have Bangladesh, Turkey, Indonesia ... I could go on. Like I said, stereotypes may be true, but they are not the whole truth.

If you live or lived in an impoverished, high-crime (or heavily policed) neighborhood that was of one ethnicity, *even your own*, it forms a strong stereotype. If you are one of the only people of another ethnicity, you will probably associate those conditions with the majority group, especially if you move out and see people of other ethnicities not living that way. If you are a member of that ethnicity, it can deeply affect how you see "your own people" – internalized racism.

Imagine being in law enforcement, placed for a long time in a neighborhood of people whose ethnicity you have no other exposure to. If your department culture follows a community policing model, you may get to know citizens as human beings. But often policing is more adversarial, seeing the role more like a zookeeper, with every person as a potential arrest, even the people calling for help. A police academy may teach its recruits not to see color, but the wrong approach in practice can set them up for failure psychologically over time – and we all pay for that.

Corrections officers have the potential for even more baggage. Imagine being immersed in an environment where you can't ever let your guard down. I'm not even talking about color at this point. I know a former CO who just could not accept the possibility that anyone in prison could be innocent, or even a good person, simply because "they" throw jars of urine at the staff.

They.

The daughter of a local block club leader tried to argue that it wasn't fair African-American families could move to her neighborhood. Their reasoning? White families who move to "their" neighborhoods have in instances been victims of arson, presumably because they weren't welcome. I asked her if she actually thought the people ("they") moving in were the same people ("they") responsible for the arsons. It went over her head – she couldn't process it.

It's probably the worst word in the English language when used this way. It is the very essence of prejudice. We may even try to fudge it by clarifying "they" only means certain individuals or parts of a group, but then will use it interchangeably for the whole group. Bigots do it on purpose, referring to a group's terrible members and the group itself to where you can't tell which "they" is being talked about at any given moment. Prejudice is the conflating of the two, sometimes knowingly. That is why I listen for the word "they" when it's used, and how it is used, and call people on it.

But that's just the outward expression of an inward error. In the former CO's mind, every person in every prison everywhere conforms to his personal experience in one corner of one facility. Anecdotal experiences become overarching truth. It's a logical fallacy, but we're wired for that, too. That's how the news evokes a warped view of reality. To be fair, the news is geared around reporting what is out of the ordinary and not emphasizing the norm, if it gets reported at all. A town with a full police blotter is practically crime-free compared to cities with papers that don't bother. But sometimes it's just irresponsible, focusing far more on dark-skinned suspects, and almost exclusively on light-skinned missing girls. This shapes our reality. It's part of our unexamined socialization.

Speaking of prisons, the stresses of incarceration bring out survivalist social psychology, which is heavily based in tribal mentalities. People of like ethnicity (or ideology) band together militantly for both protection and pecking order. Crossing lines to make friends with others not of your group carries a heavy risk. The thing is, no one created this social model – it's built into us as humans. Whether to this extreme degree, a subliminal tendency, or somewhere in between, tribalism is found everywhere there are more than a few human beings.

On a small scale, we distinguish between who is or is not of our tribe even in our own neighborhoods. I don't just mean patrolled gated communities, but even in unexpected ways. In a small town, someone laying on the side of the road may be a stranger, but locals will go to help them. The townsfolk are the only ones to help, and so empathy is acted upon. But what if it's on West 32nd Street in Manhattan? Like in the small town, the stranger may not be seen as part of one's tribe, but here it's assumed he is part of some other tribe also present – it is his own tribe's responsibility, not theirs. In one case people see a person in need; in the other people see each person as part of an abstraction of homelessness. All this happens in the gut, not the conscious mind.

On the largest scale, tribalism results in ethnic strife, and I suggest the greatest cause of it is the network of imaginary lines demarking nations. Between colonialism in the Global South and so many redrawing of boundaries in Eastern Europe and Western Asia, ethnic groups have become minorities in their own homelands. Their fate is dictated by people who do not share their language, religion, or customs. The Kurds, for example, live as minorities in Turkey, Iran, Iraq, and Syria, but "Kurdistan" – a de facto country but not a sovereign nation – may never exist beyond a common struggle for independence amidst a geopolitical mess.

Fear of one's tribe losing supremacy over a culture is almost universal. Every country fearful of being overrun by outsiders seems to have a "{my country} First" party or club. And once the intruders are here, we are worried they will start making the rules and thereby "destroy" our way of life. A few years ago one of my network associates said "They're outbreeding us like rats". Was he talking about Mexicans? Muslims? Some other fear flavor of the day? I didn't care to ask and changed the topic.

Sometimes tribal distinctions are imposed almost arbitrarily. The Tutsi and Hutu were specific ethnicities that became genetically indistinguishable in the times leading up to colonization. They were redefined in the 1920s by Belgian colonists, and anyone owning more than ten cows or having a longer nose or neck was legally filed under Tutsi. This social stratification caused some divergence by less intermarriage, but even after the Rwandan genocide in 1994, a journalist noted that two women he had met, one Tutsi and one Hutu, he would have assumed to be sisters.

Race and ethnicity are more expansive tribal constructs in America and the world at large. If it's unfair to label around a small, tight-knit group, how much more so than blanketing millions (or even billions) of people. And yet we are still prone to do it. When we treat people differently or classify them for some social, religious, political, or economic purpose, it's what we mean by discrimination.

But there is an ethical cost to prejudices, even if not acted upon or institutional in nature. Prejudice takes away the right of an individual to be seen as themselves. It's an imposition of cultural baggage, stereotypes, even fear and hate, that the individual may have done nothing to deserve.

6. (Re)Defining Racism

I was so confused. Over my lifetime I've given serious thought to the nature of prejudice, racism, and related concepts. And then someone moved my cheese. All of a sudden, it was deemed impossible for someone not-White to be racist. Okay, there's a new understanding of the term, at least by some people. In the end, I don't care too much about the semantics. It's the meaning and what is in our hearts that counts. But is repurposing words useful, or just confusing and divisive? What is that purpose? I'm still not sure, but let's get through it together and find out what is still true.

The kindergarten version of "racism" is that it is prejudice based on race. But racial prejudice and racism aren't exactly the same thing. Prejudice is the way one thinks and feels; racism is acting on it. A person can be prejudiced but actions and words can be racist, with the person doing them then considered racist because of it. This gives us a moral judgment we can make: being prejudiced is natural (or conditioned); being racist is a choice.

Of course, we don't always consciously choose to act or speak out of prejudice. But we can be held responsible for our words and actions, and therefore be considered – at least technically – racist. And that's a problem. Considering everyone a racist because we all have prejudices that may sometimes show isn't helpful. "Racist" is an ugly accusation. Admitting we have racial prejudices is like admitting we are sinners. Well, we probably all are, but it's more like seeing ourselves as inherently bad, not just imperfect.

Robin DiAngelo, the author of "White Fragility", takes on what I describe as a clinical approach. All White people are racists and always will be, and we must constantly examine ourselves and choose not to be. That's a bit harsh to have to hear even if it isn't meant as an attack. It also treats racism the way Alcoholics Anonymous treats addiction. It's an all-or-nothing view of being "racist", forever. Keep in mind her experience is in racial sensitivity training, where people need to be forced to confront their words and behaviors. It is no wonder she has a hardline refusal to accept the validity of one very important thing – intention. We will address that later.

This view that White people are racist because it is not possible to be unprejudiced would mean that *all* people are racist, as it's universal human nature to be prejudiced. Not so, according to a modern, expanded use of the term, which requires the additional criteria that a systemic discrimination and the ability to institutionally oppress is present. I thought we already had terms for that – *systemic* or *institutional racism*. But let's try to make sense of it anyway.

In 1987, the *Socialist Worker* explained it thusly:

> Racism is not simply animosity based on skin color or other physical characteristics, but a systematic, special oppression, which employers use to keep the working class divided and to forestall any challenge to their rule... Blacks cannot be "racists." They are not in a position to oppress anyone–certainly not the majority white population of the U.S.

Keeping in mind that the Socialist movement sees everything in light of a collective dynamic, that makes sense. But they aren't the only ones to take us down this path. In 2014, S.E. Smith of *TheDailyDot* says that racism "is structural, not personal." He further writes:

> In order to be racist, you need to possess two traits. The first is privilege: A structural, institutional, and social advantage. White people occupy positions of racial privilege, even when they are disadvantaged in other ways.... Furthermore, you also have to have power: the ability, backed up by society, to be a strong social influencer, with greater leeway when it comes to what you do, where, and how.

One college campus has used diversity training materials that emphatically state all White people of all circumstances are therefore racist, as a "racist is one who is both privileged and socialized on the basis of race by a white supremacist (racist) system." In that sense, being racist is inherent and not a choice. The same literature also says, "By this definition, people of color cannot be racists, because as peoples within the U.S. system, they do not have the power to back up their prejudices, hostilities, or acts of discrimination." In this sense, racism is an ability.

Also, notice the term *supremacy* here is used differently. In this context, it does not refer to hate groups or the belief in superiority over other races, but the cultural and institutional domination of a certain people over the rest. It's not a moral judgment, but a sociological reality. Because of its negative connotation, White people aren't comfortable with the word, so we should all be careful of possible miscommunication when using it.

Back to the problem. If you treat me wrongly because I am White, that is not racist because (by this thinking) it does not have the weight of society behind it. Even if I am a minority as a White person in a neighborhood or company, any discrimination I may experience is not qualified enough because society at large is the benchmark. The individuals involved and the social circumstances of any interaction are irrelevant so long as you're White in America. Sounds unfair, but I get it. No matter what word you use, the meaning has a legitimate moral value. But that's a lot of work just to enforce the use of a word that particular way, in my opinion.

The first time I had a debate of sorts about this, I asked "then what do you call it when a White person is treated that way?" The standard answer is that non-White people can be *prejudiced*. So apart from a social and cultural context, the exact same thing one person does may be *racist* and if another does it, it's *prejudice*. Maybe the reader accepts this – and I have no beef with you. But you would have to admit there is a fair argument this is a double standard.

Author and anti-racist activist Ibram X. Kendi disagrees with this redefining of racism. In fact, he, an African-American, says he has been a racist many times. Specifically, he argues that there are People of Color in power, and sometimes use that power to support racist policies and norms. In other words, at the very least, People of Color can be racist against their own people or other People of Color, participating in the supremacy of White society. So we're left with some people using the word at its literal meaning and other people adding stipulations.

What's a White person to do? I try to suck it up. If People of Color are offended by the idea they can be racist like a White person, I could stamp my foot down with logic. But I'd be arguing from a place that disrespects their everyday experience of racism, while I probably have the convenience of not having to deal with racism at all. Might it be just a rationalized, pedantic way to "stick it to the man" after centuries of being on the other end of the stick? Maybe. But again, this is semantics. And not all African-American thinkers or writers agree with any of this. The best we can do is be aware of when people use the word this way and substitute the word *prejudiced* accordingly.

People of Color might want to consider most White folks have no idea about any of this and it's not going to make sense to us. Having to explain how being a victim of racism is only a Person of Color thing can feel like a denial of whatever prejudices a White person may have experienced, however great or small by comparison. *Anyone* can be the victim of prejudice that would otherwise be described as racism. Many still remember the immigrant experiences of themselves or their families before they were considered a full member of the American tribe. In some neighborhoods, being "White" is a dangerous thing. Some say being non-Mormon in Utah makes you a second-class citizen, while being Mormon in another state may see you on the outside looking in as well. (This last example is not racial distinction, but similar in form).

I guess what I am saying is we don't need to make this a contest. Saying "my ancestors were oppressed, too" is like saying "my father died, too" when someone just lost theirs. Even if it weren't an attempt to negate the importance of another's cultural history or experience – which it often is – it is easily taken as just that. Stop doing it.

But let me wear my philosopher's hat for a moment. My problem with this one-directional definition of racism is not personal but philosophical. I posit that wisdom is the ability to make useful distinctions. I would want any given word that describes a specific concept to be fairly applied to all examples. I would want different words to describe an action versus an intention or attitude. That's how I would cut the cake with racism versus prejudice. Adding a sociological rider at the end of the contract may be prudent socially, but we need to be honest and clear that's what we're doing.

Regardless of how we use that word, the term *reverse-racism* is problematic. It was coined in 1966 after accusations of pushing out White members to make room for People of Color in a local government in Alabama. Most people think of Affirmative Action (which is in highly limited use) or the existence of race-based scholarships. We do make laws giving special designation to some people under this or that label, all under the banner of fixing inequity or protecting people's civil rights. Many White people and People of Color see how such things have a downside. It is a justification, albeit well-intentioned, for treating people according to the color of their skin. And using legislation to address social issues tend to deal only with the symptoms, not causes.

It also breeds a strange contempt from White People toward those who receive it, individually or in general. It becomes an excuse to shift the perception of social oppression into Whites being the victim. It's White people playing the race card, and it's not pretty. And even if "discrimination against White people" does exist, it doesn't justify racism or nullify it as a problem. On the other hand, racism doesn't necessarily justify reverse-discrimination as a solution, so this becomes a point of contention we have to work out.

Another problem is that racism is as ambiguous as the term race. It can include ethnic classifications, such as Hispanic, etc.. Sometimes people use the term racism to refer to anti-Semitism and Islamophobia, but then people give themselves an out, saying they cant' be racist because Islam isn't a race. So we rely on another term – bigotry.

I was taught that bigotry is incurable prejudice. It is the state of mind where one's refuses to let their beliefs be challenged. This overlaps the concepts of brainwashing and fanaticism. But in a less harsh use of it, we can use the word bigotry to cover negative prejudices against people on any grounds, including ideological ones.

There have always been religious bigots, not just against particular faiths, but sometimes against all of them in general. Still others are bigoted against Atheists. Gender bigotry includes misogyny and misandry, and being anti-LGBTetc. But we may also have bigotry against Liberals, or Conservatives, or Southerners, or Millenials, or even gun owners (decried as "ammosexuals"). Any time you have a visible, deep-seated prejudice against some perceived group, insisting on generalized statements ("they"), you are a bigot. It doesn't mean you don't have some basis for disliking the aspect or idea or practice of something, but when you take away every individual's right to not fit your mould, you find yourself back at the core of it − prejudice.

Bigotry (racism *et alia*) often has one more hallmark − dehumanization. That's where things get dangerous. Any time you hear people being called things like "animals" or "inhuman" it should be a red flag. If we can convince ourselves they are not worthy of being considered human, we can become capable of terrible things. In fact, that's what war propaganda counts on. All things considered, not many of us could straight up kill another human being. We have to feel threatened, or that there is some existential threat to our homeland and way of life. But what makes it all the easier to pull the trigger − or support a war or worse − is to not see the men, women, and children as human beings. The "Huns" in both world wars were portrayed as ogres, often with a hinting of carrying off our women, another primal trigger of racism. The Japanese were given more simian caricatures.

Even today, we are not immune to talk of genocide. Don't believe me? Check out the comments on news sites. Every single day people express how every last one of such-and-such people should be shot or ran over or bombed into nonexistence. Which targets are in fashion may change, but there's always some group of "not people" we think the world should live without, convinced they will get us if we don't get them first. In fact, that is the basis of some White supremacist groups − the idea that there will be a "White genocide" if something isn't done. It is the typical cycle of fear to hate to suffering. No one listens to Yoda.

Bigotry through fear of "other" is encapsulated blatantly in the 1915 silent film "Birth of a Nation." It depicts a Reconstruction-era where African-Americans are the nemesis of a Christian America, taking over politics by ballot-box stuffing and voter suppression, legalizing mixed marriages, and capital punishment for possessing Klan regalia. It plays on every ignorant stereotype and fear-based trope. A box office success, it was also the first American motion picture screened in the White House. Like other historical fiction, it became an interpretation of history unto itself for many. In fact, the then-dead KKK was revived into its current form later that year. We do not believe this to be a coincidence.

But let's back up a bit and hone in on White supremacy. We usually have a solitary image of what that means, but as Daryl Davis finds out, there's quite a continuum. Some ideologies are truly supremacist – they believe in the superiority of whatever they consider the "White Race", be it "Aryan" by any number of interpretations, or WASP. The basis of superiority may be beliefs about genetics, culture, or scripture. Some accept the idea of peaceful coexistence, so long as kept separate, especially by bloodline. Some groups are not even technically supremacists, but simply want "racial purity."

A new spin on this sort of bigotry has arisen more recently. The militant "patriot" group Proud Boys describe themselves as "Western Chauvinist." The media describes them as White supremacists, but they have some racial diversity, even in their leadership. So why are they considered a hate group? Because they believe in a particular cultural superiority. They are inclusive toward African-Americans and Latinx who are properly assimilated and accepting of their views. Also using the term "Western culturalists," they oppose anything that threatens it – like multiculturalism, interracial marriage, the existence of non-Christian faiths, and non-White immigration. And chauvinism isn't a sloppy choice of words either, given their stance on the subservience of women. They are the poster boys for the term bigot where the word racist simply won't do.

We are seeing a further evolution of both racism and responses to it. Born of student discontent at Harvard in the 1980s, "Critical Race Theory" (CRT) is the framing of social and historical contexts in terms of the interconnectedness of race, law, and power. Messenging of this type has been made loudly surrounding BLM protests. In concept, it's a legitimate angle to approach such things. However, it can be overbearing to those who are not minorities, and even to some that are. Some even describe it as racist, and radical anti-capitalist (Marxist) aspects ruffle yet other feathers. White people may need to hear that message, but it doesn't give much space for individual self-reflection versus what comes off as collective damnation. Making everything about race is just as much an unhelpful vice as denying it's an aspect of so many things.

All contexts are not about race, even if they may seem so. We need to admit there is such thing as race-baiting, and playing the "race card." One or two politicians have made a career out of it. But let's be clear – we should never jump to dismiss the validity of such accusations. But it does happen. Crying wolf this way in turn gives cover to denial when racism is truly present. Am I exaggerating the prevalence of this? In a defamation court case, Kimura v. Vandenberg, the opinion stated was "Accusations of 'racism' no longer are 'obviously and naturally harmful.' The word has been watered down by overuse, becoming common coin in political discourse."

And then there's another possible case, namely that someone honestly perceives race coming into play when it doesn't, or at least isn't intended. For example, I was accused of racism because I was against some social program. It infuriated me. There was absolutely no context of race from anything that was said. What I didn't realize back then was there there is in many people's minds a strong association of social services benefiting minorities. We see this a lot in political circles. Cuts to such programs are called racist, and it's hard to tell if it's a political *ad hominem* or if cuts may actually be intended to hurt or neglect minorities.

I guess my cheese isn't the only one being moved. Bigotry of all sorts is dog-whistling from behind other causes and issues, flaunting political correctness, and convincing even good people to spread hate speech via seemingly harmless memes. That is why racial literacy is essential – we need to get the spinach off our teeth instead of attacking and feeling attacked.

7. What's a White Devil to Do?

In 1988, Louis Farrakhan spoke in Buffalo's convention center for the first time. A friend at college talked me into going with them. It was my first exposure to the Nation of Islam, and it was a hard message to swallow. Much of the preaching was an enumeration of injustices against Africans and their descendants at the hands of White Europeans over the last five centuries. The slogan of reparation accompanying this message was "Add it up!" Afterward in the lobby, I felt it was directed at me personally – one of maybe a handful of people not African-American in the entire crowd. People near me shouted "Add it up!" while glancing in my direction out of the corner of their eyes.

But I had better things to do than be fearful or take offense. I was trying to process what truth there could be in the argument that White people were inherently evil. Talk about needing an open mind! Maybe I stripped out some of the meaning with the emotion, so I could at least accept the possibility that being a member of the majority by itself means something. Maybe it makes me more responsible in virtue of such power for the circumstances of those who do not have such power. Even though I don't divide society personally by race, collectively there is a "we" that held all the cards for centuries. And we still have a stacked deck.

Today, White people are being told being *not*-racist is *not* enough – we have to be *anti-racist*. In other words, we need to use our power (privilege?) to *unstack* the deck. But before we can even talk about that, we have to quell all the shouting over things like White guilt and reparations.

The concept of White guilt cuts both ways if you look closely. Racists spit out the term to ridicule the motivations of actions or attitudes that are anti-racist. Actually having guilt – or rather a heightened sense of responsibility to be outspoken or charitable toward the plight of minorities – risks taking on a White Savior complex. This can be condescending to People of Color, or at least perceived as such even if well-intended. This has played out in many ways on a larger scale.

Coming clean here, I have a lifelong hero complex. My wife says I sprout a cape anytime I see an injustice. It could be rushing to the side of someone being bullied, or insisting on taking in an abandoned kitten tossed from a neighbor's window (yes, that really happened). It means defending people who are misunderstood or being unfairly mocked, even if I don't agree with them.

Sometimes I have to remind people that I'm not partial or obsessed with this or that group being persecuted – as if I feel they are *more* important or worthy than others – only that at that time they are the ones in most need of defense. If they became the tormentors the next day, I would just as surely side with the victims of their derision. And when people are being hateful and hurtful all around, it breaks my heart. Maybe I should write a book about that. Oh, wait ...

I go out of my way to hold the door open for anyone, but do so more eagerly for people who might be marginalized. Part of it is to counteract stereotypes of insensitivity (racism, sexism, etc..) associated with my perceived group (White, male, etc.). Part of it is the way I was raised. An anecdote comes to mind of a woman who scolded a man for showing such a courtesy since she was not in need of his help. He responded, "I didn't hold it open because you are a woman. I did it because I am a gentleman."

But we do kid ourselves. We take may offense on behalf of others who honestly don't care to be offended. We speak for others as if we know their plight better than they do. (Being a know-it-all, I sometimes cross that line.) And there's the very real problem of being offended when truth is spoken to power. It is hard for people to hear about racial injustice from those experiencing it, especially if there is some element of ownership in the society that allows it. One can't help but feel accused, like it's directed at them personally rather than being a cold lesson from a textbook, or a matter-of-fact article from a newspaper. Maybe that's a form of White guilt no one talks about.

The idea of reparations offends White people for a similar reason. They don't want to associate themselves personally with racial injustice, especially one not in living history. The first defense is to simplify it to being one issue – slavery. The arguments follow from that: their personal ancestors didn't have slaves; their ancestors *were* slaves (the Irish slave myth, for example); a total dissociation from the racial paradigm ("We were all slaves at one time or another"). I myself can say my ancestors were in Poland at the time. It's truthful, but I'm not sure that it's helpful.

I've encountered an odd counter-argument to reparations I feel must be addressed. Some White people actually say they are owned big-time for all "their" blood shed to free the slaves. I can't even be sure they are taking themselves seriously. Even assuming that emancipation was the North's goal rather than an effect, America as a whole was built on slavery that was passed to all of us, not just the inhabitants of formerly Confederate states. It's not like we freed the slaves of a distant land and then left. We as colonies, and then a nation upheld slavery for over two hundred years. To say America should send a bill from some of its citizens to other citizens because a bunch of Americans freed people from bondage by some other Americans ... I just don't see it.

This brings out a more legitimate problem. Even when not misunderstood, reparation frames racial injustice as a historical construct – in the past. We should not be held responsible for the actions of our ancestors. But think of it another way. We may not be responsible for an ecologically depleted or harmed environment, but even if we drive a Prius and don't litter, can we just blame previous generations and leave it at that? This is where fault isn't the point – responsibility is. And there's still a mess to clean up.

But what would reparations even look like? Maybe a modern version of the "forty acres and a mule" plan for freed slaves? Reparations and abolitionism went hand in hand long before the Civil War, but when the battle was won, redistribution of plantation lands was an unsuccessful effort. And those plots have changed hands too many times since. Can that approach even translate to modern needs and goals? Some racists mock that "welfare" is enough reparations, but it exposes the absurdity that this might be a purely monetary question. Then again, when you consider how America's wealth and progress is in no small part due to forced labor (an estimated nearly 100 trillion dollars worth), reparations could be seen as generations of deferred wages owed.

A pertinent example of reparations that actually happened was the Civil Liberties Act of 1988. The United States government apologized for the mass internment of Japanese-Americans during World War II, giving $20,000 to each survivor. Descendants got nothing, and properties confiscated – including prime real estate in major West Coast cities – were never returned.

For descendants of slaves, there have been various proposals of financial compensation (as well as free healthcare and other measures), but it would likely involve establishing some proof of descendancy from slaves that is hard to establish. Companies and institutions who were involved in slave-involved commerce have been sued over the years, but more often than not the result was only a public apology.

Acknowledgment is no small thing, even if it is the least that can be done. And times have changed, since official apologies are a very recent thing. The states of Alabama, Connecticut, Delaware, Florida, Maryland, New Jersey, North Carolina, Tennessee, and Virginia have all issued statements in the last 20 years. In 2008, the United States House of Representatives passed a resolution apologizing for American slavery and discriminatory legislation.

Current demands include an end to the death penalty, investments in education, jobs, and mental health services. The questions about who pays for it and who receives it can be debated, and many of these initiatives already exist, but these sort of demands bring the issue forward into the present. It is easy to see how slavery gave way to a caste system that has never fully been dismantled.

Even if we could balance the ledger financially, such "transactionalism" puts a price tag on mass racial traumas. At the risk of *argumentum ad absurdum*, could this pave the way for the moral-historical equivalent of a carbon credit exchange? The nation or humanity may never figure this out, but I can hope that we as individual human beings can figure out appropriate times and appropriate ways to give personal acknowledgments. We can choose to be mindful in our civic duties to support progress that makes sense. Or at least we can stop resisting and arguing with people over it.

But is there a point where anti-racism can go too far? There are times White people, including myself, want to say "Enough!" I can tolerate (barely) a redefinition of racist to include me no matter what I do, so long as it isn't an excuse to hate Whitey or an attack on me personally. I can see why just not being racist doesn't solve the problem, which is why we are now all encouraged to become anti-racists. Unfortunately, there are those who have decided to be authoritative representatives as to what this should mean – and you dare not disagree.

I mean, I get it. If you're White, there's going to be some ignorance and you can't fully walk in another's shoes. But White people don't want to be told to stay in our lane just for having an opinion. In fact, we don't usually even know where the lines on the road are. So tell us. Admittedly, we might play the run-to-the-other-parent-to get-the-answer-we-want. I know people who scour the Internet to find that one renowned Person of Color who agrees with whatever White tropes we want authenticated. That's where honesty comes in. If we can't accept what the person in front of us is saying, why should we think another person's assertions are more representative, or the way things really are? Everyone has a different experience with race in the end, and every voice adds to the whole picture. The pieces don't have to fit each other, let alone our insisted expectations.

The problem is that when we get into the far end of anti-racism, we find constant moral extortion. (From anti-racists of our own color, we may see virtue signaling or accusations of it.) On one hand, someone may be sincere and well-meaning in their insistence you be, act, think, and talk within the confines of their paradigm. On the other, they can be vicious and based in prejudicial contempt. Sometimes there's no room at all between "stay in your lane" and "White silence is violence." Those receiving such counsel (or demands) may turn it into as an excuse to judge all efforts toward racial literacy or harmony as a battle that shouldn't even be fought. The recent presidential call to eliminate sensitivity training represents a sizable constituency who feel a reprieve from the discomfort of having to deal with these issues.

I have learned to identify extremism by the vilifying of not only those who are against you, but anyone who is not for you. The notion that if you are not part of the solution you are part of the problem is a cliche that lends itself to this. Maybe not being a racist isn't good enough if you want to spend your energies making the world a better place in that way. But not being an anti-racist doesn't make you a racist. And the idea that you are racist because you associate with racists – however particularly defined – is rationalized prejudice. If Jesus of Nazareth ate with harlots and tax collectors, I'm pretty sure you can have a positive influence on others more by being in their lives than not. Personally, I won't judge anyone for their choice, only on their own words and actions. And I say you are welcome to your own judgments.

8. The Offensive and the Offended

I can already tell you this book will not age well. Terms shift with the times. What is acceptable now could very well be offensive in a few short years, or vice versa. I remember the first time I got scolded for saying Oriental instead of Asian. I honestly had no idea that had become "insulting and outdated." I went to school a few short years earlier with Orientals, not Asians. And who knows what alphabet soup will describe the non-binary gender spectrum by next spring, but that's a whole other book. The best we can do is try not to get bent out of shape, and ask for and grant forgiveness.

Sometimes, it's a litigious battle. One of my favorite restaurants growing up was Sambo's. I still have stuffed tigers wearing t-shirts with the name. Artwork referenced the 1899 children's book, *The Story of Little Black Sambo*. The main character of that name was an Indian boy, but didn't age well, being lumped into the genre of "pickaninny" stereotypes. The name itself, interestingly, was a combination of the owner's names, Sam Battistone, Sr. and Newell Bohnett. I haven't been able to verify it at this point, but I recall the story they were sued by the NAACP which contributed to their bankruptcy. Some became Denny's. One store remained with the name until this year, in Santa Monica, where the owner was petitioned by residents to change the name. He willingly did so, and now it's "Chad's". (I hope to eat there someday.)

The most recent term I've encountered is BIPOC (Black, Indigenous, People of Color). Not sure why it's separated out that way, unless Black is no longer a color; then again neither is White in this context. And I've heard a lot of people talk about Black and Brown Americans. Here I'm trying to keep things simple to include anyone not White as a Person of Color. I generally use Black when not specifically referring to African-Americans, one being a skin color and the other of both African and American descent. People literally from Africa, even if naturalized as citizens, are not considered "African-America", as they have not commonly descended from a slave experience. I know a number of such people personally, and there are issues of cultural integration there beyond my pay grade to figure out. On the other hand, one blogger argues that Barack Obama gets a pass to be considered African-American because although his father was a Black Kenyan, his mother was a White American. Things are what people want them to be at some point. Even in the middle of writing this book,

I am finding it more and more common to see the term Black (and Brown) Americans as a preferred term.

No matter how people self-identify, it's not like they wear a nametag with this information. There are no rules in the end, and one identical twin may be offended and the other not, by any given label. But society seems hell-bent on creating a standard.

Political Correctness (PC), in theory, is a guide for people to avoid doing or saying things that offend people of particular groups. It's not an official guide written in law, but more of a concept of social mores. The problem is that it doesn't address prejudices, only particular forms. And I say "only" because it is very selective and changes with the whim of the mob. It reduces the appearance of prejudice into a sort of social fashionability. It ignores all intentions, creates double-standards with impunity, and never addresses the nature of real racism or bigotry. In fact, it often shuts down dialogue.

People who are actively bigoted in their speech rail against it, and that ironically serves them well. When they are called out on even the most egregious hate speech, they simply dismiss the accusation as not being PC. In other words, they use PC's tight correspondence to public opinion to reduce it to a totally relativistic morality. It can even be an excuse to taunt "them liberals" to boot, as PC tends to emanate from that camp.

When I was part of a "racism callouts" group on Facebook (which eventually got shut down), there were many postings of comments that I honestly had no idea why they were taken to be offensive. Once explained, I realized some of my blindness was a result of my ignorance (privilege?) about so many things that remind a Person of Color of past or present injustices or slurs. Some expressions or opinions seemed innocuous, but are used as code words for racist expressions. Did the person saying them know that? It's hard to tell. That's why it's called a dog-whistle — only those who know what to listen for will hear it. It's hidden in plain sight, taking on expressions people may use without the purpose of hate. It's racism evolved. That which was previously openly said is no longer acceptable, so it gets hinted at to avoid the recently ubiquitous stigma of being called racist.

This strays into the concept of *tone*. Some anti-racists catch people on the way they say things, their tone. The problem is that tone, especially in a written medium, or even shorter media (social media) can be easily misconstrued, even purposely. Such "tone policing" is counterproductive, making the offended appear oversensitive. On the other hand, people can be "tone deaf" and say things in ways that are truly insensitive.

Trigger words are just as subjective, but we can watch out for them. Calling people *thugs* can be considered a racial slur if applied to African-Americans, even if you just mean people engaging in brutish intimidation. Heck, I avoid using the word *picnic*, with its story of being from countryside lynchings, i.e. "pick-a-nig". I refrain from its use not because this is true – the atrocities existed but the word has no such linguistic derivation in reality – but because people *think* it's true. It's too small a concession not to make.

And then there are *microaggressions*, those everyday things that are, as DiAngelo would put it, problematic. We're talking about things like left-handed compliments. We may note how well-mannered someone is "for an African-American", or showing surprise someone Asian speaks English. Sometimes even calling attention to race or ethnicity could fall under this heading. Downplaying racial issues can be offensive from people who don't deal with them. A comprehensive list of examples would be too long to enumerate here, and Ibram X. Kendi suggests the term microaggression isn't really aggression, but abuse. It fails to call it what it more bluntly is – racism.

It is common for people to virtue signal how racially enlightened they are. Admittedly, I do a fair bit of that, and try to catch myself, but then I go and write a book! We may do it as a misguided way to disarm another's fear there is prejudice against them. It could take the form of anything from excessive pride to groveling. Unfortunately, this can cause much discomfort and a constant acknowledgment of race is tiresome. It is said that there will always be an element of being a "Black friend" to a White person instead of just a friend, as sad as I know that can be. In fact, we will mention our "friend" as some proof of our moral purity on the matter. Nevermind that we include them in our lives, but rarely ask to be included in theirs. And lastly, some of us may be seeking absolution. White people who truly care have a psychological need for a confessor, but it's not a Person of Color's job to be that person.

Being colorblind doesn't solve the problem, but in fact is a part of it, at least in the sense it can deny racial struggles. Downplaying or saying White privilege doesn't exist may preserve a White person's vision of a post-racial utopia, one they choose to see themselves living in. Saying "all lives matter" is part of that, too. But one person's ideals are another way of being racist. It looks the same on the outside.

One article I came across listed among microaggressions calling someone Black "brother" or "sister." Some friends who are Black have called me brother, and I've returned the endearment with no offense taken. But we should be mindful of it. It's harder for me personally, as I am a Freemason – I have the urge to call all men "Brother" as a sign of respect. And it is a pleasure to use this term for those I know who are Masons (and "Sister" for Eastern Star Sisters). However there is a rare jab I've heard from White Masons that Black Masons are not just a Brother, but a "brutha." Yeah, really clever. Let's let that die.

Much of this comes down to the same question: Does intention matter? From the point of view of the person affected by the words or actions, it may or may not. People have said countless things to me over the years I could have taken offense to. Mind you, they were not relating to the oppressing of a deep-seated identity (usually). They could be jokes or criticisms or sloppy words, but I would only blow a gasket if I knew it was out of intentional disrespect. If someone called me a "cracker", I'd probably joke about it, even if it were a casual slur by a stranger. A typical White person won't have any triggering from such words because they aren't associated with social oppression. But it still hurts that someone would want to hurt your feelings. I've even heard people use epithets in the heat of a moment that exceed their usual prejudices, simply because it was available verbal ammunition. I'm not defending that, just understanding it.

Using inside expressions can be problematic. "Only we can use that word." We could insert our own mocking ethnic appellation (Polack, Deigo, etc.), but you know what I'm talking about. We may consider "nigga" a separate word or a variation more acceptable, a term of endearment. But there are Black people who use the full-on n-word to describe a "lower" tier of those who share their skin color, be it due to lower social class or moral turpitude. This is the Black equivalent of White trash, something White people don't realize is based in hateful historical prejudices. Some White people argue these tendencies make it fair game to use the n-word since they use it against each other. That makes about as much sense as saying cops killing Black people is no big deal because Black people kill each other. People who would never think of themselves as racist say these things, and other White people nod in agreement without really thinking about what's being said.

Being unintentional doesn't make everything okay. You don't have to be a racist to say something racist, but it doesn't take away all responsibility. Let's agree there is a huge difference between not realizing something was insensitive and purposely attacking or degrading someone with a slur. What matters is what the parties involved do with it. The receiver of such things may know there was no ill purpose and hopefully cuts the other person some slack. Then it becomes a teachable moment or a place to initiate change.

If you say something offensive, they may choose to educate you on how they felt hearing you say it. You may even ask them to, if you realize you made a *faux pas*. On the other hand, it's all too easy to be upset for being called out, especially since being seen as even potentially racist is a stigma we can't bear to accept. Or we just shrug it off as being politically incorrect and think "how dare they!" The point is that something *can* be racist when done or said by someone who, for practical purposes, is not a racist. We need to stop thinking about this in terms of blameworthiness and focus on interpersonal and institutional solutions. It's how each of us deals with these situations that counts.

Back when I was a superintendent of an apartment complex, I told a new tenant they were welcome to barbeque in the greenspace behind the building. It elicited the sarcastic response, "You know how us folks love them barbecues!" Brief, awkward laughter ensued. We were fine afterward, but to this day I think he was pretty annoyed in the moment. Some of us might react by being offended by them being offended. I am glad I choose not to, and we became good neighbors. On a side note, like most people, I didn't think food could be a big deal as a race issue. But there is a history behind such stereotypes right down to Cream of Wheat. (Soul food scholar Adrian Miller is publishing a book on this topic in 2021, *Black Smoke: African Americans and the United States of Barbecue.*)

We must address one more thing. There can be a certain power in being offended. When being offended is the only factor in determining that someone or something is offensive – when the offended's opinions always take precedence over the alleged offender – it confers a dangerous privilege. I've seen people look for every excuse possible to be offended, just to receive special treatment, or even just to watch people squirm. It doesn't even have to be about race. It could be a veteran or senior who starts a smear campaign on YouTube because he didn't get a discount, or a "Karen" who wants to speak to the manager because they were given a table too close to the bathroom – or too far away. Any perceived excuse will do. "It was because I am a {fill in the blank}." Like people who cause trouble with fake service animals, it hurts all those on the up-and-up, and gives cover to real perpetrators of offense.

Racial and cultural literacy should be about understanding, not imposing. What is acceptable needs to be accessible. No one should have to take a college course on sensitivity to not offend their fellow human beings. And we need to be more critical of why things are or are not acceptable. But it all starts with at least trying to be aware, being honest, and communicating. It isn't easy, but it doesn't have to be hard. The conversation is the work.

9. The Polish Part of Greece

I sometimes joke that I grew up in a traditional suburban Polish household, meaning we ate Italian food. There were a few things we did heritage-wise, but not many. Polish was a common designation in these parts, so much that the adjacent town of Cheektowaga ("Land of the Crab Apples" in a local Native tongue) was sometimes called Cheektawarsaw. Many Catholic parishes have priests who are from Poland or at least speak Polish, and you may hear Polish hymns on holidays at the very least. There is a "Drive Time Polkas" show on the radio, and there are many Polish-American organizations locally. Polish culture outside of Poland is called *Polonia*, and Buffalo is one of the largest presences of it in the United States, perhaps the world.

Unlike in modern Poland, things like Polkas and Dingus Day are alive and well here. Dingus Day, the Day after Easter, was traditionally where young lasses would chase desirable young men, beating the back of their legs with pussy-willows. The lads in turn threw water on young maidens. I'm not sure how swiping right or left worked back then, but today pussy willows are more for decoration, and in Polish bars, men and women of all ages pack squirt guns. And it's not just Poles. Over the years, the East Side of Buffalo went from being predominantly Polish to heavily African-American. In fact, some of my favorite food at the "Polish" Broadway Market is at McKenzie's Soul Food Shack.

As I started to explore Buffalo (having a license and car by the time I graduated from high school), I also discovered the yearly Greek Festival. It's sometimes known as the Hellenic Festival, which is more accurate because Hellas is the name they call their country in their own language. Greek is still the more official ethnic designation, however. I blame the Romans.

I fell in love. The food. music, dancing, historical displays, artwork, Christian Orthodoxy – it was like I was in another land from another time. And since the whole world always feels like home to me, it was like a reunion with distant family I didn't know how much I missed. I went faithfully each year, and offered to donate my professional services to build and host a website for the festival. It took a year or two, but as my business card was passed around, eventually I was contacted and ended up working with their parish committee for a number of years. Web services aside, I volunteered and worked at the Plaka (food court), the wine shop (where I discovered *retsina*), and even drove the shuttle bus one year. This was a home away from home, even if for just one weekend a year, and I introduced many friends and family to this heavenly slice of culture.

Incidentally, the name of my web design and development company is "Kentropolis". I didn't realize it at first, but some assumed because of the name, I was Greek. People have even mistaken my name as "Ken Tropolis." I usually correct them, and just facetiously explain I am from the Polish part of Greece. Jerry Candiliotis, a dear friend I had made over those years, described me as *philhellene*, a "friend of the Greeks". It has the connotation of a cultural ally. In my heart, that is a great honor. It also meant a lot to me being accepted as part of the team in such a way I was never made to feel as "other". I was adopted as an honorary Greek.

Over these same years, I joined a fraternal organization called the Professional and Businessmen Association (P&BA). It was an evolution of a Polish merchant's association. I felt this would be a great way to get in touch with my Polish roots and make connections in local Polonia. And it was, for a while.

One year, I was asked to fill in for a member of the board of directors who couldn't finish their term. At one of the meetings, we were talking about how we were no longer a Polonia organization. In fact, they asserted that they never were one. This is where you can imagine the sound of a vinyl record scratching to a halt. What were they talking about? Our logo had the Polish eagle. We had events around Polish traditions. An opening prayer and the occasional anecdote or joke was often told in Polish. It even said on our membership application that members agree to support Polish culture.

Apparently, I didn't get the memo. Over recent years, more and more people not of Polish descent had joined. We just had had a president who was Italian (though married to a Pole). It never crossed my mind this would be an issue either way. But those new members didn't perceive the ethnic aspect as part of the group's identity. That's not why they joined. The new generation sees the association as a purely business networking club that happened to be almost entirely Polish in demographics. After all, they were given applications to join irrespective of their last name.

The whole thing really irked me, and I know I wasn't the only one. The argument was that the association was never limited to people of Polish descent. My rebuttal was, so what? If most of the volunteers at the Greek Festival weren't Greek, should they just stop making it about Greek culture? What would be the point? No one seemed offended non-Poles were members, so why assume they would want us to give up our unique ethnic identity?

Heck, the chairman of the Christmas party for many years was Jewish and he didn't care it wasn't a generic "Holiday" party.

Times change, I suppose. New generations of Something-Americans, farther displaced from the old lands, don't seem to place as much value on ethnicity. Or is it the "patriotic" stigma of that damned hyphen? There are still ethnic festivals of all kinds, but is a club with an ethnic label becoming taboo, even if it's inclusive? Maybe when the traditions aren't living anymore, those who do them will be seen as ethnic reenactors, like dress-up Vikings.

But what of deeper things? Are there things we can discern as cultural values? Reading articles in the local Polonia newspaper, the *Am-Pol Eagle*, and talking with people from Poland, I realized where I got some of my values from. Being landed is a big deal, so much so that Poland was the only Communist country to allow personal property. I always had an itch for a square of land to call my own. Tenacity bordering on downright stubbornness runs deep with me. And then there's the sense of nobility in work.

The big thing that caught my eye was tolerance. Poland was the America of the Middle Ages, having open arms to all. There's a reason more Jews lived in Poland than anywhere else in the world until the Shoah. In fact, when the Internet was young, I discovered people with my surname in the 1800s that were Jewish, and a potential *shtetl* namesake was the site of a massacre under the Nazis. The official religion was Roman Catholic, but there was no tiering of rights based on one's faith. Even pagans were allowed to own land. The Inquisition across the rest of Europe was not instituted in any real measure, except under the invading Teutonic Knights. Poland even refused to participate in the Crusades, although the official reason given by King Casimir was that there was no beer in Jerusalem. I can't make this stuff up.

Admittedly, not all Poles I know curb their prejudices, but succumb to typical White American socialization. However, I did find something interesting – an African-American connection to Polish-Americans. The first time I saw my mother's maiden name, Wysocki, in the news, it was from a California newspaper, and the person was a Black football player. My family found it interesting, and we assumed he was adopted. I didn't give it much thought, being adopted myself, and there was no positive or negative value in it for me. Years later, I saw a photograph of Polish-American airmen who went to fly with the Royal Air Force before the United States entered the war. Every last one of them had a Polich name, and every last one was Black. The article where I found it, in *Polonia Today*, explains:

... In my personal opinion, they were sons of mixed Polish-African marriages, which were not so uncommon when the first wave of Polish immigrants reached the American soil. There was a dramatic shortage of Polish brides and Poles were very often called "white niggers" by the WASPs, settlers of White Anglo-Saxon Protestant origin. Hence, the Poles often chose Black women, sharing almost the same social status. Those Poles, the earliest emigrants, were mostly simple farmers for whom black women, born and raised on the cotton fields, were the perfect match.

It continues on:

The word "racism" did not exist in the Polish mentality. Poland was bordered by Christianity, Russian Orthodoxy and Islam. Poles, Russians, Cossacks, Tartars, Turks fought together and they lived together for centuries. They had learned to respect each other's ethnic origin and understand various religious beliefs. The 18th-century Polish Constitution of the 3rd of May was more democratic than the U.S. Constitution of that time. Everybody, no matter what God they prayed to, no matter what the color of their skin was, all had the same rights. There was no Holy Inquisition in Poland; no one was burned at the stake for his own belief in God...

Would I be more protective or prideful of my heritage had I not been adopted? The truth is I have never given thought to biological parentage and I even forget I'm adopted. I once went on for ten minutes about my family's medical history before realizing it wasn't helpful. So I doubt it. Does my globally-inclusive tolerance and appreciation take away my identity as Polish? Does it have to? I still insist on holding Wigilia (Christmas Eve dinner) and break opłatki (a wafer similar to that used in Communion). I even try to sneak in other traditions I researched that had not been passed down to me. We always get our Easter baskets blessed (Święconka), containing the foods for the following breakfast. It's a tradition that has become so popular, non-Polish Catholic churches have started doing it. Sometimes the non-Polish priest could use some counseling on how it's properly done, but appreciation for the effort is granted just the same.

I never did learn more than a smattering of Polish. My parents understood it but did not speak it, even though it was taught in grade school in their days. In choir, my wife and I couldn't form the words fast enough and faked it with a series of retroflex affricates. No one seemed to notice, although there was much debate over the pronunciation of some words given that some ladies descended from speakers of Warsaw Polish, while others were from other dialect regions.

My most interesting discovery was that Polonia culture in Buffalo was different than that of Dunkirk, or at least what I knew of it through my family. All my immediate ancestors had settled and lived in Dunkirk, New York. It's a city the size of Depew (population 12,000) about 40 miles down the coast of Lake Erie from Buffalo, and I spent nearly every Sunday of my childhood there, visiting relatives. Attitudes seemed different, especially with respect to one particular word – "Polack". I grew up where it was a friendly pejorative term of endearment. If I wear a mismatched shirt and pants, I am "such a Polack" to my wife. But as a temporary board member of the Buffalo-Rzeszów Sister Cities program, one of the other members was shocked when I used the word. He explained that it was hurtful, as it was used to demean him as a child growing up in the old Buffalo neighborhood. I apologized, admitted my ignorance, and shared my difference of experience.

The lesson I learned is that the same word that is blunt to one person may cut another, sharply. It's another way subjective reality is still very... well, *real*. Words themselves are just letters and sounds, but the weight of it, great or small, is personal, even if spoken by one's "own kind".

10. Choice and Appropriation

The BBC had called me from London. They had come across an article I had written four years earlier, in 2011, titled "Ethnicity Is a Choice." Moments later, I was being interviewed live on world radio, along with Camille Z. Charles, a professor of Africana Studies. Born of one Black and one White parent, she chose to self-identify as Black, which she explained was based heavily on how others perceived her. I believe I was included to provide a counterpoint.

We were put on the air because of an odd incident at that time – the head of an NAACP chapter was "outed" as a White person "passing" as Black. What would I do? For the record, I do not believe in deception. If one self-identifies, they should be honest about what that means. If I would have been asked to be president of my college's Black Student Union or Latin-American Student Organization, I would have turned it down. I would not consider myself capable of fully representing another's ethnic experience. I would fear it would cause confusion, suspicion, and be complicit in the derision of others toward myself and my friends – my "people" in a deeper-than-skin sense.

But I am not in the controversial woman's shoes. It's not my place to judge. If we want to impose limits on ethnic identity, what shall we choose? The quadroon yardstick, which serves race activists and bigots alike? Is it really any better if people already under a label make such rules who must wait outside?

Oddly, we didn't talk about the incident in those brief moments, but were set up for a debate. There was common ground. We concurred that ethnic identity isn't rigidly genetic. The opposing assertions were that ethnicity was primarily self-identified or a matter of strict social distinctions. For a start, I mentioned that such labels are amorphous and ever-changing.

When I suggested that people self-identify all the time, the radio host laughed incredulously. I gave the example of someone adopted into a family of another genetic heritage, and living in a neighborhood of a third culture. How are they supposed to identify? Don't they have choices? But that's an uncommon example. Most people self-identify in some basic way, but it does not seem so because it is rarely questioned.

We may have a specific nationality (a legal-political distinction), but any number of ethnicities. Sometimes people change nationality and embrace a new ethnicity. Some are adopted and claim ethnicity loosely but not in practice. For example, I had to remind a young lady I know that she was Polish.

The fact she was adopted from China was irrelevant – she grew up in the Polish-American ethnicity and didn't know a lick about Chinese culture. And that should be okay. In contrast, I grew up Polish (adopted from an unknown lineage) but embrace a combination of cultures, including Chinese. If I had been adopted from Kenya, I'd still be Polish by name, Black, and might take up the bagpipes and eat haggis. Well ... maybe not haggis.

In America and other countries, people self-identify on the census their race and ethnicity, choices being what they may. This also applies to religion, which is an aspect of ethnicity. If you choose to see yourself as a Jedi, it's your choice. In fact, numbers for Jedi rank between Jewish and Pagan in Great Britain's census. Admittedly, someone dressed as Obi-Wan on the weekend for a charity gig (done that) isn't a challenge to society. Someone who didn't grow up a particular ethnicity who wants to be a leader in a self-advocacy group based on it may have trouble.

It can be a hard reality for countless people of "mixed parentage" where both ethnic groups shun them for not belonging. They can't get past the bouncer at either door. My Native-American-slash-German stepbrothers are a perfect example. And sometimes it's a win-win. Both "Asians" and "Blacks" claim Tiger Woods as "one of their own". On a less coloured note, my daughter is mostly Polish by percent and slightly Irish by blood, but sees herself as mostly Irish – as is the neighborhood she grew up in. She's also Jewish by birthright, and could explore that with impunity, but then anyone can convert even if they didn't trace it back on their mother's bloodline.

Ethnicity is collectively defined and redefined, being partially or even not-at-all based on historical fact. For example, the movement in Southwest America called "National Council of La Raza" calls for the reclaiming of whole states by Mexico – on the grounds of aboriginal bloodlines. Never mind the whole Cortez thing. I wonder if those claiming Toltec heritage will want all of Mexico back if La Raza succeeds in taking back lands they consider theirs. This whole thing cannot logically be about blood – there are many, many Americans who (allegedly) have a Cherokee or two among their distant ancestors. And yet few consider themselves Native by ethnicity. My step-family is Seneca. They don't speak the tongue, wear the clothes, live on a reservation (currently), or go to Longhouse. They are as Baptist as La Raza is Catholic. And the Aztecs didn't speak Spanish as their first language last time I checked. La Raza is an intentional ethnicity at its heart.

And what of Kwanzaa? The holiday didn't exist before 1966. It's based in African principles, recreating meaning from a lost heritage. It's an intentionally created ethnic schema. And I think it's great. Someone has to start a tradition, even a family tradition, at some point. And Christmas? That combination of pagan holidays and rituals from across Europe? Heck, we might not have Christmas trees as a thing in America if it weren't for a German Prince Albert marrying Queen Victoria of England!

The lesson here is that we create and mould our culture, both individually and collectively. It happens over generations and centuries. Nearly everything comes from somewhere else, or many places. We can resist change all we want, but it will never be exactly the same from generation to generation. We may as well appreciate that and participate in the process.

But some things are not only about how one sees themselves, but how they are viewed by society. From Negro freemen to dark-skinned Europeans or Asian Indians, skin color is the visually obvious distinction and first impression. And yet the appellation "African-American" only applying to longstanding descendants of Africans and not newer immigrants is a recent yet real phenomenon. If one is from Haiti, maybe it could go either way if the French part of one's accent is suppressed. Or maybe you could just say you're Creole and fit in finely in some parishes of Louisiana. These become almost arbitrary distinctions in some situations.

However, we should not forget that being African-American is intimately tied with the "Black Experience" – one that has been dictated directly and indirectly for too long by White society. There are African-Americans that in isolated cases have had little such experience, and some "outsiders" actually have. But the point is that in general, all Black people are treated similarly by social convention. But why should we accept any of this just because it is currently so?

Accepting the judgments of the larger society to dictate one's ethnicity is a set of mental chains forged within. Sharing a common hardship is apparently why some People of Color will acknowledge each other in public, even if they've never met before. (Then again, according to my wife, so do people wearing Red Sox jerseys.) But it's more than that. Concepts of race not only reflect aspects created through circumstance by White society, but are policed and enforced from within. A social worker friend of mine at the VA recovery center where I teach Tai Chi bared his soul on this. He grew up and lives in the African-American community, yet he is shunned because he is (gasp!) Republican. Being Catholic instead of Baptist doesn't help, either.

My friend Alexander, who I met years ago on the set of a movie we were in together, confronts a version of this. When people hear he is from the

East Side, they assume he has connections for drugs. When other African-Americans learn he's from "the hood" but doesn't share the expected inner-city accent, some question his Blackness. Many are scolded for not "being {insert race or ethnicity here} enough", or even accused of trying to be White, however that may be defined. Truthfully, many White people think "improving" the Black man's conditions means making them more like him. Many of these divisive conventions have been internalized from generations of oppression. And it's natural that any Person of Color would learn to self-identify primarily with their personal traumas unique to their experience of place within society.

The question is to what extent there is a choice. We cannot blame people for falling into social expectations and longstanding identities. But we must expose them for what they are and allow people such choices. Perhaps ethnicity not being experienced as a choice but an unavoidable fact is why some are territorial about it.

British nurses doing their version of a Māori haka (a war chant of sorts) against COVID-19 went from inspirational to apologetic the moment someone accused them of appropriation. There is also a concern about facets of this currently-trending culture being used for product advertisements. As ethics are contextual, these are two very different uses, but you can see this isn't simple.

Chinese families own most of the Buffalo-area restaurants featuring Eastern Cuisine, be it Korean, Japanese, Mongolian, and of course, Chinese. Then again, the Greek festival has served shishkabob, but don't you dare bring up its Turkish origin. Every aspect of a typical country's culture – food, music, dance, architecture, language, customs – is influenced by and influences other cultures. Arabic numerals are almost universal, as are word-forms for "taxi" and "coffee". Reggae rhythms are derived from beats used in traditional West African dance. To be against appropriation altogether is to convict most of humanity over most of its history for just being human.

But not all appropriation is benign. Blackface has a long, winding history. The minstrel shows were definitely crude, even mocking caricatures, but then there became a demand for Negro culture on the stage and screen. Sadly, this demand wasn't for actual Negroes, but – like men taking on women's roles before they were allowed to be thespians – White audiences were entertained by White approximations of the Black man's singing and dancing. In 1933, Mickey Mouse and friends were portrayed in a blackface animated production based on Harriet Beecher Stowe's "Uncle Tom's Cabin". Eventually, styles were co-opted altogether, with a White Elvis basically cashing Little Richard's paycheck.

The People's Republic of China is an example of one-sided appropriation standards. Recently, a professor gave out gifts of chocolate turkeys to celebrate American Thanksgiving. That didn't go over well. He apologized, but peers argued that China embraces the notion of Chinese Lunar New Year being celebrated abroad as a "Chinese cultural export" – why not allow imports? The answer is ethnocentric political pressures couched in condemnation of decadence and religion. Perhaps only mainland China would consider Thanksgiving too religious.

Bruce Lee was the barrier-breaker for Asians to come onto the big screen and into livingroom TVs. But even he was replaced by David Carradine when it came to portraying *Kwai Chang Caine*. Almost 50 years later, we are having a discussion about voice actors portraying other ethnicities in animated works. I'm not sure if that's taking it too far, but at least we are trying to be respectful.

Maybe I shouldn't talk. I've been a cultural magpie my whole life. I was into the whole ancient Egypt thing in early grade school, but I mean living cultures. In a way, learning French fits this discussion. I chose it (after taking Latin) because I figured a lot of the world knew it (much of Africa, Southeast Asia, etc.). However, what I hear from travelers is that unless you do it flawlessly and to someone in a charitable mood, it will irritate people in France, or among Québécois. I have not experienced this personally, but it seems the opposite end from talking in Japanese, where the slightest honest attempt will be met with gratitude and encouragement. Appropriation seems invariably subjective.

Since high school, I've loved Asian culture, particularly Chinese and Japanese. I study martial arts closely derived from them. We decorate for Lunar New Year in our house and we have door guardians (nicknamed Bill and Ted). I've worn Chinese outfits over the years, even for my wedding. My wedding was quite eclectic, with music in Latin, Polish, and English, and the Kyrie... well, in the obvious tongue for that. Is this appropriation? Must I be Scottish to wear a kilt? (Asking for a friend.)

I also took on an African name for a while. I warned you in the introduction that I have no sense of where inside or outside the box is, so bear with me. The first wedding in which I stood up, or actually even attended now that I think about it, was for my friend Janet. We lost touch when she graduated, but we shared many a meal in the Porterview Room (as the dining hall at D'Youville was called back then). I remember one time her coming up to me, upset. She said that "people were talking". Apparently loaning her my car a number of times provoked a rumor we were sleeping together. It wasn't true, but I honestly had no idea why we should care – or why anyone would care. Only now in writing this book do I wonder if it was her being Black, rather than an older woman (no offense if you're reading this Janet). On a side note, I recently found an editorial I wrote for the school paper that mentions comments made about an interracial couple at a school dance. A copy is in the back of this book.

Anyway, it was a huge wedding party, but someone didn't show up so I filled in. The officiant was an "African priest", meaning of an African aboriginal faith tradition. His name was Kenyatta, which he informed me was Swahili for "piecing spear of fire". It was his first name, though it is more known as a respected surname. I used it so much it ended up on mailing lists for years – magazine subscriptions, even credit cards. Not sure why I stopped (sometime in the 1990s), but part of me still feels like it's as much my name as Ken or Kenneth or Kenny. Definitely more than Kenny.

America itself is a massive appropriator. The national anthem is an English tune (and in English nonetheless!), the Statue of Liberty is French, and Country Music without Spanish guitar ... well, you get the picture. At least we have Levis, Football (ahem ... *American* football, not "soccer"), processed cheese, and pretty much invented the Internet. But who's keeping score? Almost every invention or discovery in history happened first in China, anyway. But this is bigger than the American melting pot, or British footholds in every corner of the globe. In the end, aren't all achievements a collaboration of the sum of mankind's collective knowledge?

Sometimes appropriation is for profit. That's a different situation ethically, or at least more complicated. There's a backlash, for example, of White people doing and teaching Yoga. Like many martial arts, these practices were sometimes borrowed and imitated rather than handed down. It's no coincidence Karate came to America after World War II and Tae Kwon Do after the Korean War – it was brought back by members of our military stationed there. Sometimes it wasn't authentic, or was piecemeal, or modified to military attitudes and American tastes. Of course, there were and are traditional teachers available for these. These may be honored by such interest, or feel cheated personally as a businessman or culturally on behalf of their heritage.

I don't have a solution, but clearly, honesty of provenance is important. My first martial arts teacher opened up a world to me and was extremely skilled. But the story of how he learned changed over time into utter fantasies about being a Shaolin priest. Years after I dissociated myself from him, I found him claiming to be a Tibetan Lama. After investigating the claims personally and even talking to his family and friends growing up, I found it all to be a lie. But his *kung fu* looked good. It worked. And it makes up some of my central skill sets. So when I teach Chinese-style martial arts, am I a fraud if I'm honest that I have no direct lineage? I make it a point to be transparent about my various teachers and their credentials. And I encourage people who want to go deeper into more traditional aspects to seek and find a lineaged "master" – a title I myself eschew for the reasons above.

But in general, almost every culture plays some part in American culture. No human experience is separate from World history and culture. From Immanuel Kant to the Hague Convention, all heritage has been declared Human heritage. Sadly it's human to be territorial, hoarding our culture, or denying ourselves a larger identity for fear of losing our specific identity. Am I any less Polish for embracing Chinese culture to the point I wore a *darn jian* and red outfit with frog buttons at my own wedding? Or am I better off, taking a fuller advantage of the diverse richness of human culture?

Yes, more and more, ethnicity is a choice, conscious or not. Not only do we accept or reject any particular identity (or identities) but establish and help mould existing ones by our own individualism – our choices. What about myself? Ultimately I am a citizen of the world, and every people's story is my story. It's OUR story. So if ethnicity equals culture, and culture truly is a choice, mine is for all-you-can-eat heritage buffet. Not a bad choice, I think.

Even so, ethnicity is also a matter of pride, however one chooses to slice it in one's favor. Tiger woods is Black to African-Americans, and Asian to people of Far Eastern descent. Obama is revered in Hawaii and Kenya alike. My brother has a friend at work who is Dominican. He makes it clear he is Black around African-Americans, but *not*-Black around White people or Latinx. He's like the Korean shopowner in Spike Lee's *Do the Right Thing*. I'm not sure if a joke about having your cake and eating it too fits, but that's the malleability of ethnicity, even if you look and are treated the same on the macro-social level.

Ultimately this isn't choice about how to define ethnicity, but who gets to do so. Who we are individually helps collectively define the ethnicity itself. That's why it's ever-changing and often confusing. But if we do not choose, the choice WILL be made by others. So make it a good one.

11. What Privilege?

Nothing triggers my White friends more than saying the words "White privilege". The immediate response, if they are willing to continue the conversation at all, is "What privilege? I had to work hard for what I have!" I can get some of them to nod in agreement with every aspect of what it really means, but the word has such stigma. When not understood, it feels like an assumption and accusation against the individual, and all White people.

I was first exposed to the phrase not long ago. The concept has been around forever, but that term became a thing, along with "male privilege", thanks to women's-studies scholar Peggy McIntosh in the 1980s. But like most scholarly ideas, the general public doesn't really care or talk about it, and it's considered something only taught in the college classroom, if at all. I never even heard the term (or noticed it?) until a couple of years ago.

Most people take offense because (to them) it implies they had some advantage in life others did not. And that's hard to swallow if you've had a hard life and had to claw your way to any level of financial security. Color had nothing to do with that from their point of view. However, we would probably all agree that rich people often had some advantage, being born into a "privileged" household with no question of better education, access to connections and capital, or even just the whole silver spoon inheritance paradigm. So when WE are told we have it – and it does feel like a dirty accusation – it puts the shoe on the other foot.

It bothers me for a very different reason. Maybe it's my philosophy degree. Justice in a sense is giving everyone their due. Privilege implies I'm being given something extra. That might not be fair, but it's not the same as taking away from someone else. So what are we talking about? I do not consider it a privilege to be treated like a human being instead of a criminal or animal by strangers, banks, law enforcement, or employers. I consider my opportunities and ability to participate in my community and economy a right, not a privilege. And taking away that privilege, if we use the term this way, doesn't help those who do not have it. It almost makes me feel like I should be ashamed NOT to be oppressed, going back to White guilt. So what was I missing? Is the term just a way to blame people like me for someone else's less desirable station in life?

It doesn't feel right, so we look to rationalize it away. Those not born into affluence yet attained it must have pulled themselves up by their bootstraps. And any anecdote of a Black man "rising from the ghetto" is seen as proof of the American Dream, with a fair meritocracy clearly in place. Any challenge of that is a slap in Uncle Sam's face. Or maybe it's an excuse to avoid considering there may be a real disparity of opportunity. Most of us probably haven't given thought to it, or just have an opinion and dig our heels in.

But even that isn't how the word is actually used in everyday life. I was shocked at how simple it was once I looked into it. But please don't judge White people too harshly. The million little things we White people take for granted are truly invisible to us. Do we have to look for a special section to buy foods we grew up with because they are considered separate ("ethnic")? Can we easily find a doll or action figure that is our child's skin tone? If we go to a social gathering, is there a chance of being the only person of our ethnicity? This isn't the White man's fault in any direct way, but the result of being in a majority. It's like doors opening a certain way that benefits right-handed people and is harder for the ten percent who are not.

These aren't vicious acts or bad intentions but thoughtless oversights. There is much room for consideration on the part of corporations and institutions to fix that. It's very much like countering ableist privilege by making sure there is proper public access to those who are physically diverse, such as those who use a wheelchair or read braille. In the case of race, most don't even try, or are only making inclusive options available recently. And hey, a bunch of White folks invited a Person of Color to a gala to begin with, right? How nice. But then someone assumes they are "the help" and hands them their coat.

Let's look further. Are you watched with suspicion when you go into a store? Did the Supreme Court have to decide you have the same rights as other people? And what about "hate crime" laws? Shouldn't illegal actions just be illegal? You'd think that's an advantage to be a special "protected" class, but what kind of world do we live in where such a thing is even necessary? Maybe it is more than what is realized by those of us who don't live with it.

Affirmative action helps in some ways, but not as much as people think and has drawbacks. In practice, such policies rarely apply or are rarely contested, and the biggest recipients of such consideration are now White women. But there's still a consequence. Will your co-workers assume you got the job because of pressure to hire a minority? Will someone wonder if you only got into a good college because of a diversity initiative?

Even if a White person has not missed an opportunity personally, they are convinced other White people are losing jobs and other opportunities. And this goes back farther than people realize – all the way to the Reconstruction. Some of the hate groups from that time had White employment as a significant concern. But today, the odds of missing out based on being White is pretty slim. Where companies have very tight hiring systems, such as the local car manufacturing plants, your only good chance to get hired is to be related to someone who already works there (or so I am told).

But isn't affirmative action racist, or at least unfair? It depends how you look at it. Supreme Court Justice Harry Blackmun refuted the idea that affirmative action constituted unacceptable discrimination, saying "In order to get beyond racism, we must first take account of race. There is no other way. And in order to treat some persons equally, we must treat them differently." This is the equity versus equality argument and would be considered anti-racist by Kendi's model, where adjusting toward equality supersedes maintaining a status quo that results in overall inequity.

Before giving it thought, my naive self argued that instead of giving bonus points on entrance tests and job applications for being a minority (or woman), we equalize the education system so that there is an equal chance to be equally qualified. After all, hiring quotas as a goal isn't unreasonable if the purpose is to have employees that fairly represent the community they serve. This is especially important in the area of law enforcement.

But I'm not naive anymore. I know that education and intelligence tests have some degree of cultural bias, and that less qualified candidates are still statistically chosen over minority applicants. There is what can even be described as occupational segregation, and not just in fields like STEM. If you have a restaurant with only one African-American employee, the odds are they are the dishwasher. Please tell me I'm wrong.

And things aren't getting better. For this and other reasons, African-American wealth has decreased over the last three decades to a level lower than during the Civil Rights movement of the 1960s. Affirmative action is at worst a band-aid effort to artificially even the odds. It's philosophically and politically problematic, as best expressed in The New Yorker:

> [The] paradox of the civil-rights movement is that outlawing racial discrimination made it harder to remediate its effects. Once we amended the Constitution and passed laws to protect people of color from being treated differently in ways that were harmful to them, the government had trouble enacting programs that treat people of color differently in ways that might be beneficial. We took race out of the equation only to realize that, if we truly wanted not just equality of opportunity for all Americans but equality of result, we needed to put it back in.

This is one more example of where colorblindness doesn't serve us well. It makes hiring and firing about race enough that in some companies, it is the knee-jerk accusation for being let go, regardless of an actual offense. This further hurts perceptions that fuel racism. In a twist of consequences, some manufacturers lobbied against getting rid of affirmative action. The (predominantly White) seniority system of unions was preventing the hiring of much-needed workers. On another positive note, affirmative action fits into the schema of anti-racism in that at least some effort is being made instead of just hoping at being non-discriminatory.

Another argument against privilege is that "we've all been discriminated against." This may mean historically, which doesn't calculate, since we're talking about the present. My father was openly warned at his first job that he would never become management because he was Polish. I can't imagine that happening today, openly or otherwise. Maybe I am missing something, but I really have no idea where other White people are coming from when they say things like "C'mon, you're Polish – you should know better than to think privilege is real."

Other aspects of privilege are about tendencies of disadvantage. Did you grow up with both parents present? Was either of them heavy drug users or alcoholics? Have any of your immediate family members been incarcerated? Have you ever went to bed hungry? The list is longer, but let's stop there. Take almost any two groups of Whites and African-Americans and compare the prevalence of these things. It's like we're living in two different Americas. Take any given individual and you may not see it; take a survey of more than a few and it's clear cut. Realizing this, White people have to decide if it's due to some matter of cultural deficiency or superiority, or if there is some system in play, intentional or not, that "keeps the Black Man down".

But aren't there dirt-poor White communities who suffer these characteristics? Some. We might even consider generational poverty in these areas to be systemic, and a form of intraracial prejudice – against those "on the wrong side of the tracks". But that would be apples to oranges. If a White person moves *across* the tracks, or better yet to another town, they are more likely to have a fresh start. Hiding their previous address is not the same as hiding their skin color.

The other day, I was reading an old issue of *Smithsonian* and came across a snippet about the paper wasp. Like all social insects, they have two castes, the reproductive and non-reproductive members of a hive. They have very different distinct functions and privileges, and yet are genetically identical. As an occasional beekeeper (and being honest here have more book knowledge than experience) I know that the way a queen is made is by feeding an ordinary female larva a bee-produced substance known as royal jelly. For the paper wasp, all of the female larvae could become queens, but adults beat on the nest walls with their antennae. This vibration inhibits a larva's fat storage, which guides their genetic expression into that of a worker.

I keep thinking there's a metaphor to be had here. In what ways does society give off "vibrations" that inhibit the advancement of some "castes" of people? Does this happen before one's birth even? Forget whose fault it is. Society often runs on instinct and auto-pilot inertia. But only if we can find ways in which this is true, can we intelligently talk about dismantling the structures that preserve this arrangement.

12. Music and Language

I must have been four or five years old. It was a particularly long line to get on some ride in Disney World, and a crowd within the line formed a circle of sorts. I have no idea who they were or where they were from, but they started chanting and clapping and dancing to pass the time. I couldn't help but dance, too, to my mother's embarrassment. The reassurance of one of the women who noticed this was clear: "Let him dance!"

I've always loved music, but mostly as a listener. I didn't take well to the accordion, practicing on the one my father used as a youth. At age 11, he was the first person in Dunkirk to play music publicly during Lent, in a bar no less. Very little of what he played was polkas. One time I came home to what I thought was a recording at first – my father playing *Flight of the Bumblebee* on accordion. But I never took to it. I even tried the violin for a bit, but it seemed like an hour of surgery just to tune and rosin it. To this day my wife forbids me from bringing my harmonica while camping. But I do love music – all genres, all cultures, all time periods. Growing up, I basically listened to whatever was at hand, and followed my father's tastes more than my schoolmates. My grandmother would complain about the "boom-boom-boom" of the music played by Puerto Ricans two doors down from her house, all the while my father and grandfather tapping their feet under the table. He had a Gloria Estaphan phase and whenever I hear her music, I think of him.

We may say music defines a culture, but how can it define people, especially in America? I remember walking down the streets near my college dormitory on the West Side. Within a single block, I could hear Spanish horns, Rap, and Classic Rock. There are origins, influences, and crossovers in "American" music, if there even is such a thing. And we might say certain ethnicities listen to music from their origins, but even that can get muddy. For example, Polkas are associated with being Polish, but not in Poland (they prefer pop and swing from what I hear), and it's mostly "old people music" unless mixed with Rock flavor in bands like Those Idiots or Weird Al.

Some people frame the morality of African-American culture on the merits of "their" music, but what does that even mean? Are we talking about Lionel Ritchie? I know, the target here is Rap, or Gangsta if you want to get specific. The argument is that "their" music sets the tone for immoral, criminal behavior. Maybe there's a tiny bit of truth to that, even though parents have been complaining about their kids' music and its effects since Rome tried to outlaw the lute. And that Negro music that became "Rock and Roll" (slang for copulation) was definitely a bad influence on all our grandparents.

Joking aside, I don't buy it. Because I know.

I'm the guy who always surprised people when I finish lines to "their" song lyrics. I followed "Black music" since my interest in breakdancing in the early 1980s. Before that, I scoured my parent's music collection, which included artists such as Nat King Cole (on vinyl) and Dione Warwick and Diana Ross (on cassette). But even rapping didn't register as a race thing. I still remember most of the lyrics to Debbie Harry's "Rapture", and I didn't give it a thought to her being White. And this music certainly wasn't unknown to White folks, even before the Run DMC / Aerosmith crossover, "Walk This Way". Then again, MTV rarely played artists of color, arguably because of how they defined "Rock", until Rick James and David Bowie called them to task. Michael Jackson and the reception to his music blew that door open for good. As a teen, I was oblivious to the politics of all of it. It was just music to me.

I never thought of Black music as separate from the rest of the music of that time. Sure, Motown was a genre along with what eventually gave way to Hip Hop, and I may have come across tiny hints of history about that at most. It was really when I started driving after high school and listening to the car radio regularly that musical segregation took form in my mind. Why? There was an unabashedly African-American station, WBLK 93.7 FM, that quickly became my favorite preset. It still is, actually. However, at one point they seemed to back off from the format and I was getting more of the "Black music" I wanted to hear on my second-favorite station, WKSE 98.5 FM.

In edginess, some of the music went beyond LL Cool Jay (and way beyond Ton Loc) to strong messages, like "Pump Your Fist" by Kool Moe Dee. I often got my fix from classmates from "The City" (New York City), as WBLK was more Black pop artists. The messages weren't aimed at someone like me, but I recognized and appreciated it as a voice I wouldn't ever hear in my existing circles. By the time Gangsta hit its peak, I wasn't listening to much radio unless someone else had it. Maybe something softcore like "Hey, ya!" by Outkast (André 3000) would catch my eye on MTV, or I'd discover Digable Planets on a boom box while working in a warehouse. But otherwise, I either dug into my New Age MP3 collection at my desk, or became second-hand fans of my daughter's music as she blossomed from boy bands to modern folk. Christina now writes and performs, and her first album will come out if we ever get over COVID-19. One of her showstoppers is a Regina Specktor-esque version of "Slim Shady" by Eminem.

A few years back, I got to talking music with a vet at the recovery center. His name was Jerome, which was easy to remember because it's my father's name and my middle name. People are sometimes amused by that, as it's a name more common among African-Americans. Anyway, I found out he was a DJ contractor with the Department of Defense. Somehow we got to talking about rappers from Long Island, like EPMD and LL Cool J. (I've actually been to the Brentwood-Islip area.) That might be a bit obscure, or a random coincidence of shared experience, but it's one more friendly place we could connect.

My dearth of Black music ended a few years ago, when I did some driving for Lyft in my spare time. Ridesharing is one of the most fun things I've ever done. My daughter talked me into it, knowing I loved driving and loved meeting people whenever and wherever I find them. The radio was on once more. And my two tried and true stations were still there.

On a side note, in my discussions with other rideshare drivers, I found that many avoid Buffalo's "East Side", considered the "bad" part of town. They express their choice in terms of not wanting "problem" passengers, or may even whisper (dog whistle?) about fear of crime. You can guess the demographics. But I never had a problem. I'm not a fan of the trademarked version of the *Law of Attraction*, but when you have a positive mindset, and treat others with respect, people do respond to it. It's hard to be upset with someone serving you when your sincere care for them shines through. And if you expect trouble at every turn, people feel that, too. Personally, I go out of my way to work in that area because I know it's underserved – not just because of fearful drivers in ridesharing, but as a community in general.

One of the easiest ways to start a conversation and even develop a bond is talking about music. What I found was that passengers had very little predictability in their music tastes based on race. Many African-American passengers, especially older ones, didn't like Gangsta or Rap currently on the charts (I did). One young African-American woman asked to listen to the Country Music station, WYRK. Some liked classic Rock. Only those wearing headphones seemed to be into harder Rap, and kept it to themselves.

To be clear, I don't feed off the negative messaging that does clearly exist in some music. But I can still appreciate it like a really good actor playing the bad guy in a movie. And sometimes we have to stretch the shadows of our personalities and just enjoy it. That's my excuse, anyway. Thanks, Carl Yung.

Justin Easton, an international booking agent and tour manager, gave me some much-needed education about skinhead culture. Contrary to popular notions, it has roots in Jamaican Reggae music, a heavy influence to this day. The stereotype of being racist didn't happen until the late 1970s or early 1980s. As a response, "SHARP" (Skin Heads Against Racist Prejudice) was formed. Many British and American skinheads were vehemently anti-fascist, as their fathers and grandfathers had fought in WWII. (This is a conflict even among people in the Aryan Front, who were not all skinheads and included many politicians and pastors.) To this day, Easton says, "If a Bonehead (racist skinhead) shows up, it's gonna be a bad time ... it's gonna be a riot." But the stigma of the racist element prevailed in today's extreme anti-racist sensitivity. Roger Miret of Agnostic Front, after the last show before COVID-19 lockdowns, had a skinhead forehead tattoo removed.

Another tangent I'd like to mention that's not specifically about music is Skateboard Culture. A lifelong skater I know (more of a cyclist these days) told me how the White skaters from the suburbs had an alliance of sorts with African-American skaters on the other side of the city line. In addition to a common passion or sport, they were all targeted by police for the usual loitering, trespassing, etc.. It turns out skateboarding IS a crime in some places, either codified or de facto, but also transcends race.

Something special happened last year that brought back music memories. My daughter got hired to transcribe a book for lifelong music promoter and artist, Gene "Poo Poo Man" Anderson. He was there at the very beginning of Hip Hop, and it was a pleasure to talk with him about things that were going on behind the scenes of the music I grew up with. I would have never known any of that. Most people still don't, so I'm giving a shameless plug here for *The Birth of Hip Hop – Rapper's Delight: The Gene Anderson Story*. He talks about the culture of the industry when he started and pushback against Hip Hop until it was too hot to *not* handle. It was working on that project where I discovered my wife can recite all the words to *Rapper's Delight* by the Sugar Hill Gang. I thought she was only into music like The Police and Peter Gabriel!

When my daughter transcribed the book and I was chosen as the publisher, I had to make a call about the language used. Calling his wife "a little thang" is not the same as saying she was a little *thing*. Should I "clean up" the grammar to make it conform to formal English? We decided against it, the reasoning explained in the back of the book:

> This particular book was written entirely through voice transcription, and every effort was made to be true to the unique voice and intention of the author with only the most necessary edits. There will be no

apology for what some may consider improper grammar, as the language preserved here is a legitimate and longstanding American dialect, as important to the times and culture of the subject matter as any other detail.

Like culture, no one owns language. Even the dictionary is not supposed to be an authoritative standard, but a *description* of how language is currently used. That's why they add new words and change old ones. It's because they are being honest and observant, rather than some imagined political pressure against "correct" English that needs to be avenged. Some do believe language should be defended as culturally immutable. Any evolution or impurity or foreign influence is anathema.

France comes to mind, where language has always been part of their politics. French is their official language, and they codify right up to their constitution what other languages are recognized or allowed in some settings. Things got much more complicated with the forming of the European Union. But it's the strict preservation of French by the likes of the Académie Française I'm talking about here. They were founded in 1635 as an official authority on the language, but people do what they want to do. Culture waits for no one's permission, as hard as some try. They are also responsible for almost ridiculous efforts to prevent the Anglicisation of French, scolding anyone who dares to say things like "*ce weekend*", or more recently, "*un selfie.*" I'm sorry, but "*le sandwich*" just makes more sense than "*quelque chose au milieu de deux morceaux de pain*".

America has no official language. Our culture is English-speaking dominant, and Spanish is the next common language in various parts of the country. English speakers may get bent out of shape having to "press one" but we are unique in that respect. The joke goes that if you speak two languages you are bilingual; if you speak three or more you are multilingual; if you speak only one language you are American. And language is one more way we want to define America in only our image, telling people who speak in other languages to "go back where you came from" – even if they are Native American.

We have many dialects, collectively known as "General American English". It is distinct enough from British that some companies serving American consumers have moved their call centers from places like India (with their British colonial accent) to the Philipines (a former protectorate of the United States). The attempt at an "average" that all Americans can understand most easily is the "Broadcast English" taught and encouraged for radio and television. Also known as Network English or Network Standard, it avoids the peculiarities of any regional accents, not sounding like you're from anywhere in particular. It's perhaps closest to how English is spoken in the Mid-West. An acquaintance of mine, Bob Lewis, was the voice of the Emergency Broadcast System as well as other radio announcing, and can turn off his Southern accent in favor of Broadcast at any time.

But what about Ebonics? Is that really a thing, or is it made up to justify bad grammar? I tend to take on the accent and mannerisms of the people around me. I was once told a friend was impressed I spoke "Jive". I do slip into that frame of speech, but try not to, as it could be taken the wrong way. However, it is NOT a poor, uneducated rendition of English – it has its own distinct, consistent rules. The verb constructs come from West Africa, actually. It's a composite of that and Southern American Colonial English. Its linguistic name is African American Vernacular English (AAVE), also known as Gullah. It's actually in the same ballpark as Creole. And its continued existence around the country (instead of an isolated region) is a testimony to lingering segregation. African-Americans are judged by the presence or lack of this accent, both from without and within. As a whole, America sees this in need of correction in our schools, in favor of what one friend of mine calls professionally expected "interview English".

With further regard to language, our diversity of immigration can be problematic. We deride people for not learning English, forgetting our great-grandmother only spoke the language of the Old Country. After a generation or so, all people learn English. In the meantime, we have people from all over the world speaking in their native tongues. Being employed may require an employer's patience, an interpreter, or working with other employees who speak the new person's language. This happened to most of our ancestors, and it works itself out in the end.

Language, ancestral or currently used, speaks to each person's identity. Sharing these differences can bring people together. My wife takes the stance that if you want to come to America, you should be expected to keep up your lawn and teach her how to cook your cuisine. Like family recipes, even a swear word or two can be passed between neighbors on the back deck over a beer.

To put out the welcome sign to all those who pass my house, I have a Peace Pole in the front yard. These markers with the words "May Peace Prevail on Earth" in multiple languages can be found around the world (including my alma mater's campus, where I found the idea). I thought about having the phrase in Gaelic, Polish, and others, but in the end, I chose the four languages actually spoken by people in my neighborhood, English, Spanish, Arabic, and Chinese. You can find out more at WorldPeace.Org.

I think I need to explore more languages, and not just linguistically or for scriptural exegesis. When I can, I converse a bit in French online, and yet I'm more likely to run into someone speaking some form of Spanish in real life. But it seems language also segregates people, as I have found myself, without trying, in almost exclusively English-speaking circles. Let's see what the upcoming years hold for me, and for America.

13. Dimensions of Faith

I went to Saint Mary's High School, a private Catholic school in Lancaster, New York. On a wall in the foyer was an African art version of a crucifix. I thought it was neat, and figured there was no harm in anyone depicting a religious figure or deity in their own cultural style. But as much as it seemed out of place to a student body nearly devoid of ethnic diversity – and did elicit a few comments or ignorant snickers – we never questioned our own depictions of the Christ. Interestingly, the earliest images of the Good Shephard were in Greek catacombs, sans beard. The Renaissance took anachronistic liberties – paintings featured Medieval clothing and architecture. To be fair, Jesus of Nazareth probably didn't look like Chaka Zulu, but he didn't look like Ewan McGregor as Obi-Wan Kenobi from the prequels either.

I went on to become a trained catechist and taught religious education ("faith formation") to teens in preparation for their Confirmation as Christian adults. I was surprised by what I got away with, as I had no qualms about allowing other viewpoints and sharing ideas from other faith traditions. I always say there are two types of Christians, hypocrites and heretics, and I ain't no hypocrite! One thing I learned early in life was the gulf between what we know of other traditions in theory and how they actually are practiced. In the spring, I brought in my friend Larry to do a proper Seder (Passover meal) for my class. Before this time, I had been to ones put on by my religion teachers, but they turned out in retrospect to be vague approximations, and not just the Christianized versions. (I personally love having Ceder and have thought of making an interfaith version of it for my family, if such a thing can be done without losing its unique spiritual and emotional content.)

One of my students, Michelle George-Yates, went on to become a Unitarian Universalist minister. Her great-grandmother was a Jewish immigrant. When she settled in Holland, New York, attending a Christian church was her way of assimilating. And it's interesting to note that many Jews celebrate "Christmas" as an American holiday, often with a tree, or "Hanukkah bush". Michelle's matrilinear status qualified here for a free trip to Israel under the birthright program. (My own daughter qualified for the trip via a distant great-grandmother, but Judaism was never part of her identity and she had no interest at the time.) From her balcony, Michelle had an experience I would hope to have someday. One evening, she could hear Jewish dancing, a minaret's call to prayer, and Christian church bells, all at the same time. Three religious cultures, separate but present. Unfortunately, the geopolitics isn't as simple or idyllic as that, but we can at least linger on the hope of it all.

In America, Freedom of Religion is a cornerstone of our culture. But here is another place reality doesn't match our intention or principles. Many groups came to the New World to escape religious persecution, and then promptly imposed it on their neighbors or excluded others by law. Before and after the Revolution there have been massacres between Protestants and Catholics. The Philadelphia Bible Riots combined religious intolerance with nativist anti-immigration sentiments. Mormonism, a truly American-born faith, had its adherents chased across the continent and almost ceased to exist after the "Utah War".

There have always been varying degrees of anti-Semitism, especially during the Great Depression. The term "Semitic" refers to a Middle-Eastern language group that includes Hebrew, Aramaic, and Arabic, and was hijacked into attempts to classify race. Sometimes you will hear that anti-Semitic includes prejudice toward Muslims, but the term in use today specifically refers to Jews, whereas the term Islamophobia has filled in the other space.

We have to realize that Jewish and Muslim are religious *and* ethnic labels. Most Jews are Jewish by birth, but many are Jewish by blood only (not adherents of Judaism) and others are converts. Being Muslim is defined by faith, not blood, but is ethnic in a more general way. Contrary to popular notion, only about 12% of all Muslims are Arabic. The culture itself is actually many diverse cultures across many continents. In America, we perceive and treat Muslims as a single group, and in being treated as such, they have become so in a way. Language and religion are ways for diverse immigrants to find social support where they might otherwise be none. And even the deep schism of Sh'ia and Shi'ite are left at the door, as most mosques in America make no such distinction.

American Christianity, on the other hand, makes *lots* of distinctions. On top of numerous larger denominations, vast numbers of churches make up the religious fabric of America. There are over 45,000 member churches in the National Association of Evangelicals spanning 60 denominations. There are even more that are completely independent. And there have always been "Black Churches" on top of this. Well, not always. Particularly in the early South, Negroes were forbidden to have their own churches, though "Invisible Churches" of secret religious practice did exist. On the other hand, attendance was encouraged to hear White preachers teach the virtues of obedience and a bit less attention put on the universality of God's children. This is an area I would have hoped to study more before writing this book, as there are conflicting narratives of religion used for unity on one hand and another tool for oppression on the other. I heard it suggested by more cynical voices that formal religion provided a means of control to replace the plantation. And it's hard to ignore there is more than a little historical and political overlap between American Christianity, particularly Evangelicalism, and White Supremacy.

More traditional denominations, such as Orthodoxy, Catholicism, Episcopalian, etc., tend to be more liberal, i.e. concerned with social justice. But even then, the age of an institution often corresponds to its slowness to change. Only this year do we see the first African-American cardinal in history, Wilton Gregory of Washington, DC. And then there is "liberation theology" as an alternative to the kind of Christendom geared toward "saving" People of Color. Mostly prevalent in Latin America, this approach to the Gospel focuses on humanitarian efforts, and was even discouraged by the Vatican for reasons too complex to address here. The big question for People of Color is if Christianity is the "White Man's religion" or if they can make it their own. It seems many have.

"Segregated Sabbaths", as Pastor Miles McPherson calls it, is the norm today. Only one out of five American churches have less than 80% of its members of a single ethnicity. In his book, *The Third Option: Hope for a Racially Divided Nation*, he uses the phrase "Skittles Churches" for those more diverse. But we're still a melting pot, so any given church may be an unexpected experience. Within Catholicism, you would hardly believe the difference between a Latinx church and a German one, in spite of the same ritual and script. When going to services with my dad and stepmom in Las Vegas, there was an exuberant Gospel choir at the Catholic church on the Strip, and a marching-band vibe at the Baptist church. It was unexpected, but all good.

Religious pluralism as an American value was borrowed from Freemasonry, where people of all faiths were welcome to work together and govern themselves in toleration and equality. We see this in the concept of separation of Church and State, but sometimes it goes to extremes, meaning removing faith from the public sphere altogether, or insisting it be part of it. When we peel back the facade, we may find the latter is a continuation of (White) Christian dominance. If we are a Christian country demographically, the argument goes, "In God We Trust" should remain on our currency. But if you ask about changing it to "Allah" in a hypothetical future where America is predominantly Muslim, you may not get the same answer. How do I know this? When French Muslims block intersections in Paris with prayer rugs to fight for the right to pray in public, the same Christians who believe in prayer in schools condemned them as criminals for blocking traffic. Perhaps the bar for martyrdom is a bit lower in the Bible Belt than it used to be.

Like White is the default for color, Christian is the default for religion in America. Blue laws, holidays, and the schedules of commercial establishments are perfect examples of Christian privilege. It's not as much these days, but the default for where I live is Roman Catholic. Until recently, real estate and rental descriptions worded location in terms of the nearest parish.

I have never seen discrimination against Atheists, but like race, I have no business to think it doesn't exist. In fact, I believe it does because I know others who have experienced it. I find it weird that theism would even be an issue outside of one's personal life, but apparently America's diversity of ideas extends equally far in its prejudices.

We can see the battle of belief in a roundabout way. When I was growing up, Atheists lobbying to remove "In God We Trust" from our currency was the debate. Now we hear about the "War on Christmas". Jesus is the reason for the season – for some. Even among Christians, it's more secular (commercial) aspects take precedence. And every year people lament and take a stand for their right to say Merry Christmas instead of Happy Holidays, though I honestly don't know who is telling them they can't. If it's in the course of serving the public, then it would only be reasonable and polite not to assume the customer celebrates Christmas. And Happy Holidays is a shortcut to include New Year's. I would hope the average person wouldn't take offense if they were wished Merry Christmas (or Happy Hannukah, etc.) but to say it's supposed to be specific makes a real case for being offensive. I keep everyone happy by saying "Have a Blessed Holiday Season!" It speaks to the religious and secular alike.

But the more "foreign" a religion is, the more it creeps some people out. Some people think Yoga is evil because it's related to Hinduism. I remember a news segment on Christian radio where one of the commentators even felt Indian music was "demonic". The other commentator wasn't convinced but backed up the rest of her judgments. To extremist Christianity, anything not clearly Christian is the same as being against or harmful to the Church. I've studied cult phenomenon on and off most of my life, and one of the main characteristics of cultism is a highly judgmental separation of identity from the in-group and everyone and everything else. It is ironic that many "anti-cult" endeavors in America are actually Christian apologists targeting and judging others as "cults" based on nothing more than not conforming to their highly particular brand of soteriology. If anything, a group doing this makes *them* a cult.

As far as actual cults go, if we define them by dogma, then opposing them is religious bigotry. And the denotation of the word as a small fringe religious group is useless in a meaningful, modern context. By cult, most people mean a group that has a high degree of psychosocial control over its followers. This paradigm is totally different. Individual people or beliefs cannot be cults, no matter how bizarre to us. Organizations and tightly-knit groups, even non-religious ones, can be cults.

This brings me to my experience in Anonymous, specifically my involvement in Project Chanology. Censorship efforts by the Church of Scientology triggered a spontaneous response from the Intenet, spawning a movement to bring attention to the human rights abuses and other criminal aspects of the organization. In February 2008, the first online-organized protests in history took place in over a hundred cities in countries around the world.

The Church of Scientology attempted to frame us all as religious bigots. I can tell you that the accusation was not entirely false. Many in the movement indiscriminately attacked their belief system with the CoS itself – it was all the same to them. Still opposing the organizational practices and actions, I defended people's right to embrace the belief system of Scientology. Many ex-Scientologists were in the movement, and many (but not all) of them still believed to some extent or another in the principles or "tech" of L. Ron Hubbard. It was the organization and the way it *used* its beliefs, not the beliefs themselves, that enslaved or abused people.

I made friends with a number of can't-use-the-trademark-but-practicing Scientologists, including Trey Lotz, the most experienced and trained auditor (counselor) in the history of Scientology. I even did a series of interviews with him as part of my Interfaith work to talk about the belief system in relation to psychology and other issues. He's a brilliant man, and like me has a Philosophy degree. You can only imagine our conversations.

But what if you can't wrap your head around another belief system? A healthy approach is to not burden yourself with the notion you need to make a judgment. A friend of mine had just become Born Again and asked me about Buddhism when I had casually mentioned it. Soon, he was struggling to know if it was or wasn't compatible with (his notion of) Christianity. Its very existence seemed like a challenge to his faith, which was not at all my intention. Buddhism, like other Eastern faiths, doesn't proffer itself up as a one, true religion, or decries other religions as wrong or less true. But in the West, we like our Greek Logic either/or constructs. I suggested what others believe doesn't have to support or negate his own faith journey. Why judge at all? I had no reason to convince him of the merits of Buddhism, and it wasn't his responsibility to evaluate other beliefs as good or bad just because he found his own path. He let it go and was happier for it. Not everyone can accept ways of seeing the world foreign to us, especially if we're dogmatically conditioned not to. And if we can't, there's no need to treat all else out there as a threat.

It's so easy to lump people together on the basis of religion into a huge "other" that is all the same in our minds. We (wrongfully) assume they must all believe this or that, and think we know what their scriptures mean better than they do. We look at the most fanatical believers and say, "That's who they really are!" and anyone who doesn't match our concept is not a "real" believer. It's a terrible prejudice. In an opposite sort of way, it's just as bad as telling a Person of Color they are not like those "other people" of their race or ethnicity. Don't do it.

Some people hate Christians, the largest faith-label of people in the world, making summary judgments against them as a whole. If someone I know says they are Pagan or Wiccan, I am hesitant to say I'm Catholic or Christian because of potential knee-jerk recoil. I've seen it. Being anti-Christian is usually the result of real or perceived persecutions done under its banner. It's not made any better by assertions American is a "Christian nation" and the rest of us are just "other". It's usually not people's objections to the faith itself, but that it often comes from an attitude of supremacy. I get why there's a bumper sticker that says "Lord, save me from your followers!" Prolific stereotypes of intolerance, not unfounded, have hurt us all. Christians are often judged by what a televangelist or the Pope does and says. They may not represent Christians as a whole, but that's what is broadly visible. I go out of my way, when talking about my Catholic-Christian identity, that it does *not* involve condemnation or judgment against anyone. Not all Christians or Catholics feel the same way, but others need to know we are not all the same. Such a discussion breeds trust that will be passed into future interactions with people of different faiths.

Some people reject all religion. But even "they" are not homogenous. Some just don't like the trappings of organized religion, recognizing that as a social, historical phenomenon religion is arguably a means of control. Further down the line are people who don't put any credence in the spiritual of any sort, or partake in atheist reductionism. Even farther are those who agree with Marx that it's an "opiate of the masses" or even Mao that it's a disease, describing theism as a delusion of sorts – an intellectual deficiency. Somewhere between recognition of its faults, and intolerance for its existence, the line is crossed. Those who insist belief is incompatible with healthy human existence and work toward irradicating whatever they think religion is are bigots.

We may point to "religious wars" and see the evils of colonization and even slavery in the context of religious belief. Religion and religious power have been used to motivate and justify many evils. But more people died under non-religious, political ideologies in the 20th Century than all others. Staunchly atheistic Stalinism tops that list. This is a perfect time to learn that fanaticism is the cause of evil, not belief. When belief requires the vilification of other beliefs, that is where fanaticism begins.

Whereas many saw 9-11 as an indictment against Islam, militant Atheist Richard Dawkins widened the blame to religion itself. He seems to have missed the mark his whole life, confusing belief with fanaticism. He tries to focus on the particulars of theology, and even misunderstanding these badly. Again, we can find world-scale heinous acts done in the name of theistic and nontheistic ideologies alike, but many share his view that "religion" is inherently evil. This is the broadest form of religious bigotry possible.

But it works both ways. There is prejudice and even active bigotry against Atheists, with all the same kind of projected misunderstandings. The only difference is that the Atheist derides the intelligence or sanity of the believer; those with faith lament for the nonbeliever's soul. It's pointless as a serious debate unless we realize we are speaking different languages about different frames of reference for understanding Life, the Universe, and Everything.

Ecumenical and Interfaith efforts and dialogue have grown much over American history. Our slow advance toward our Constitutional ideals in that respect could almost be described as "fake it 'til you make it." But we aren't quite there yet. The National Day of Prayer I went to one year in downtown Buffalo featured a Catholic priest, a Protestant minister, and a rabbi from a Messianic Jewish temple. It was mild weather for that time of year, and I was invited by Joe and Judy Kulbacki. (Joe, a former Buffalo Bill from the 1960s. had written a book, *America: A Nation That's Lost Its Way*, which looks at America as a civilization from a religious perspective.) I appreciated the invite as I always meaning to attend one, but I was disappointed. They couldn't even get a non-Christian rabbi? By contrast, the Dalai Lama had visited Buffalo and the Interfaith service included non-Abrahamic faiths, a Native American blessing, and secular humanist poetry. Some of us are content, even adamantly so, with American as a Christian Nation. But the latter experience is the reality of America in the totality outside our spiritually gated communities. What I would like to see is an "American Day of Prayer and Reflection" across the country that includes as much of each community's diversity as possible.

Seriously, that should be a thing.

PART II
TWO WORLDS

14. Stand in the Place Where You Live

Why does it seem that half the country has attitudes and viewpoints that make no sense to us? Do some regions deserve to be known for certain things? Are some places inherently more racist? If so, why?

If you overlay a map of all the counties of the United States and divide them between high and low population density, it will be almost the *exact same map* of Blue and Red counties politically. In fact, an analysis of the 2012 election by Dave Troy measured this. The crossing over point between predominantly Democrat and predominantly Republican voting was 800 people per square mile. This is only distorted by gerrymandering, which is often crafted on the basis of race, not just party, and these distinctions greatly overlap.

What I've pointed out for many years now is that population density profoundly affects personal world views in understandable ways. This is why some political and economic ideologies make sense (or don't make sense) to people living in those areas. You may have heard chatter about the "urban-rural divide" during the election coverage. That paradigm seems to be more on the radar the last year or two, not just in America, but around the world.

Urban areas are much more Democrat/Liberal; rural ones are Republican/Conservative. I know, these terms aren't perfectly aligned, and any given issue at any time may mean all bets are off. And they may mean significantly different things in other countries. But there are general underlying values and assumptions we can pin down, so hold onto your seats here.

In rural areas, there is understandably a higher value placed on self-reliance. This puts an emphasis on personal rights and responsibilities. Living in a packed community where everyone is more deeply connected, there is a natural tendency to focus on collective efforts and communal responsibilities. At one end I may want to be left alone my whole life, pay taxes for the mail to be delivered and the borders defended, but not care much about government or other people so long as they stay out of my way. On the inner side of the suburbs, it takes a village to raise a child, and every bill that becomes law affects you or people you know, or at least someone who lives in your community. This is why we argue so much about individual rights versus collective housekeeping. This determines how we feel about the role of law, government, the whole shebang. The wearing of masks during the pandemic also plays out according to this model, with people weighing personal choices against collective good differently. Such deep-rooted value preferences can even override the pertinence of facts and common sense.

Whatever our view is, we will often defend it as what the Founding Fathers wanted – the "real" America. In the larger scheme of things outside one's head, it's actually a balance of the two stances with a lot of haggling room. Being for smaller government and private solutions to social problems, my bias may is more toward a primacy of individualism – I did grow up at the far edge of the suburbs, after all.

But what does this have to do with race? Two things, actually.

The first is sociological. It's understandable that people who value self-reliance believe if you make it or break it, that's on you. This assumption fosters the notion that if you can't get a good job, or a better house, or become an addict, or get in trouble with the law, it's unequivocally your fault. (Affirmative action feels like an affront to that.) This is all about the America we want to believe in, the one where anyone can make it. We don't blame television or "The Man," though perhaps bad parenting. Blaming society seems like a cop-out because people in the country are more displaced from any imposing concept of "society" – such influences feel like they are less of a measurable thing, or far more at a distance.

But faith in the principle of self-responsibility is a positive attitude to have, even if the reality has some cracks in it. One of these cracks is empathy's natural limitation to that which we can see. Another study from the time of the 2012 election correlated racism with people's contact with diversity. In a nutshell, it was easier for people who never or hardly saw People of Color to have opinions of them as a group – and not usually good ones. They are outsiders, and the introduction of any people identified as "those people" would bring social discomfort. It may even feel like an invasion. However you may feel about forced integration (busing, etc.) and its troubles, it arguably did a lot to move that needle in many communities. Visibility and proximity drive how we are aware of, and therefore care about, the plight of others. After all, it's human nature to assume everyone has the same challenges and experiences as ours. Sheltered White people have no other frame of reference, and therefore judge People of Color's success based on their own access to the American Dream.

The American Dream is a wonderful ideal. It was best described by the Swedish economist Karl Gunnar Myrdal, a 1940s-era Tocqueville who wrote *An*

American Dilemma: The Negro Problem and Modern Democracy. He states that with all our diversity we can coexist because we share a common cause – an "American Creed" – based on individualism and equality of opportunity.

People point to the success stories of immigrants who made it, and wonder why some of the "new" ethnic groups don't have the same success. Actually, I don't think there are any statistics to even quantify that belief. Besides, it's apples to oranges all around. Every wave of immigration had different circumstances, support systems, access to capital, levels of acceptance, etc.. But it's a valid point that people have overcome all sorts of diversities, so why can't everyone? (Ironically, we could also turn around and ask why *we* aren't rich, complain about how the system isn't always fair, and be prejudiced against those who are more successful.)

If you search hard enough, you will find People of Color who assert that the influence of racial privilege is overrated. And White people furnish such attributions as examples to prove that point and not look racist. These tend to be those who *have* made it, of course, and are most often conservative. When I hear this, I probe deeper for details when people tell me of that Black person they know that made it "out of the ghetto" and have kids who are doctors and lawyers. The descriptions are so similar I must wonder if they are all talking about the same person. Regardless, going to a better school seems to be the common denominator.

Speaking of school, there is also a general difference in educational values between rural and urban families. I'm not buying into city folk being smarter or better educated here. But I would suggest that *trade school* education being more valued makes sense in communities that proportionally require more physical infrastructure (and therefore skilled laborers) per person. Urban environments, at least in this day and age, are service economies, with concentrations and higher competition of intellectual, non-laborer professionals. But again, these are generalities, not hard and fast rules. And the passing on one's profession to their children isn't anywhere near as common as it used to be.

The second thing population density has to do with prejudice is psychological. Most people who live in the burbs or country (mostly White) have a hard time thinking in terms of race because they see people as individuals. That's a good thing, right? Well, it doesn't seem to be an issue until you interact with people who don't have that experience – those who are very much considered and treated as part of a group. And if you "ain't from around here", pretty much everyone else is part of some "group". And that's another reason to see people in your "in-group" as individuals – things like White are the "default" setting. We folks don't see race between ourselves any more than fish thinks about water – until we find ourselves out of the water.

This sameness is more common in rural areas, but wait, there's more! When people have enough space to "mind their own business" (and expect it of others), they can maintain the appearance of *sameness* even when there is not. You can ignore the migrant worker, the person who attends a different church, the one "Coloured family" who lives on the next hill. And if someone's son is gay, you don't talk about it, or probably don't even know. It's unlikely the average village or town will have a pride parade. But then you turn on the television, and these things are visible. Very visible. Demographics that were underrepresented (or not represented at all) are now sometimes over-represented. Or at least it feels that way. Attempts at inclusion and diversity can even feel like it's being shoved down our throats.

Let's chew on a particular example and how it plays out. The stock photos of scientists in some children's textbooks show people of every color but White. Does a White person notice it? Does a Person of Color? Does it bother someone who is White? Now (un)turn the tables: would a White person notice if everyone in the pictures were White? How would a child – a Person of Color – feel about seeing only people who don't look like them?

Maybe it's forced. Maybe we're going to the opposite extreme. But is it really hurting us who are not minorities? Do we really feel like we're losing control of "our" world, or that our "normal" way of life is being persecuted? Even if not consciously, the answer is usually yes. We don't have to be proud of that, or apologize for it, but we White folks should *own it*. Only then can we consciously decide what to do with it, and do the right thing.

Let's do two things here. First, let's admit there are some people who militantly want to wave their flag in people's faces, especially if it was previously (or currently) oppressed in some way. There's always a pendulum swing about such things and people will publicly display how they feel. If we believe in a free society, we're good. We don't have to judge them for it. It doesn't require our opinion or response. Second, let's not qualify every exposure to a demographic foreign to us as flaunting or attacking our own. Seeing other ethnic people doing other ethnic things may not represent our neighborhood, but it probably does represent someone else's. We don't have to be in the parade. But if you ask and are willing to expand your world a bit, you may find yourself welcome and learn it never was about being against "your kind".

Here I want to add a note about the word *urban*. It literally refers to life in a populated area, but it has connotations and uses we need to be aware of. When we refer to urban culture or urban music, or urban wear, we mean something that is predominant within African-American circles. Sometimes it's a codeword for Black, even a dog whistle where people mean Black but don't want to say it. Just like "gentrify" can sometimes mean to expand a neighborhood's whiteness, people often use "urban" to mean the part of a city that is heavily African-American – where a White person doesn't want to invest, shop, or park their car. The distinctions between "good" and "bad" places to send one's kids to school or buy a house are also a subconscious battle of defining quality by the absence of Color. A White person may never give such language a second thought, but even if they don't mean anything by it, a Person of color may find it unpleasantly suggestive.

Interestingly, gentrification battles over park use are becoming common in some cities. By this I mean White people moving into neighborhoods that up to that time were mostly African-American. Newcomers generally want more dog parks, while existing residents want to keep their playground space. It's hard to believe, but even our pets influence segregation and conflict.

I myself *prefer* the term urban, not as a cultural distinction, but as a composite demographic of all people who live in the "inner city." Okay, maybe I'm mincing words here, but I don't care for the term "hood" or "ghetto." I'll be specific: There is a distinct thing as a low-income, poor-infrastructure, underserved, low-opportunity area in most cities. You can almost draw a red line around it on a map, and in fact, that's where the term red-lining comes in. Discriminating against neighborhoods, particularly on the part of financial institutions, has been illegal for some time, but it still happens. Even pizzerias selectively skip ZIP codes for their delivery service.

Going with this definition, urban neighborhoods are often assumed to be high-crime areas, even though they are often not. They have very little owner-occupied housing, in part due to generations of discriminatory denials of lending to minorities. The dominant demographic is African-American, and often Latinx, but there are residents who are White. They all go to the same underperforming schools, have the same trouble scrounging the food desert, and are also looked down upon by others for where they live. Even if there are additional obstacles for minorities, all who grow up and are socialized in that environment share a certain experience. That is partly why there have always been White rap artists, Hip Hop dancers, and those who dress in a way they're called "wiggers" ("White n-s").

Most of what we associate with African-Americans, particularly negative things, are founded in the circumstances of that very particular environment. Nearly all of Black and Latinx America lives in, or are from, inner cities. This has created stereotypes that are based in a harsh reality, yet still a lie. It says nothing about those human beings themselves. Even before the 1960s Civil Rights era, African-Americans proved they can excel in every field, not just athletics or music, the two fields most open because it lucratively entertains the rest of us. These individuals often had to make extreme sacrifices and overcome obstacles that simply do not exist for others, and it is realistic for the average person to rise above basic things like poverty and a justice system that's arguably out to get them. In fact, studies as far back as the 1950s show that middle-class African American culture is almost indistinguishable from that of White people both in educational capacity and perceived family morality.

This is where the Department of Labor report by Daniel Patrick Moynihan comes in. Published in 1965 as *The Negro Family: The Case For National Action*, the statistics showed that the Black family was falling apart under "stress and urbanization". In the context of these times falling apart meant a rising number of out-of-wedlock births. It argued that the function of Black men as authority figures was impaired because of the matriarchal structure of African-American culture. And the resulting "culture of poverty" resulted in a culture of crime.

People drew very different interpretations and conclusions from it – ones that fall along the battle lines of who is to blame, society or the individual. Sound familiar? But a lot of this seems to fall on the subject of "fatherlessness" – in which we appear to have been dead wrong. Half of all African-American children today are born outside of marriage. This is twice as much as in 1965. But then this is much more common today across the board. And people assume this means uninvolved fathers. A study done in 2013 by no less than the CDC paints a very different picture. Two-thirds of African-American fathers live with their children, and even when not, record more parental involvement than any other race or ethnic group. And this is on top of all those "missing" through mass incarceration. Michele Alexander, author of *The New Jim Crow*, says the War on Drugs "is a big part of the reason that a black child born today is less likely to be raised by both parents than a black child born during slavery." We can still argue that fatherlessness has a negative impact, regardless of blame. But an oft-repeated myth of 70% fatherlessness, and being the cause of all ills in the African-American community, is busted.

The nuclear family as a norm is also a prejudice of our socialization. It's a relatively modern, Western construct. In some places in Africa, a woman will copulate with several males she admires for various qualities she wants to see in her child. I know, gene transfer doesn't work that way, but the belief of having many fathers translates to benefiting from many desirable, active role models. Even if we think of the woman with several children all by different fathers as an African-American stereotype with some truth in it, does that have to be bad? Perhaps that's too foreign a concept to digest, but having a step-family isn't uncommon these days. So I argue there is no causation of poverty or crime based on family structure, but there is poverty and crime in the neighborhoods in question.

So why don't African-American neighborhoods clean themselves up? The truth is, it's not their neighborhood. They do not have their own governance or infrastructure or law enforcement, and are subject to the surrounding municipal administrations and services. They do not have an independent economy, and few financial institutions, though some promote buying within the community instead of letting it all go out of the neighborhood. So what would an African-American community of their own look like? First, let's look to the past. We know (or should know) about "Black Wall Street" in Tulsa. We should know why Rosewood, Florida was abandoned. These are among many examples of how success was thwarted from without, ever since "Freedom Towns" were founded after the Civil War.

Today, Atlanta (54% Black) is considered to have the most thriving African-American community, with Washington, D.C. right on its heels. Less than 20 American municipalities with a population over 100,000 have an African-American majority. The print would have to be small, but the list of all others of *any size* would fit on the back of a t-shirt. Therefore, the nominal integration of America doesn't give us an economic or social petri dish to examine today. What this tells me is that solutions must include all stakeholders, and all stakeholders must recognize that it is not a problem of certain types of residents, but neighborhoods that are not equal.

15. America Unfurled

Journalist John Howard Griffin considered himself an expert in race relations, but soon found himself admitting he knew nothing directly about the Black experience. In writing *Black Like Me*, he opened the door for people to at least try to know. It was the strangest sort of expose. It wasn't written to fill us in on secret gatherings at Negro night clubs, but to be around White society in the light of day. Didn't White people already know what it was like for African-Americans to be around them? An entire existence was right under their nose – heck, shining their shoes – and yet it was a massive revelation of another America, hidden in plain sight.

That was another time. White people as a general rule wouldn't listen to other people speak of their plight; African-Americans knew there would be consequences if they spoke truth to power. We had pre-written scripts about how those "other people" lived, how they felt, and who they were. And many of us simply didn't care. From the other end of the stick, there was a lot of animosity, even militant detestation, toward the social class responsible for slavery and continuing to support, or at least rarely challenge, a racist status quo. White people tuned out the message along with the anger they did not want directed at them.

Today there is no need for anyone to "infiltrate" the world of Color in this way. Music and food and even the bonds of marriage are open to everyone regardless of ethnic identification. Wholesale segregation and discrimination have been taken out of the equation, at least in theory. There are more bridges, relationships, and access between people of diverse ethnicities today. We can actually talk as a friend and confidant to people different from ourselves, so long as we possess an honest desire to listen to things that may not be comfortable to us. Doing so with empathy and without judgment may be difficult, but is not impossible.

But cries that the job is done and the mission was accomplished in the 1960s are gravely naive. Sure, we've made outward progress in terms of codifying equal protection under the law. This is perhaps ironic given so many of us grew up believing this was a founding principle of our nation. But a reaffirmation of these principles in the Civil Rights Act of 1964, *et alia*, began a more rigorous application of this ideal in practice. I say began because the need for it did not end there. And it may have even been a setback in one particular way.

I attended a marriage equality rally not long before it became lawful in all states. A number of speakers said their pieces, news cameras rolling, and each of them used certain wording the irritated me. They were demanding rights. At face value, that was the whole point. But my memories harkened back to Gary, my coworker in the plastics industry whose *Challenger* newspaper I used to borrow and read. He had made the shocking statement that passing the civil rights laws was a bad thing. This, coming from an African-American! But it was obvious once explained. If you can be given rights, they can be taken away. And in the spirit of "certain inalienable rights" that are endowed by Deity (or inherent by nature if you prefer that route), the government can only legislate *protections* of existing rights. They are not to be granted or not granted, but can only be acknowledged or not acknowledged. I think most Americans get this wrong, and by fighting the wrong battle, give too much power over things that should never be put up to a vote.

This is actually at the heart of many political arguments – what the government should and shouldn't keep its hands off of. The main difference between conservative and liberal stereotypes are which rights should be regulated and which ones are sacrosanct. When it comes to voting, we feel pressed having to choose one set over the other, and that's why 40% of Americans don't identify with either party strongly. Here's the rub: different people define America such that people with different beliefs are un-American. Just like liberals and conservatives try to make Jesus Himself in their own image to justify their brand, they do the same with the Founding Fathers. And that's a problem, since even they had to make many compromises to accommodate disparate views. I would guess none of them would fit nicely in either party if they lived today.

So who owns the Red, White, and Blue brand? I could rouse a tear saying it belongs to all of us, but it doesn't. We can speak of brave men and women who shed their blood for the freedom of all Americans, but that's more a religious belief, not a literal truth. The vote of self-determination started only with male landowners. Until after the Civil War, defending our way of life including slavery. It was legislators, not doughboys that granted suffrage to (White) women. So many atrocities and other unrighteous things have been done under our national banner. And bigots will fly the Stars and Stripes at least as often as the "Rebel Flag". Many supremacists proudly use both, along with Christian crosses, as their brand. It's always been about what any given group or person wants America to represent, or what they think it does, or what it used to.

It only makes sense that the Flag brings out conflicting, hard feelings. In the military, you are compelled to accept it as a sacred object. I can't address that as I did not so serve, but I get why any perceived disrespect isn't tolerated. But even veterans can share in feelings that "the Republic for which it stands" no longer exists, or never truly existed, or perhaps it represents an ideal we just don't live up to. Is the Nation, the United States of America with its federal and state governments, the same as our Country, the people and her land and principles and dreams? Does the Flag represent a government that will send a generation to die in rice fields for some vague ideological goal? Or does it represent our freedoms and the pursuit of happiness? Yes and yes. (Personally, if I wanted to burn something representing the government, I'd use dollar bills. It would be a more honest representation of our political vices.)

One of my dear friends and Lodge Brother, Russ, fought in World War II. Generations apart in age, we had common interests, particularly in aerospace. He worked at Bell Aircraft on early experimental projects and my father worked in the industry while I was growing up. A year or so before he passed away, I took him to the Niagara Aerospace Museum. When browsing all the achievements of the Space Age he commented that he wished "that football player" could see it and realize how great America is. I knew immediately he was referring to Colin Kaepernick, who wouldn't stand for the national anthem. Russ, Heaven rest his soul, was a sweetheart of a man and I know he meant nothing ill by it, but I surprised myself with a spontaneous response: "That wasn't his America. There were no Black astronauts in those days."

Maybe that was a bit much; the conversation moved to other topics. And it was a bit misleading when you consider that NASA was progressive compared to the rest of society with regards to having People of Color in the agency. The space program brought together America, and even Humankind. But the feat of Sputnik was a mere decade before, the year "Balck Like Me" took place. We were a contradiction of amazing achievement and petty tribalism.

I show respect for the Flag in customary ways. In high school, I was in charge of raising and lowering it every school day. In the local chapter of the Order of the Eastern Star, I have been Color Bearer more years than not. My eyesight disqualified me from service, but I did consider the Army, though as a chaplain or medic so I wouldn't have to take a life. Regardless, my wife says I bleed red, white, and blue. I've worked with recovering veterans with all sorts of physical and psychological challenges for nearly 20 years now, and it's been one of the most rewarding things I've ever done. But I've had my limits. During Desert Storm, I waited for the patriotic backdrop to be taken down before couples photographs at a semi-formal dance. Just or not, I don't think we should glorify war in our daily lives. And it annoyed me how people were suddenly "patriotic" in times of conflict. I was used to being one of the few with the Flag hanging off my porch, but after 9-11 it felt like a bunch of people saying they like some band they don't listen to just to hang out with the cool kids.

Conversely, others turn their backs on the Flag. Some even burn it. It just doesn't mean the same thing to them as it does to me. I would never do it, and it makes my skin crawl knowing how much the Flag means to others. But I get it. At the very least I know why some do not show respect the way we demand of them by sitting out the Anthem or not saying the Pledge. Lack of respect is not the same as disrespect, and being offended is a choice at that point. Vilifying such people bothers me. Just like I don't care for fashionable. fair-weather patriotism, I find compulsory patriotism a contradiction in a country that claims its citizens are free.

Let's be clear about Kaepernick. He is a professional athlete and therefore a financially endowed man. When he took a stand (or kneeled rather) against inequality and police brutality, he was told by many he had nothing to complain about. He was even raised in a White family. But he probably dealt with his share of racism just because of his skin, identifying as African-American. But what if he was White? Are we going to judge the validity of his views based on if it affects him personally? How many social justice advocates are not victims? Does it matter? It's ... problematic ... how White America treats African-American athletes. They were among the first People of Color to be welcomed into our homes, even if only through the television. So when a Minnesota senator cited athletes (and Obama, of course) as examples of how African-Americans have equal opportunity, there was much eye-rolling. We've heard this too many times, where sports and music are the only notable contributions to our culture (and we even argue about music). We talk about how they (specifically non-White athletes) should be *grateful* to be sports celebrities as if bestowed a privilege by a White and fair America. A complaint against their benefactor insults White "sensibilities" we honestly don't realize we have. I'm not saying the person holding this book feels this way, but that there's something to his, and this is how it feels to Black America.

When any "privileged" Person of Color speaks out about inequality or injustice, it really sticks in our craw as White people. If someone downtrodden complains, we can always find a way to blame them for their circumstances. If a White person does it, we can chalk it up to White guilt or being a bleeding heart liberal. But people like Kaepernick pose a unique problem. "We" (the

Americans we choose to identify with) gave him everything he could ask for, so he's either an ungrateful jerk, or maybe there's something else we just don't want to see. We rush to other *People of Color* for a second opinion, or a third, and there are a few who will tell us everything is fine and we can go back to watching the game. But there's another way to see this. What if there are issues so deep and real that those who are in a position to use their success to bring our attention to it, well, do just that?

Believing there are issues in America isn't threatening. But to see a high-profile person make a symbolic gesture to blame America itself for failing in some fundamental way? That's too much for some of us to handle. If there's such a thing as "White fragility", this could be called "American fragility". A version of patriotism where America is and always was "great" can't coexist with such criticism. The idea we do not all have the same opportunities feels like admitting America failed, or even an outright lie. Frankly, it's kicking their stars-and-stripes baby Jesus.

A humanist author on *Psychology Today*, David Niose, writes:

> [T]hose who question authority or longstanding cultural flaws are quickly branded subversive. Thus, many well-conditioned citizens will rush to the defense of the Establishment if someone raises objections to ... mistreatment of minorities at home or other grievances. With one side seeing themselves as the "real Americans" and opponents as something less, polarization is assured.

This is exactly what we are seeing with the current protests and our country's response to them. These people aren't burning flags, but it's hardly a symbol in their fight. Being branded as being unAmerican is further reason to not want to be associated with a "patriotism" that appears to be founded on preserving or ignoring racial injustice. I've even seen the term "superpatriots" used synonymously with White supremacists, further confusing the difference between healthy patriotism and heavy-handed nationalism. In recent years in particular, those claiming to be patriotic are in fact creating a model of America that excludes People of Color – and anyone else who has cultural or religious or ideological differences. And the Flag, like the Rebel flag in the 1950s, has come to represent to many of us something we don't want to be associated with. And it breaks our hearts. We want our Old Glory back.

This is where the "Love it or leave it" paradigm hammers down. I see this mostly with older people, but it goes with any flavor of patriotism to some extent. The problem is it denies America's forgotten greatness as the Grand Experiment – a work in progress where every generation can move us forward into a place where our ideals are real, for everyone. Frankly, when people pull this card (and I'm feeling ungenerous), I just say I was born here and maybe *they* should leave. America doesn't belong only to those who have the luxury to feel their country is perfect. And we shouldn't have disparate Americas.

Black History, Women's History, Native American History and other categories are all part of American History. Having a unified America is a nice platitude to work toward, but these all exist to overcome their previous neglect. America can't be whole when it's missing pieces. And it's political all around. Is Confederate history American history? Of course it is, but do we include the CSA president Jefferson Davis as an "American" president? We don't even include the nine presidents *before* George Washington under the Articles of Confederation. Slavery and genocide against Indigenous Peoples happened and we suffer the scars of that. And we never fully divested from those trajectories. The sooner we own that, the sooner we can reconstruct a divided America into a united future.

I do not write this book posing as an "insider" like Griffin. I'm not a rich or famous Person of Color. I grew up privileged, not having any idea what that meant. I never really saw color and don't know where the lines are. But I've cared enough to know through other people's eyes and stories that there are at least two Americas, divided any number of ways. We don't all have the same relationship with Betsy Ross or Uncle Sam or society at large.

We only have one excuse to not know how the ethnic "other half" lives, and it is just that – an excuse. People not of Color want to believe we live in a post-racial world, and everyone else should just "get over it". We believe since we are not personally racist in our own estimation we have no responsibility to deal with this, even when we admit it's real. Broader injustices, such as disparity in education and vastly disproportionate incarceration rates, are things we might agree are a problem, but don't see or pursue opportunities to address them. We find an easy answer and excuse them. Even in the most mixed neighborhoods, schools, workplaces, and churches in America, we still have a segregation of the mind.

16. Whistling Dixie

I remember praying over the infantrymen before they went onto the field. I can't remember what I said, but it was crafted to be pertinent in two worlds – for the challenges of our modern times, but also for the time and place it represented. It was at Letchworth State Park, on a weekend, and it was our turn to lose. They were not reenacting any particular battle, but we were the Confederates, and I was their chaplain. Near the end of the battle, I solemnly stepped across the field, bodies all around, asking if people were alright. I knew it wasn't real, but to some part of the back of one's brain, it is. When the last soldier fell and the gunfire stopped, I took off my hat and hung my head. Taps played in the distance.

Many Civil War reenactors are descendants of soldiers from that time, very often having ancestors from both sides. It wasn't just a country divided, but families torn apart. Over time a (somewhat) united nation (mostly) healed. At the very least, it all became a part of our common history, even down to family stories. Today, these stand-ins for their distant fathers have a solemn respect for each other, even forming color guards of blue and gray, together, for memorials. I've seen this firsthand. For me as an American, there is a profound emotional potency of that great schism and repatriation. I can imagine the ghosts of over a million Americans from the North and the South walking each other home.

That was the only time I reenacted, but I knew some of them from the Buffalo Guards Chapter of the Sons of Confederate Veterans. Historical researcher Steve Teeft, founder and director of the only Civil War Museum in New York State, asked me to be their chaplain (in real life as an actual minister). I accepted. I was an honorary member, of course, as my ancestors came from Poland in the early 20th Century.

To help fill the role, I read "Faith in the Fight" by Ben Maryniak, a Civil War chaplain reenactor I am honored to have known personally. The most interesting thing from his book I can relate here is the theological split between churches in the North and South in the generations before the war. Southern Theology focused on individual salvation, whereas in the North, social justice was heavily preached. This is consistent with the rural-individualistic versus urban-collectivist social psychology discussed earlier.

On this basis, we find a reason other than economics why abolition was more popular in the more city-dwelling North.

This was a while ago – the chapter no longer exists. I believe my last act was in 2004, performing a memorial service at the POW camp in Elmira, New York, where hundreds of Confederate soldiers had been interred. History tells us that a single man, "Reverend Eddy", chaplain of a Texas regiment, committed these boys and men to the next world in the Christian rites. John W. Jones, a freedman and sexton to a local church, dug each of these graves, up to 48 burials in a day. Some say he acquired a hefty sum of money by the end of the war by doing so, but others note that he gave extra assurance that the burials were properly and reverently conducted.

Unbeknownst to me, the SCV at that time was going through internal battles and becoming more political on the issue of flags. Up to that time, they – often working with the Sons of Union Veterans of the Civil War (SUVCW) – focused primarily on preserving American Civil War graves, monuments, and markers. They advocated the protection of battlefields from becoming shopping centers and subdivisions. What made me feel I had a useful part to play was their anti-hate policy. The image of a Klan hood in a circle crossed out was on all the literature I saw. As their chaplain, I wrote a few articles for the chapter's newsletter, reiterating this virtue of tolerance. Were there bigots in the group? I honestly found no reason to believe so. Did they feel they were associated with slavery and supremacy by historical proxy? Absolutely not.

I was a bit oblivious to any social pressure at the time against things associated with the Confederacy. I grew up watching the *Dukes of Hazzard* and was surprised when they took it off the air and models of the *General E. Lee* no longer came with a flag decal. I didn't connect the dots as to what was going on in the big picture. The Charleston church shooting in 2015 prompted the change, and anything related to the Confederacy in American culture has been more and more contentious since.

I once combined my personal summer picnic for my old community education students and friends with that of the Buffalo Guards. We were both small groups, it saved cost on the shelter, and we got to share the frontier-style dutch oven delights of our common friend, Hyde Hitchcock. A neighbor brought her African-American fiancee, who raised an eyebrow at the display of the SCA flag, modeled after the iconic battle flag of the Confederacy. The Confederate National flags – the Bonnie Blue, 1st, 2nd, and 3rd National – may also have been displayed. I don't think any conversation about it came up. My wife recounted recently to me she remembers a Black family in their car driving slowly past, eyes on our presence. I honestly was oblivious to it all, and at the time subscribed more to the "I'm offended that you're offended" camp, and even a regrettable "If you're offended you need a history lesson". I didn't realize how much negative baggage such symbols have. I never had a conversation about it with People of Color. I had only discussed it with those who, in my opinion, were honestly upset they and their symbol were being unfairly judged.

It's hard for me not to see both sides. On one hand, I believe that intention matters. And I believe people should have a right to what a symbol means and represents *to them*. And those things may be sacred to them and not include those bad things it represents to other people. On the other hand, it is hurtful to others who believe it means something hurtful. And there is good reason to believe that, since it was used that way, and sometimes still is.

Let's talk specifically about the flag I'm referring to. Some call it the "Rebel flag" or "Dixie flag". It is the one with white stars on crossed blue stripes on a red field. Sometimes it's mistakenly called the "Stars and Bars", the name of the 1st National flag. But it's not a national flag at all, even though the design can be found within the 2nd and 3rd National flags. It was proposed as a national flag, but ended up being used as General Lee's battle flag (the Army of Northern Virginia). Sometimes known as the "Confederate Flag", it never officially represented that nation or government. Mostly it is the recognized symbolic flag of the region of the United States that once contained the Confederate states – the "American South".

But it's not that simple. It was one of the symbols of the "Lost Cause" – the continued desire to go back to antebellum life, which very specifically included the "right" of slaveholding. And this is where monuments and statues come in. Most Confederate monuments were placed in a resurging fervor for this Lost Cause long after the war, in the period just before Birth of a Nation in 1915. It was about propaganda, not honoring the dead. But that was forgotten over the years, and only recently become a talking point in the discussion. To many average townsfolk, it represents their ancestors, not the cause. But it was used prolifically by opponents of civil rights up until the 1960s. It even became part of Georgia's state flag when forced segregation began. The connections cannot be ignored except by force of will.

Southerners, or anyone who appreciates Southern culture, are in a predicament. Symbols, such as flags and monuments, are part of its heritage. Attacks on those things – just like perceived disrespect toward the American Flag – is an attack on their identity as Southerners *and* Americans. Remember, we each tend to define America by the experiences and surrounding we grow up in. To some, Country Music is the epitome of Americana; others think it's just a Southern White thing. And we have to wonder if going after symbols we can argue are associated with slavery and racism might actually be prejudice against Southern culture altogether.

According to an article in USA Today in 2013, an Arizona high school decided to have a "Redneck Day" that "encouraged classmates to dress – and spoof – accordingly". This sparked debate over "free speech, social stereotypes and good taste." But the cries of racism weren't by Southerners concerned over ridicule or admiring fans of Duck Dynasty. It was African-American leaders in the community equating these caricatures with racism against them. So who is driving the negative stereotype here? "Redneck" is often a self-described label of pride in backwoods, earthy, typically Southern culture. Or is it a derogatory term that is transforming into a blanket for White, gun-obsessed, NASCAR-watching, "un-edumacated", and in particular, racist "South Shall Rise Again" types?

Whether being a redneck is an ethnic designation or a lifestyle choice, why is it acceptable to generalize it in a way that breeds contempt and discomfort? If anything, people who consider themselves rednecks should be offended, or honored, or amused accordingly. But assuming racism in rednecks is like assuming criminality in African-Americans.

Even if the meaning of redneck and the Dixie flag are used and defined in part by White racists, should they be just as easily defined by the offended? Is having people dress up with camouflage and long beards carrying banjos really making African-Americans uncomfortable? This would be like Jewish people throwing a fit over Oktoberfest. I'm not trying to be harsh here. The Dixie flag is often compared to the Nazi flag. In Germany, there is a common sentiment that it's not the same country as back then. If by "country" they mean nation (a political entity), that would be correct. But it's not like everyone left and new people moved in with a totally new culture. To some Southerners, the Dixie flag is akin to the German flag, not the Nazi one. In fact, some military units in World War II had Southern nicknames and used the Dixie flag (unofficially) as their emblem. A marine even hoisted one atop a castle in Okinawa after its capture. Only in 2020 was the use of this flag banned by the military. Personally, I can see how the "Rebel" fighting spirit would be emulated, keeping in mind those using it saw it as a military symbol, not a political one related to slavery.

But any rationalizations aside, we can't ever fully decouple America from it's past, in whole or in part. We have to own it and figure out what to do with it here and now. In a recent survey done by YouGov, over 40% of Americans say the Dixie flag represents racism. Many are undecided. But a third of those surveyed – mostly older, rural White Americans, maintain it is a symbol of heritage. Let's assume the latter group is honest in their assertion. The question then becomes one of offending your neighbor, or feeling bullied into putting aside something you may hold dear.

A lesser-known flag, the Bonnie Blue may be the answer. It also represents the Southeastern states of the United States, but its history and use are not solely tied to the CSA. It also has not been used with any frequency in White supremacist circles or to intimidate neighbors. This is probably due to its obscurity. The problem is that it could quickly be used by bigots as a socially acceptable substitute, and anti-racists could target it among public sentiment as one more symbol of hate, to hate.

I don't think the existence of Southern culture – whatever that means – needs to divide America. Regionalism and localism can be healthy, and people from the South share commonalities of cultural experience the same as African-Americans, or New Yorkers, or people from the Southwest, have theirs. There's room for pride in your region or state or city as well as your country. Southerners have to find that line between pride and prejudices that still exist. And with the recent change in the flag of Mississippi, we find a willingness today to shelve symbols that, regardless of fault, no longer serve us. And even if we can't resolve this in the next generation, I hope we can disconnect Southern culture from its chains instead of disconnecting it from America.

17. Rewriting History

History has been written and rewritten many times. And I'm okay with that. In fact, how the telling of history changes over time and from different perspectives reveals more than the historical dates, people, or facts themselves. I call it the "5th dimension of history" – going beyond the where and when to studying the evolution of contextual historiography. Orwell warns us, "Who controls the past controls the future." And we often hear that history is written by the victors. (More accurately, a nation's textbooks are written by the victors, while serious histories are often written by the conquered. But that's a discussion for another book.) So how we choose to see history is important. These battles for the past are actually a fight for perspective. But it shouldn't be a fight. There is no one "story" in history, and the deeper in detail you go, the more you can see that none of them are watertight or uncontradictory.

The traditional bias in American history classrooms is Eurocentric. If we want to peel back a few layers, we find it a most specific story that follows Biblical (Judeo-Christian) history ending with American supremacy. We begin with the prehistoric Middle East, a mention of Egypt, and preach a foundation in Greece and Rome. Ignoring any mention of Islamic civilization, we then fast-forward to the Sistene Chapel and an Age of Exploration to the "New World" where America surpasses Britain's role as a world power, defeats the bad guys in two world wars, and wins the Cold War for the Gipper. Half the world's population has always been in China and India, but those only come into play in scant episodes where they meet the West, be it Alexander the Great or Marco Pollo. We teach as if sub-Saharan Africa and even the pre-Columbian Americas didn't even exist until the tallships found harbor there. Well, not even then. When I reviewed some the earliest known maps of the continents at the local Karepeles Manuscript Museum, almost every single one was in Arabic. And yet all the explorers famous to American grade-schoolers are Spanish, Portuguese, English, French, Italian, or Dutch.

A counterbalance to this skew is Afrocentric history, part of a larger American Afrocentrism movement. It challenges the undue weight and even myths of Eurocentrist approaches, but also has its own biases as per the opinions of both White and African-American historians. Its political roots stem from a legitimate need to recreate historical context for a people displaced and cut off from their past through colonialism and slavery.

But, like Eurocentric models, not all beliefs are not founded in fact. Egypt is part of Africa, and so there's a strong association with its achievements and claims to ancestry. However, it was genetically very diverse and distinct from the rest of the continent. I've heard the ancient Egyptian term *Kemet* "Black Land" as referring to skin color, but its counterpart is *Deshret*, or Red Land, referring to dark, fertile soil versus desert, respectively. I really don't care what color they were, as race had no such meaning back then, but let's be honest this is a belief system more than a science. Sometimes it's outlandish, such as claiming the Japanese Samurai were Black in ancestry. Humans as a species did expand from Africa. The legend of Eden hails from Mesopotamia, but mitochondrial Eve may have lived in Tanzania. But just as I've found that Europeans take credit for countless Chinese and Indian advances, I've seen Afrocentric writers claim a lot of things trace back to Africa with no evidence. It's like the running joke on Star Trek where Chekov claimed everything came from Russia. Then again, I prefer Shakespeare in the original Klingon.

I don't mean to mock here. Remember, I believe that collectively and individually we all have a say in our ethnicity and what it means. If African-Americans consider themselves descended from the kings and queens of Africa, then let's accept that. In fact, let's honor them as such. There's probably truth to it in some way, and the real value of our ancestors is in our hearts, not our genetics.

Less scholarly or strict narratives can be meaningful even if not true at all. Earlier this year, the Federation of Italian American Societies took down the Buffalo statue of Christopher Columbus for preservation outside the public's view. This was likely over the recent fervor to topple or vandalize monuments across the nation. Apparently, they commissioned a replacement statue named "La Terra Promessa" ("The Promised Land"). which will depict an Italian immigrant family. As more factual (and darker) chronicles of the man's escapades is becoming widely known, municipalities across the nation are replacing Columbus Day with Indigenous People's Day. I get it. The holiday itself was advocated by President Benjamin Harrison in 1892, likely a reparative gesture to an immigrant population that suffered the nation's largest lynching the year before. And before politically correct history lessons went mainstream in favor of the myth, few people cared or gave it a second thought.

Like many a saint whose life may not have been quite as stainless as our nuns told us, Columbus's story served a purpose. The ghost of the flawed human that inspired it only haunts us if we let it. Many other monuments suffer such double jeopardy under popular opinion, even Founding Fathers who were slaveowners. Locally, President and Buffalo Mayor Millard Fillmore is being tried for his support of the Compromise of 1850. Most people probably have no idea what that is until we're informed why we should be offended.

I think two types of criticisms against removal are legitimate, the first of which is that these are only token gestures, while actual living people are being brutalized and killed without consequence. The second is a matter of principles, perspective, and opportunity. Should we remove our historical human failings from sight, when they could be object lessons? Where do we draw the line as to what is a monument representing slavery versus its literal representation of a statement caught in the mix? Some of these statues have nothing to do with slavery except by being a leader or soldier on the side that had (more) slavery. And we know that many who fought for the South had no interest in the slave issue or were against it and fought as a matter of state pride, believing they were truly a reiteration of the American Revolution. Also, insisting on that standard would invoke the near-impossible removal of George Washington's omnipresent images and namesakes.

I personally don't see the need to defend statues if at some point we agree we no longer wish to honor people connected to the abhorrent parts of our past. I'm not convinced it's erasing history to remove them. But historian Camille Agricola Bowman takes a very sensible approach I can respect. She calls for "redefinition" rather than removal, meaning the placing of historical interpretation placards to give them a meaningful context that honors both meaningful and offensive views. Explaining who and why a statue was erected could be a powerful move toward reconciliation with our past. Her focus is on planning and community considerations rather than reactions that can't be reversed from a preservation standpoint.

Demonstrators damaged or tore down nearly 40 memorials around the country this year. I'm not going to judge them, but we have to admit these were somewhat unilateral decisions, whereas many more have been taken down (or planned to) via a municipal process involving citizen input or consent. Like residences hanging the Dixie Flag, we must weigh the value of these icons to some against the negative things they represent to others. Agreement may not come in any particular circumstance, but attempting a more community-involved process will probably result in more acceptance of removal than the resentment it was done without consent. Then again, maybe that's been tried and unresolved, or deferred repeatedly to preserve the status quo.

I'm more for adding to, and not subtracting from, our visual heritage. We've named a tremendous number of places and buildings after Martin Luther King, Jr., for example. And we could do so much more than commemorative stamps or naming an asteroid after Rosa Parks. But these shouldn't be appeasing gestures for "those" people or neighborhoods. I'd like to see it all – the good, the bad, and sometimes the ugly – accepted as a common heritage, not a perpetuation of race politics. MLK is my hero, too, and for years it was my tradition to donate blood on his holiday. But why are his namesakes only in certain communities? It shouldn't be about appeasement. Also, more and more people have ancestors from proud heritages that are in conflict, evoking shame or stress when the past is given too much weight. We do inherent the tribulations and sins of our ancestors in some way, but I'm not sure that sort of trauma is healed by lessening opportunities to talk about it.

Right now, all these attacks on symbols and the past feels more like a purge. In our fervor to address racism, everything becomes a potential target. Cancel culture takes few prisoners, and people and institutions are tried and convicted in the court of public opinion like never before. Between this book and things I've written over the years (even though my positions have evolved), I know I will be in someone's crosshairs for one thing or another. What concerns me the most is the at present time, you can't bring moderation or challenges to these strict interpretations of history without seeming racist. You can't defend legitimate perspectives based on solid facts if it contradicts the small range of acceptable views. History is in the hands of the mob, and accusations of who is rewriting history are probably justified in all directions.

"No one can question that the [American] Civil War was about ONE thing – slavery." That's what an acquaintance said across the table at an event where the Rebel flag issue was being hashed out. Like most such instances, one thinks of a snappy comeback no more promptly than the next day. And in my imagined version of the evening I would have said, "Wow, I cannot believe I am sitting with the person who has finally ended a century and a half of debate."

Don't get me wrong. It's an odious lie to say the war was *not* about slavery. It was front and center in the issue of states' rights, and most wars are only fought when platitudes about home and hearth intersect with large-scale economic interests. (Overthrowing a dictator intersecting with securing oil supply rhymes with this.) But to say that was *the* reason for the Civil War and call it a day? That would be as oversimplistic and only slightly less honest than Columbus discovering America.

Downplaying the role of slavery may assuage an ugly past that modern, not-so-racist Sounterners want to have some pride in. Others want to whitewash slavery itself. A hundred years ago, The United Daughters of the Confederacy were busy helping erect many monuments to the "Lost Cause", but as late as 2018, their website stated that "Slaves, for the most part, were faithful and devoted. Most slaves were usually ready and willing to serve their masters." They also endorsed a "Measuring Rod to Test Text Books and Reference Books," to influence the inclusion of their version of history. Many textbooks before my time even referred to slaves as servants, and had passages such as "Enslaved people were happy to be in Virginia and were better off than they would have been in Africa." Even recently, slavery is sometimes referred to as "forced migrations" and slaves as "workers", which are technically true, but nothing more. This is surely tied to the same Southern pride that carefully narrates the "War Between the States" in some books almost to the point of denying defeat. Generous euphemisms and whitewashing still exist. Such wording is more comfortable for some, but is taken as an offensive denial of a hurtful reality by others.

Sometimes the half-truth is the worst. There were, in fact, slaveholders who were far less abusive and arguably "took care of" slaves under their control. But focusing on that rarity misdirects attention from the fact these people were still being used and not free to live otherwise. Even if a man took a slave for his wife and sent their children to Northern schools to avoid continued slavery, such an anecdote – if it existed – is a tiny splinter in the massive beam of the institution. Even calling it an institution is hard to chew, as it was a collection of ongoing heinous acts I shouldn't have to recap here, nor do I have the stomach to.

That is why portrayals of slaves or even Negroes from that time in any other light is offensive. A young boy, maybe nine or ten years old, wanted to be his hero musician for Halloween. His parents helped him darken his skin, as he was White and Sachmo was Black. Now we may wear wigs or cross-dress or do all sorts of things for costumes, but this was problematic due to the history of blackface. Nothing was meant by those not sensitive to it, but it feels like a slap to others who knew the backstory. Lawn jockeys are a toss-up because there are several questionable myths as to their origin and use, and even those who believe it's noble aren't sure if it is offensive or not to those who don't.

You can't get Disney's movie *Song of the South* in the United States. I had seen it as a child, but we got our VHS copy from a friend who visited England. This 1946 film, familiar to most by the song "Zip-a-dee-doo-dah", was criticized for its idyllic portrayal of plantation life after the Civil War. It was progressive in its portrayals of genuine friendships between races, but the problem was exactly that – it was dishonest or misleading in its historical context. (Worthy of note was that the award-winning lead actor, James Baskett, wasn't allowed in the Atlanta theater where it premiered.) There were also accusations of African-American tropes of dialect, though faithfully derived from the (also criticized) Uncle Remus children's stories by Joel Chandler Harris, who was White.

Whoopi Goldberg, who played a leading role in *The Color Purple* with Oprah Winfrey, advocates its return to start a conversation about these issues. My wife and I have sometimes watch banned cartoons, many of which are offensive for good reason. They tell a story about the times and their prejudices that should not be forgotten. And even things like Aunt Jemima Syrup and Uncle Ben's Rice can be an opportunity for us all to have a much-needed talk. Some of us grew up with these icons not seeing it as problematic and feel that's going too far. Just switching the packaging, even if a good idea, may be missing an opportunity to expand the story instead of cut it off.

But the simple story we have taught our children about the Civil War hides an ugly truth. Slavery was an *American* institution, not merely a Southern one. We inherited it from European imperialism and didn't let go of it when we declared ourselves "free" in 1776. In fact, a writer n *The Challenger*, a local African-American publication I used to borrow and faithfully read from a coworker in the 1990s, suggested it was the Revolutionary War that was fought for slavery, not the Civil War. His argument was that the British Empire was outlawing slavery (the slave trade ended in 1807 and all slavery in 1833), and we didn't want to give them up. At least some of us.

Thomas Jefferson wanted slavery condemned in the Declaration of Independence. The final version omitted it, as the economy of the colonies was dependent on it. And unifying the colonies took precedence over basic human, moral concerns. After independence, and a Constitution that formalized how slavery would be handled on a federal level, even New York started out as a slave state. Abolitionism was a movement around the world since the 18th Century, and the people of our new nation was divided, even down to towns and families. Americans from every state argued for and against it.

Perhaps that is why the hamlet of Town Line seceded during the Civil War. It's a tiny municipality in New York State. I've driven through it many times ... don't blink or you'll miss it. To this day, no one remembers why they voted to do so. But to be honest, no one cared, and everyone had forgotten about it after the war until a news article surfaced in 1946, at which time they voted to repatriate. Having been known as "the Last of the Rebels" or "Last Confederacy", their fire department's uniform still features the Rebel Flag from what I hear.

The question of slavery even ripped apart the Anti-Masonic Party, the most successful national third party in our history. It had its roots in Western New York, a few hour's drive from here where the Morgan Affair took place.

Most (but not all) the Northern States had by the start of the Civil War outlawed slavery as an institution within their respective borders. The federal government didn't start seriously crafting national abolition until after the war started. The 13th Amendment was put before Congress just before the end of the war and ratified later that year, months after Lee surrendered to Grant. That's why Lincoln carefully worded the *Emancipation Proclamation* to not jump the gun. It only applied to states in rebellion, which technically he had no control over anyway. Delaware and territories not in rebellion were not so compelled. (Another interesting omission in most classrooms is that the proclamation demanded those freed not to engage in violence.)

The state constitutions of the rebellious states all mentioned slavery explicitly. It was a raised fist to the Union at the very least. Slave ownership was nearly exclusive to the one-percenters of their time. Many a poor Confederate soldier lamented they were fighting a "rich man's war". However, it had the general support of the people, even after the war. But not by everyone. There were definitely Southern abolitionists as surely as there were supporters of slavery in the North. And During the war, the rhetoric of the Confederacy was all about being free from tyranny; the rhetoric of the Union during the war rarely mentioned abolition, but focused on unity as integral to American strength. The war may have been started by powerful men over slavery, but the man in the field was hardly fighting to keep or liberate slaves. This is usually an argument to downplay slavery. I say it is even more damning, expanding the indictment to all of America.

The most damning fact is that the Underground Railroad didn't stop in the North. The final destination was Canada, not the Mason-Dixon line. With the Fugitive Slave Act and other similar legislation throughout the 19th Century, those who escaped slavery had to be returned even if they were in states prohibiting it, and that ran right up until *after* the war. Some slaves went to Mexico, often accompanying migrating Seminoles. Mexico's Congress abolished slavery in 1837; their Constitution of 1857 granted freedom to any slaves who entered the country. But law enforcement in all the states of the United States was tasked with the capturing and returning of slaves. There were stiff penalties if they didn't. In at least eleven sites in Buffalo, New York, escaped slaves hid as fugitives from our own police and sheriffs. Let that sink in.

The friction of the time was from states wanting to maintain their sovereignty, especially over this "peculiar institution" we are talking about. In our time we saw such a battle over marriage equality. Would a state that doesn't recognize Gay marriage recognize a union done lawfully in another state? There weren't armed border skirmishes over that, but then again, whole economic paradigms and the fortunes of powerful and wealthy plantation-owners weren't at stake.

But even if we accept the war was about slavery in the South, it most certainly was not in the North. Lincoln represented his constituents' general priorities by saying, "If I could save the Union without freeing any slave I would do it, and if I could save it by freeing all the slaves I would do it; and if I could save it by freeing some and leaving others alone I would also do that." As with writing and ratifying the Constitution, the union (and its economic prosperity) was more important than getting rid of a horribly inhumane institution.

Going back, we have to wonder if, without slavery, the South still would have seceded. There were already basic cultural schisms in areas of religion, not just economic regionalism. It's where we get things like "Southern Baptist". And these distinctions have an impact on the psychosocial demographics of racism today (discussed earlier in the book). Secondly, without secession, would slavery have continued? Like same-sex marriage a few years ago, abolition was reaching the tipping point in terms of state support to make federal action possible. How much longer could slave states have held out? I will leave that to more specialized historians to guess. But what if there was no federal impetus?

The visiting Frenchman, Alexis de Tocqueville (Alexis Charles Henri Clérel), suggested slavery couldn't last due to its economic inefficiencies. But as dispassionate as he tried to be as an observer, moral questions stuck in his eye.

> I am pained and astonished by the fact that the freest people in the world is, at the present time, almost the only one among civilized and Christian nations which yet maintains personal servitude ... An old and sincere friend of America, I am uneasy at seeing Slavery retard her progress, tarnish her glory, furnish arms to her detractors, compromise the future career of the Union which is the guaranty of her safety and greatness... I am moved at the spectacle of man's degradation by man, and I hope to see the day when the law will grant equal civil liberty to all the inhabitants of the same empire, as God

accords the freedom of the will, without distinction, to the dwellers upon earth.

Those were prophetic words given what occurred generations later between North and South. (He also predicted the rise of the United States and Russia as superpowers.) If he were to have visited us, say, just before the Civil Rights Era of the 1960s, or today, would he conclude we have prevailed against this great American contradiction? Slavery is no longer an institution, but since the beginning of the Reconstruction, African-Americans have been disenfranchised or marginalized as much as the law would allow, and often more.

Making racism out to be specifically a Southern thing gives the rest of us a free pass we don't deserve. Sure, racism has been more visible in "those parts" with Jim Crow and all. But I have heard time and again from people who've lived on both sides of the Mason-Dixon line that racism in the North is more insidious, with its facade of outward civility. This is even evident during the Civil War, where popular sentiment placed the Negro as inferior and therefore could not be a good soldier, given mostly to menial tasks. A number of Negro Union soldiers even refused their pay for over a year to protest the highest of their wages being half that of the lowest-paid White soldier. Southern Nergoes, freedmen and slaves, volunteered and were conscripted, and some did serve as soldiers with guns. It was a controversial move given fears of an uprising. But that is too complicated and convoluted a topic to get into here without being misleading, overgeneralizing, and distracting us from the big picture.

This brings us to another prejudice we avoid talking about – that against Southern ancestors who fought for the Confederacy. It makes sense for us to focus on slavery as the elephant in the room. But learned historians would also know the men in gray were not personally fighting for slavery anywhere near across the board. The diaries of Confederate soldiers and officers tell us many didn't give a damn about the slave issue compared to protecting what they saw as their freedom and way of life, and like their Union counterparts, coming home. We can say not all Confederates supported slavery, just as not all German soldiers were Nazis. (And even then there is an occasional Buddha of Nanking.) We can agree that arguments to downplay slavery aren't helpful, but it's wrong to put words in their mouths or intentions in all such men's hearts.

We are left with guilt by association, all being held responsible for the political intentions and injustices of its national leaders. Perhaps that's why so many people were harsh on Vietnam veterans, simply for participating in a war the public despised. So many were spat on for the atrocities of a few. And that wasn't right either.

Confederates were not always seen as or hated as traitors. If that were true, so many army bases wouldn't be named after them. After the war, there was a general amnesty. Pensions were set up for all veterans, though administration and funding for Confederate soldiers and sailors were the responsibility of states rather than the federal government. However, recent rumors that Confederate monuments are officially considered and protected as federal war memorials have been found to be false. The point here is that we have forgiven soldiers of countries that are no longer at war with us. There are even reunions of Axis and Allies veterans who made friendships after previously shooting at each other. To all-of-a-sudden regard all Confederates in the same light as Nazis makes little sense. But the association with slavery is so strong today that arguing over fact serves little purpose, and the discord from it can bleed into real, current racial issues.

The real danger is to package up inequality and oppression into geographic or historical boxes so we can hide them in our cultural attics. What we can label as "in the past" in "those parts" of the country gives a false sense of American innocence, and anchors us less in a world built upon, and is a continuation of, that history.

That's where the 1619 *Project* comes in. Developed by the *New York Times Magazine*'s in 2019, it's a telling of American history from an African-American perspective. It's a work in progress and includes framing current events as a continuation of the aftermath of slavery. It doesn't sugarcoat anything, even Lincoln's problematic words and actions inconsistent with the one-dimensional storybook version we've been taught. Is it biased? Of course it is. The value is that it counterbalances existing biases we've taken for granted all these years.

But it isn't without backlash. A Senator from Arkansas proposed the "Saving American History Act of 2020" to strongarm schools out of using it in their curriculum. Soon thereafter, the president announces an executive order to form a "President's Advisory 1776 Commission" charged to codify "the core principles of the American founding and how these principles may be understood". He even defended the Columbus myth as being what "we grew up [with], you grew up [with], we all did, that's what we learned". The Onion parody site hit the nail on the head, chiming in with the headline, "New Patriotic 1776 Commission Struggling To Find Ways To Improve Upon

Education System's Existing Propaganda". It's all politics battling over history in the context of a larger, unnecessary war of American culture and race.

We are entering a place in America where we can no longer acknowledge shades of grey in our quest to either purge all evil or maintain nationalistic beliefs. It never turns out well when anyone wins such a polarizing game. I applaud those who want to bring balancing perspectives that address real cultural flaws. But my suggesting the historical narrative is greater than a rigid, politically correct one puts me at risk for appearing a slavery apologist. The whole thing has become off-limits at times. A friend of mine, Tom Schobert, runs the town of West Seneca's historical museum and portrays in costume various figures. Just after the Charleston mass shooting by White supremacists in 2015, an appearance as General Robert E. Lee was canceled. He's now retiring that uniform.

History has always been a collection of interpretations, even ones we don't like or agree with. It gives us something to debate and explore, never being satisfied with one pat answer. I know we have to teach our kids a watered-down version, but we as Americans need to grow up. We have to stop pretending anyone owns history, and that we all share in it. To make it a battle disrespects each other's narratives. And we need to hear them out if we are going to make peace among ourselves as Americans.

18. Brothers in Arms

In line at a supermarket (in a not-so-racially diverse suburb), a World War II veteran was checking out in front of me. I don't recall what got him riled up, but he started complaining about Obama, who was in office at the time. He said something to the effect of "I didn't fight a war to have one of his kind be president." I was shocked and speechless. And when he left, the woman behind me said, "He was only saying what the rest of us were thinking."

In hindsight, I should have said, "No, he was NOT saying what I was thinking. I'm not a bigot." But the cashier and I just stared blankly and completed the transaction. The regret of my silence will haunt me for the rest of my life. And from that moment on, I realized that not everyone or everything about "the Greatest Generation" was great.

In fact, White-American and African-American troops were in pitched battle AGAINST EACH OTHER in a small town in England during the war. The "Battle of Bamber Bridge" started out with tensions between MPs and Black soldiers, with the Army failing to impose segregation between Black troops and Brits. The British were so offended at their attempts that they marked the town pubs "Black Troops Only". During arrests, Private William Crossland was shot in the back and killed. These servicemen of color had fears they were all going to be killed. Although they were assured the MPs would be held accountable, the MPs rallied and ambushed the troops, resulting in a night of shooting and injuries.

Military command determined the incident was the result of violent MPs, poor leadership, and racial slurs, prompting some organizational changes, including racial integration of MPs. However, the only court-martialling was the conviction of 32 African-American soldiers for mutiny and related crimes. And this was only the worst of several such incidents. (These scenarios and their details may be eerily familiar to some in 2020.)

Also notable during this time was the most decorated unit of the war, the 442nd Infantry Regiment, made up almost entirely of Japanese-Americans. Nicknamed the "Purple Heart Batallion" (over 4,000 awarded), their medals and other awards are too numerous to detail here. Thousands of these men volunteered from, and thousands more had family in, the American concentration camps set up by the federal government upon alleged fears of domestic sabotage. No incident had ever occurred and no Japanese-American or non-citizen immigrant was ever found guilty of any such act, and every investigation and detail indicates internment was based solely on regional racism (mostly the West Coast).

And yet I have met people old enough to remember this as it happened who believe it was justified. It took many years since then just to overcome euphemisms that whitewashed it all, as well as ongoing debates if "internment camp" is accurate enough. The musical *Allegiance* was made to express what the experience was like, along with conflicts of identity in a country they loved that didn't trust them. It's based on the childhood of George Takei, the actor who played Sulu on Star Trek, having lived in the Heart Mountain Relocation Center in Wyoming.

In addition to over 110,00 men, women, and children of Japanese descent, many Germans and Italians were detained and deported. Anti-German sentiment seems to have been much greater during The Great War (WWI). Countless business and surnames were changed. It was perhaps the start of animosity toward the concept of hyphenated-Americans.

Times are, for the most part, different now. For nearly 20 years I've taught Tai Chi to veterans at the local recovery center. Most are from Korea, Vietnam, and Desert Storm, but I've known a few from World War II when I first started. I've gotten to know many of them, spending extra time after class playing pool, working on jigsaw puzzles, or just sitting and talking. Most of the racism they experience and share with me is outside military and veteran circles. The military isn't segregated anymore, but it's not without problems.

In 1972, racial violence on several United States Navy ships occurred in spite of two years of reforms to tackle discrimination. A 2011 Pentagon study recommended improvements in diversity and inclusion. Yet even today women and minorities are underrepresented among officers, more so as you move up ranks. People of Color now hold high positions in the armed forces and have for some time, but accusations related to advancement clearly exist and the numbers support that.

The veterans I know say bigotry isn't tolerated within the ranks. Their attitude is they all bleed red and having each other's backs is all that matters. My father, the bookkeeper and a bartender at the West Point officer's club, recalled an incident just after the Korean War where an officer was removed for racial slurs. It just wasn't tolerated. This is consistent with what I hear from many other veterans. But the stories I've heard are anecdotal, and there are other facts to consider.

Around the end of the Vietnam War, Ku Klux Klan meetings were hosted at Camp Pendleton. A decade later, Marines were photographed at a White supremacist rally in Klan garb. These may have been isolated incidents from the past, but the US Naval Institute writes today,

> White nationalist recruitment campaigns have had increasing success within the military... Junior servicemembers are the prime targets for such propaganda, and thanks to ever-sophisticated algorithms and the addictive nature of social media itself, white nationalist recruiters can overwhelm a captive audience with crowd-tested racist propaganda.

This is yet another reason White Nationalists are considered at least an equal threat to America as groups like ISIS.

But our perception of history is full of contradictions. We revere the Tuskegee Airmen and Navaho Code Talkers with much lip service, while a large number of forts and barracks are named after Confederate war figures. My wife finds it strange we were only taught in school the name of one victim of the Boston Massacre, Crispus Attucks. He was of Native and African descent. He the first casualty of the Revolution as per the national mythos, or perhaps noteworthy as a symbol due to his racial identity. Let's apply the 5th dimension of history to this and see what reveals itself.

After the incident, no less than John Adams successfully defended the British soldiers from murder charges, with only two being found guilty of manslaughter. He denounced Attucks as a wannabe hero and the rest as, in today's vernacular, thugs. It wasn't until 1858 that he was acknowledged, in Boston, with a day in his honor. Those who established it were abolitionists. A location marker was placed in 1886 and a monument in 1888, but the latter was opposed by the leaders of the Massachusetts Historical Society and the New England Historic Genealogical Society. Some would say he was added later into the American Story. Was this to shine an example of at least one Person of Color playing an active part in the first chapter of the American story? And so what if it was? Would he have otherwise been forgotten if not for abolitionist fervor?

What I find most interesting is that we were taught it was a "battle", but it seems history rhymes once again with familiar themes. He and others confronted redcoats (the law and order of the time) over some little injustice – the payment of a haircut. Things escalated to snowball throwing, the (alleged) swinging of a stick, and ultimately gunfire. We could say the American Revolution started with a Black man being shot by persons of authority who mostly got away with it.

19. The New Black

"Please don't let them be Muslim."

This is the common prayer of American Muslims every time some shooting or bombing takes place, even though statistically such things are rarely done by people who are Muslim. Individuals, community centers, and whole communities have been targets of harassment and violence by people who believe Islam is some imminent ideological threat or behind an impending culture war. It's been difficult to educate people out of such notions. Trust me, I've tried.

Around a decade ago, a friend on social media asked me why I was so intent on defending Islam. Around a decade ago Muslims were the most common target of prejudice in America. That is my answer – I defend whoever needs defending. It's part of my hero complex. Like any hot topic, at least since the advent of social media, we all become experts overnight by watching YouTube videos. When a wave of Islamophobia swept in ten years ago, propagandists were eager to get our eyeballs and fill in the blanks for what we didn't know about Islam. People fell for it. After all, most people don't know Muslims (or don't realize they do), so it's easy to become misinformed.

Is Muslim the new Black, so to speak? It's not a coincidence they are sometimes referred to as "Sand N*s". I was even at a community meeting of block clubs around that time when a man – an African-American who made it known he was a veteran – stood up and talked about those "Ay-rabs" running corner stores. The inflection of his voice was unambiguous in its contempt.

From France, we heard news of riots and violence in one or another Muslim *banlieue*. The word denotes a suburb or neighborhood, but in this context means *ghetto*. The conditions in those places parallel what was experienced by African-Americans in our own cities, and to similar results. People assumed it was about religion. Well, partially it was, in the sense of religious persecution in a highly secular country. But Americans, without knowing the context, saw it as a Muslim issue.

The Internet turned into a battleground over what version of Islam people should believe – the monolithic one based on propaganda, prejudice, and examples of extremism you may see on TV, or the incredibly diverse one lived by over a billion people across the world, including a million of our American neighbors. When someone brings up Sharia, I have to ask "which one?" as there are nine major schools of thought on that, none of which live up to people's fears. Obscure theological points are turned into misrepresented, major doctrines that in real life most Muslims may not have even heard of. The worst part? Misinterpretations of *taqiya* (lying to save one's life from persecution) make all Muslims out to be religiously-mandated liars, meaning if we ask them what Islam means to them, we can't trust their answers. This blocks off any counter-criticism or productive dialogue where Muslims can't even defend their own faith. That brainwashing tactic is why so many today have become incurably ignorant on the subject.

Some play whack-a-mole with their bigotry. When pressed, they claim they are only against radical or militant or political Islam, yet will prove time and again by other statements their disclaimer is a sham. I've even seen acquaintances of mine do this, if not about Islam then about African-Americans. "I have friends who are Black and I don't mean all of them are bad, but ..." It's the creeping equivocal "they" we talked about early in this book. But their agenda is clear when those things that define Islam broadly are attacked, such as Muhammed or the Quran. And we hear one-sided or puerile historical quips like "those people have been fighting for thousands of years" like it's in their nature. When you hear (as I have had) that violence is "in their blood" or they are "born with it" it's hard to walk it back by saying "only those who do bad things".

Fanatical tribalistic fear of losing one's own cultural identity had gone mainstream in America, as was growing in Europe, mostly over huge influxes of refugees from Middle East conflicts. In the process, bigotry became acceptable, justified. Many have even taken to the notion that Islam isn't a religion but only a political philosophy, so as not to see themselves as religious intolerants. People who wanted to vilify it on religious grounds catapulted a myth it is not even Abrahamic, but that they worship a "moon god". Nevermind that Moses (Musa), Jesus (Issa), and other familiar names are in the Quran. Heck, Mary (Maryam) is mentioned more in the Quran than the Bible!

With regards to Muslims in America, one word crops up time and time again – assimilation. Some Americans have this weird fear that if people from other cultures don't conform to "our" ways, we will have to conform to theirs. The funny thing is we characterize certain cultures as not wanting to assimilate, not realizing they already have. Where I live, for example, you may occasionally see a family where the women are covered head-to-toe, and they may speak in Arabic. But here's the secret: we've had Muslims in America for hundreds of years. Most of them we don't even think of as Muslim. Why? Because they dress and speak just like you and I. The only ones you "see" are the ones that you can pick out for their differences. These are usually that first generation who just came over. And what if some maintain their language and visible aspects of their culture? It's still alright to wear a kilt, right? And we can let the Amish be the Amish, too, I would hope. My point is that the desire for others to assimilate and the fear of them not doing so isn't rational.

We also try to judge cultures by our own measuring stick and miss the mark. Traditional Middle Eastern Islamic coverings such as burqas, niqabs, or hijabs (most common among younger folks) are assumed to be for the oppression of women. They are in fact an interpretation of modesty, and not specifically outlined in the Quran. Some countries are strict with the dress code for the purpose of public decency. Turkey, on the other hand, is quite secular and restricts wearing headscarves in some public contexts. This actually caused a backlash by women, who wore them defiantly, as a form of Feminist religious empowerment.

The social mores of some predominantly Mulsim nations is modern, but in others, is akin to America a few generations ago, or even farther back to Puritan America. The role of women can be anywhere from not driving cars and having separate amusement parks in Saudi Arabia, to having women as heads of state. And there is a huge Women's Rights movement in Islam worldwide. Egypt-American journalist Mona Eltahawy is perhaps the perfect example of such advocacy in America. She's an amazing woman – look her up. But don't make assumptions about what you see. A woman walking behind the man doesn't imply property, but protection, the same way I can't help but walk "on the outside" next to my wife. Gentlemen know what I mean.

If you are not of Arabic tradition, there are a few things you need to know to not be disrespectful. These may not apply at all, as customs vary greatly, but you can play it safe anyway. If you are a man, do not speak to or interact with a woman more than necessary unless you can tell she initiates it. Speak with the apparent man of the household, careful to avoid phrases such as "Dude, it's so cool you are married to a ninja." Seriously, though, if they make eye contact, you probably can too. But be warned – I saw a woman fully covered to where I could only see her eyes; if hiding her beauty was the intention, she failed.

Of course, a lot of Islamophobia has to do with terrorism. There was a cartoon during World War II depicting Japanese (buck teeth and round glasses to boot) lining up in California to get sticks of dynamite, a sentiment some fear-mongers have pushed with regards to Muslims in America today. Islamic sleeper cells are poised and ready to take over! Actual Muslims, when told of such nonsense that Muslims were planning to make their move around the world, had reactions from incredulity to laughter. "Will there be some kind of Bat Signal? What are you talking about?" Indeed.

We hear the words "Islamic Terrorism" or wonder why some politicians won't say the word "Islamic" in cases where the actors purport to be Muslims, albeit fanatic. In fact, discovered search histories of terrorists show that "Islam for Dummies" is quite popular among that crowd. Like fanatic Christians or any other flavor of extremists, the religious fervor component of radicalization has little to do with the core substance of the religion. And radicalization can't exist without a target or purpose that gives wind to its sails.

I would think most people agree there is no excuse for heinous acts, but we cannot say there is no cause, nor afford to be ignorant of such causes. Organized violence doesn't happen in a vacuum of the personal life of spiritually scarred or stressed individuals. Terrorists, not too unlike regular armies, are pawns played by the princes of the world. The possibilities of their existence are predictable reactions to the lamentable policies of powerful nations, including America. Sometimes it's just about power, pure and simple, but persecution, real or perceived helps. Extreme acts are answers to extreme circumstances.

Terrorism may be fueled in part by the belief there is no other option, but no matter how (poorly) thus justified, it is actually a fruit of bigotry. The innocent are taken with the guilty. Islamists would lump all Westerners into one category, holding all responsible for the injustices of politicians and general prejudices. Our complacency to allow our country to participate (or interfere, rather) in foreign matters is not without consequence. We may have reasonable justifications, but we need to understand the opposing point of view and address it rather than let it fester.

And bigotry breeds bigotry. Westerners are all alike to extremists; in turn, all Muslims become the target of blame for specific acts. Our arguments sound different, but they are the same. We blame culture, religion, and insist it's the fault of "all of them" because they are not magically stopping the evils of people under the imaginary banner of "them". It's like wanting to take all Catholics to task because of scandals within the clergy, or all African-Americans for a heart-wrenching crime. It's not one person's job to apologize or condemn another person's acts just because they are in the same group. In fact, many Muslims refuse to accept that terrorists are true Muslims. Good people don't see bad ones as having any relation to them. Regardless, there have been countless condemnations of terrorism from Muslims around the world. It just doesn't get the same press as the crazy imam who few people listen to anyway.

This is the most important thing to understand: Islamists (adherents of radical political Islam) and Islamophobes think the same way and want the same thing. War. Revenge. Genocide. Repeat.

We cannot control what is in the hearts of others. But we choose our response to it. And why not take responsibility for the part we may play? Perhaps we consider it a weakness, but the narrow path is to defend ourselves without hating our brother. We can choose not to give wind to the rhetoric of other people's sails. And there are countless ways we can go out of our way to build bridges rather than blow them up, personally and collectively, figuratively and literally.

20. Weaponized Bigotry

Sunando Sen was pushed to his death in front of a subway train. The woman who did it proudly confessed, "I pushed a Muslim off the train tracks because I hate Hindus and Muslims – ever since 2001 when they put down the twin towers, I've been beating them up." She is probably deranged, but more concerning, perhaps she is not. The notion of "other" is psychological, not rational, and people speak and act on that in all sorts of ways. If you wear a turban, that might be close enough to trigger someone with visions of Arabians flying airliners into buildings.

After 9-11, hate crimes against Muslims sharply but briefly spiked. But the above incident was in 2012. The trend of higher numbers of such crimes started in 2010, over a very specific controversy. Here I bring you the tale of two very different mosques in Lower Manhattan.

The first was a proposed mosque, one that would look down on Ground Zero, close enough to be built over the possible remains of the victims from that fateful day. The radical imam behind it was connected to Jihadists, running an organization named after a famous conquest of a European city by Muslims. The purpose was to place it there as a sign of victory for militant Islam, slipping under the wire of guaranteed American religious freedoms.

The second was a proposed cultural center with space to be used sometimes as a mosque, replacing a building already being used for such religious services. It would be over a football field outside the area where remains have been found and not anywhere near within sight of Ground Zero. The imam behind the project worked with the federal government to fight Islamic extremism around the world, and his organization is named after a European city that under Muslim rule was a center for learning with peaceful co-existence between Christians, Jews, and Muslims. The top of the proposed structure would have a 9-11 memorial.

What is the fundamental difference between the two? The first one DID NOT EXIST. It was the purposeful fabrication of a fringe bigot blogger, Pamela Geller. Referring to the actual, second mosque, she painted a picture based on assumptions, half-truths, and rhetorical implications, none of which when scrutinized have been found to have much truth. So how did this cause such a stir? A local television station of a national affiliate interviewed her as an "expert" without checking her credentials. And this took place many months after the locals knew about the proposed center with no concern or controversy. Quickly it became a hotly-debated, national urban legend.

Geller and her ilk leaked into mainstream consciousness. Her blog articles went viral and blatant hate sites, such as JihadWatch.Com and ReligionOfPeace.Com, became constant citations for people's fears of an impending "Islamification" of America and the whole world. It became all the rage to quote pseudo-historian authors, misquote the Quran, and any video someone could make "exposing" Islam was guaranteed vast viewership. People and organizations that would otherwise be written off as no better than the Klan were no longer an embarrassment to talk about or even support.

One site, FaithFreedom.Org, purports to be run by ex-Muslims. It puts Muhammed in the same boat as Hitler. Jumping on the bandwagon against "unlimited mosque construction", they made their own Hitleresque intentions clear: "Islam can't be reformed, but it can be eradicated. It can't be molded, but it can be smashed."

Sometimes we catch it in time. A friend of mine unknowingly became a fan of Dutch politician Geert Wilders, with his public, mutual support of Geller's agendas. That was until she realized what she was sharing on social media was propaganda from a man considered the most dangerous neo-fascist in European politics.

But what I found most disturbing was the web of connections between these people and groups. Each organization or person was found to be related to another, and within very few degrees all came to the same people. And the most centrally connected to them all is anti-Islamic David Horowitz. (A former liberal extremist turned conservative extremist, he should not be confused with the consumer advocacy show *Fight Back! with David Horowitz*.) JihadWatch is associated with Horowitz's "Freedom Center" and run by Robert Spencer, a blogging partner of Geller. And Horowitz is always on the attack – anyone who challenges his own prejudices is promptly threatened with being marked an anti-Semite.

One video purporting to be a documentary about "Sharia Banking" featured a banker who talked about the horrors of Islamic law with generous images and video of violence and gore, never even explaining what Islamic banking actually is. The organization that made the video traced through association easily back to Horowitz. Other pieces of the puzzle include David Yerushalmi, who runs the "Society of Americans for National Existence", an anti-Sharia not-for-profit, who has represented and worked with Geller.

A strange thing occurred to me I didn't notice right away: all the prominent voices against Islam were Jewish. That didn't seem right, so a deeper investigation revealed they were specifically ultra-conservative Zionists. Many were or have direct ties to Israeli intelligence. Those few that were not are all staunchly pro-Israel, such as author Brigitte Gabriel. A racist against Arabs in particular, she lived through the Lebanese Civil War as a child. The hate and resentment half-world away between the State of Israel and its neighbors has for years been templated upon America as *our* cause. Our changing views of Islam are being written by people with not only grave bias, but an agenda worthy of a conspiracy novel. I was going to make a map of these people and groups, which I call the "Hate Club", but someone beat me to it. You can see their interconnections at IslamophobiaNetwork.com.

The attacks of 9-11 put an exclamation mark on existing sentiments and politics influenced greatly by the Arab-Israeli conflict for half a century. By the time of the rise of the Taliban in the 1990s, the target of propaganda broadened the idea of Arab adversaries to include all Muslims. America uniquely finds the acceptance of this simple narrative not only palatable but as a sacred duty. This is not metaphorical. An extremely large proportion of private financial support of the State of Israel is from Evangelical Christian groups. Modern-day Israel is equivocated with the Israel of the Bible, including its role in Revelation with regards to the end times. "Whoever blesses Israel will be blessed, and whoever curses Israel will be cursed" is repeated constantly on news site comment sections, mixed in with platitudes about Jesus being the only way to salvation. This a pervasive Christian-American perspective, and not just among Millenialists.

Efforts at early Zionism in the mid-1800s almost placed a Jewish refuge here in New York, a half-hour drive from my home. Mordecai Noah would call the settlement "Ararat" and invited Jews around the world to migrate there. This colony was to be "under the protection of the American Constitution" but have a "Hebrew government". He had much local support, even a lavish parade and ceremonies to commemorate its start, but no one showed up. There is still a cornerstone marker for it, but since has moved across the Niagara River to Tonawanda. Not to play into alternate history games, but some suggest that if early efforts at such things had succeeded, many families would not have suffered the Shoah. Then again, American intelligence had some idea what was going on under Hitler, yet turned away a ship of almost a thousand Jewish refugees, many children. So many what-ifs haunt us.

Like the term Feminism, Zionism has a wide variety of meanings. It's most often equated with the establishment of a self-governed nation of Jewish people. Some don't see a homeland as necessarily a political entity, or at least not embodied by the relatively recent State of Israel. Prime Minister Netanyahu invited people from Europe to move to Israel over anti-Semitic crimes and attacks in 2015, saying "Israel is your home." Some did move; others were not impressed and thought his invitation presumptuous.

Fanatical and militant forms of Zionist belief do exist, even ones that are arguably racially supremacist. That may be one of the reasons it is given a bad wrap by conspiracists and anti-Semites in general. (I am careful to avoid using the term Zionist by itself as derogatory or meaning its radical versions.) If you look, you will find a full continuum of Zionist views in Israeli politics, fighting many of the same battles over liberal and conservative values and policies that we do. In other words, Israel as a country should not be seen with prejudiced eyes as all Israelis supporting every action of their government or wanting supremacy over the Holy Land. Neither should we judge all those who are Jewish anywhere else in the world, any more than judging your Arabic-speaking neighbor as supporting terrorism.

There are clearly Jews (and non-Jews) who support Israel, those who don't, and those who support Israel but not its policies. Some of it is generational, with older folks lamenting the younger generation's lack of homage to what they consider their homeland on a guttural level. And as Palestinian rights intersect Black Lives Matter, things can get even more complicated for those who feel they must choose sides. A recent survey by the Mellman Group showed that a majority of American Jews support Israel but at the same time do *not* support its policies. Prime Minister Netanyahu is a globally divisive figure that has escalated tensions and worse, and his coziness with the American head of state, a Republican, didn't win brownie points with a predominantly Democrat Jewish demographic.

Let's be clear: anti-Semitism in the Middle East today is most accurately anti-Zionism. This hatred stems from the creation of the State of Israel being perceived as a continuation of European colonization from which the people of the region had just thrown off the shackles. People don't understand that it has nothing to do with Judaism versus Islam – at all. Jews had always lived in the Levant, but then a large contingent of European Jews (Ashkenazi) basically staked a claim by force, and ... well ... the rest is a highly contested history that isn't relevant here. Let's just acknowledge there is SOME overlap between Zionism and anti-Semitism, but it's not the whole story. Most of the world agrees with claims of illegal occupation, settlement, and human rights violations against the Palestinians. Regardless of our personal determinations of truth, there are many people who love Isreal but believe this injustice exists, even Holocaust survivors, and they are in a difficult social position because of it.

A peaceful movement denouncing Israeli policy is growing within Palestine, Israel, the United States, and around the world. Many Palestinians and Israelis have banded together. Of course, you don't hear of such things in the news because violence gets attention, the effectiveness of which becomes a sad, self-fulfilling prophesy. In spite of this, the movement has loosened the stranglehold over the conflict's narrative and other voices are now being heard.

Israel is a very political issue in the United States, given they are considered a strategic ally and receive more foreign aid than any other country. Support of the State of Israel is a third-rail topic in America if ever there was one. Until very recently, any lack of total, unquestioning support – devoid of all criticism, especially over the Palestinian question – meant political death. Pro-Israel entities have successfully branded Israel as the Jewish People and the Jewish People as Israel. To be against one is to be against the other. There has always been prejudice against Jews, and by extension Israel, but now we see utter vilification of all who oppose Israeli actions or policies, even if it has absolutely nothing to do with Jewishness. If such a critic is not Jewish, they are publicly and loudly branded anti-Semitic. If they are Jewish, they are degraded as a "self-loathing Jew". There's no other option in such thinking, and I know people who are permanently hard-wired into this either-or fallacy.

There's no need to debate or agree on the particulars of Israeli politics here. What we are concerned with is the weaponization of accusations of racism or religious bigotry. Ironically, the Jewish Anti-Defamation League (ADL) has done many things that could be described as racist, and is a sworn enemy of their Islamic counterpart, the Council for American Islamic Relations (CAIR). Nearly all Zionist groups reject comparisons or connections to White Supremacy but there have been collaborations in Islamophobic propaganda in some circles. There are networks of organizations (some overlapping the "Hate Club") devoted to crushing people and groups – even Jewish ones – who speak out against Israel's occupation and policies in Palestine. Lobbyists are constantly pushing to outlaw boycotts related to Israeli economic entities.

Smear campaigns abound, such as the Canary Mission, which publicly lists and defames student and professor activists as anti-Semitic, even if they are simply anti-occupation. Under pressure from such groups, Arab-American studies in universities are downplayed or even scrubbed in whole or in part from curricula. Even mention of Palestine is forbidden in some cases. The organization Jewish Voice for Peace is mocked as "Jewish Voice for Hamas" and criticized, like other Jewish anti-occupation groups, as being made up of large numbers of non-Jewish members. Some of them are, and I'm not sure that's damning.

Because of pro-Palestinian Rights groups, and growing bad press from particularly problematic events in recent years, times are changing. Rashida Harbi Tlaib is now the third Palestinian-American to serve in Congress, (That doesn't sit well for some propagandists who preach that Palestine is not and never was a real country on the grounds there was no political nation-state by that name.) And yet censorship legislation moves forward, and the American Israel Public Affairs Committee (AIPAC) remains perhaps the most over-influential lobbying group in Washington.

In recent years, the International Holocaust Remembrance Alliance (IHRA) adopted a working definition of anti-Semitism that is being codified as law in some places, such as in Majorca. The United States, a member of the group, may follow suit. Much of it is sound, excerpted here:

> Accusing Jews as a people of being responsible for real or imagined wrongdoing committed by a single Jewish person or group, or even for acts committed by non-Jews. ... Holding Jews collectively responsible for actions of the state of Israel.

This accurately describes prejudice similar to what I wrote earlier in this book. Well done.

> Calling for, aiding, or justifying the killing or harming of Jews in the name of a radical ideology or an extremist view of religion.

This describes religious hate speech. Good job. Then it goes into murkier waters of free speech, condemning any "myth about a world Jewish conspiracy or of Jews controlling the media, economy, government or other societal institutions." Okay, such a thing has and does cause anti-Semitism. Holocaust denial is listed, but that is a matter of ignorance, not necessarily prejudice.

Accusing Jews of loyalty to Israel (versus the nation of their citizenship) is a common prejudice, much like accusing a Catholic of political allegiance to the Pope. However, this makes it more difficult to accurately describe the unique fealty expected within pro-Israel sentiments. Context matters.

It also includes the interpretation of historical views. That's where things get dangerous. Describing (or not describing) the nature of the existence of Israel or the state's policies as racist is a matter of ongoing debate. There are vehement objections to it from many quarters. If it wasn't for US veto power, half a thousand resolutions condemning actions by Israel would have passed over the years, many on the basis of racism, apartheid, etc.. Again, the reader does not have to take sides on the issues themselves. The fear is that this definition may label NGOs such as Oxfam, Human Rights Watch, and Amnesty International as anti-Semitic on allegations they support the BDS (Boycott-Divest-Sanction) movement.

Conflating Israel with Jews as a whole we can agree is a prejudice, but it is exactly this prejudice that is used by supporters of Israel as a shield. It also ethically contradicts another part of the definition IHRA lists, "Applying double standards by requiring of it a behavior not expected or demanded of any other democratic nation." There's no point in debating what that even means except that there is no logical justification for lumping the political expectations of even a theocratic nation in with guidelines for determining ethnic prejudices. Iran's nuclear program, similarly, doesn't have anything to do with being Muslim or defining what anti-Persian means.

It's imperative we untangle these things if we wish to be able to have an open dialogue. We should recognize that being Jewish or Muslim in America is impacted by these geopolitics but must rise above them. We need to recognize what is and isn't bigotry and hate speech, regardless of any perceived special status due to politics. We don't need a hand-crafted definition for each group, just an awareness of backstory and baggage, good intention, and some patience.

I have written many articles condemning hate speech over the years, not just because words matter, but because they have real-world consequences. We all have to take some responsibility for the part we play in that, even if it's sharing a meme that we should have looked at twice before posting.

The latest spike in Islamophobic crimes was tied closely with the rhetoric of the presidential election in 2015-2016. The spike included 12 murders, 34 assaults, 56 acts of vandalism, nine arsons, and eight shootings and bombings. At least one incident was tied to White Supremacy, but most appear to be by everyday people, such as a road-rage incident in which a Palestinian-American was killed by a man telling him to "go back to Islam." A wave of opposition to the construction of houses of worship and community centers swept the nation, with bigots reframing all such things as "terrorist training camps on American soil".

When a powerful public figure even suggests not allowing people into the country based on religion, or warrantless searches and surveillance of houses of worship, or that people of a certain faith be required to carry special identification cards, that should scare the hell out of us as the greatest affront to American Liberty of our time. No such person should ever be given a platform to speak, let alone public office. What we found was that even for many People of Color, bigotry and xenophobic policies aren't a deal-breaker over other perceived reasons to vote for someone. Regardless, we have to readdress the question if the influence of religious supremacy on our society is compatible with our purported ideals and the future we want.

21. Freemasonry

I don't know where to begin with this one. I could start before the Revolutionary War where Black men who became Freemasons were turned down in their request to have their own Lodge (local chapter of Masons). I could get right into how a hoax pamphlet a hundred years ago spurred on anti-Semitism and even the Holocaust. Or I could start with my own journey of becoming a Freemason in 2011.

There are plenty of sources where you can find out about Freemasonry: how it's the oldest and largest fraternity in the world; famous people who were Freemasons; stuff about philanthropy. It's no secret there are hospitals around the country that care for children (at no charge) run by the Shriners. They are all Freemasons, known also for their circuses and tiny cars. So I already had some idea what Freemasonry was. But I also came across (questionable) stuff like Illuminati connections and accusations by some Christians of how evil it is. I also knew there were "Prince Hall" Lodges that appeared to be for African-Americans. But like anything on the Internet, I didn't know how it chalked up to real life.

Personally, I wanted to be part of the local community, do some charity work, and be part of something with a living-history tradition. I wanted to be around people who shared my own values of tolerance, friendship, morality, and the desire to be better versions of ourselves. And I did find all those things.

But it might not have happened.

The few times I had seen someone with a Masonic ring (with the Square and Compass symbols), I asked about it and was given the cold shoulder. Most of those times, looking back, the person was African-American, but I didn't recall that until much later. I was curious but just figured there was some reason, such as having to be asked first (which is not true). When I finally found someone who was willing, even eager, to tell me about it, I had some hard questions before I would ever commit to a "secret society". I asked if we were keeping secret knowledge from the world. Nope. I asked if there was any allegiance required toward particular political views. Absolutely not. And I asked about Prince Hall.

Prince Hall and fourteen other free Black men, after being turned down to become members of a Boston Lodge, received the ceremonial initiation to become Freemasons from a British regimental (military) Lodge. With some difficulty, they formed the first Lodge of Black men in America. For years they suffered somewhere between toleration and non-acceptance with other Lodges. In 1808, they formed the African Grand Lodge, independent from the others. (A grand Lodge is a governing body connecting Lodges within a geographic area. Today, most countries or their individual states and provinces have their own independent Grand Lodges.)

Long story short, African Grand Lodge helped form what are now the Prince Hall Grand Lodges across the country, independent and separate from the predominantly White "mainstream" Grand Lodges. For almost 200 years, "White" Lodges wouldn't recognize (acknowledge) "Negro Masonry", which basically means we couldn't even visit or work with each other.

Here's a grand contradiction – Masonry teaches toleration for all people as brothers and children of the same Heavenly Father. I was told Lodge is a place where people of all colors, creeds, and ideologies pray and work together in peace. And we (mostly) live up to that. A common view in Evangelical circles is that Masonry is wrong because it does not subscribe (enforce?) a very particular view of salvation. How dare we pray together with "unsaved" people of other faiths? Ironically, that was a selling point for me, another reason why I joke that I was always a Mason but didn't know it until now. But then we are faced with a truth voiced by a Masonic author that it was not the Church (Christianity), but Masonry, as the "most segregated institution in America". So my deal-killer question was if we had racial exclusion in membership and did we still shun Prince Hall Masons. The answer, thankfully, was no and no.

My wife had wanted me to become a Mason since we were courting 25 years ago. If I would have had this conversation before 2003, that answer would have been different. I would have walked away before I began, perhaps forever. Fortunately, the "mainstream" and Prince Hall Lodges in New York now have full recognition of each other. Most of the various Grand Lodges are now accepting of each other; some still are not. Decades earlier, a mainstream Grand Lodge who dared to recognize Prince Hall Lodges would be shunned as well. It was a very long path. I personally know some of the Brothers (on both sides) who fostered this reconciliation around 2003. And there were false starts in the preceding decades, with perceived discourtesies and misunderstandings that still stick in a few craws of those old enough to remember.

One of the missteps was out of eagerness. When my Grand Lodge found out Prince Hall wanted to establish relations, a "unity" committee of sorts was immediately formed. But that wasn't what our counterparts wanted. From the mainstream, and frankly, White perspective, integration was the obvious choice, overturning over 200 years of separateness. That would also solve questions about territorial jurisprudence we need not get into here. But the fact is that Prince Hall Masonry has acted, and continues to act, as a social pillar in urban communities and play a particular role in African-American culture. To be "swallowed up" and become a minority, in addition to losing self-sovereignty, would disturb or destroy such benefit. A desire to merge may have been well-intentioned, but it was offensively presumptuous.

I have to be honest here. The animosity and prejudice of the whole thing is a deep stain on what we profess as Freemasons. And some Brothers on both sides are still resistant. Not to be morose, but like change in society itself, we may have to wait for some of the older, more prejudiced generations to age out. And there are still a few states where it may as well be 1860. An ancient institution tends to change slowly and lag behind the times, and American Freemasonry is a microcosm of the American journey, not separate from it.

To be even more honest, I would have hoped, or even expected, that Freemasons (of all flavors) would have led the way in civil rights. After all, we created the template for Western Democracy, and it's no coincidence that the Bill of Rights reflects Masonic principles that did not widely exist in politics before that time. But there is a reasonable excuse: Masonic Lodges cannot participate in politics. We can take a stand as individuals, but not in any capacity as Freemasons or representing our Lodges.

Many famous politicians across the globe have been politicians, from many of the Founding Fathers to Senator John Lewis. We should be proud of that. But it's too easy for a member of the Fraternity to attribute their own political stances (or those of their local fellow Masons) to Masonry in general. We forget that nearly every general in the Revolutionary War was a Mason – on *both sides*. We laud Davey Crockett (or more accurately the legend of him), but American Masons never talk about Brother Santa Anna.

There is one Masonic figure that is perhaps the most controversial with regards to race, Brother Albert Pike. He was a poet, author, orator, and as a jurist fought for Native Americans in the courts. But he is most famous for being the only Confederate general to have a statue in Washington, D.C. – until this summer. Gifted by the Scottish Rite to the city, it wasn't a military statue, but his statue was still a prime target for toppling. He was racist, anti-Catholic, and against post-war suffrage. He may (or may not) have resigned from his commission because he didn't want to defend slavery. He may (or may not) have been involved in the early years of the Klan. Either way, some of us Masons whitewash his record or dismiss his prejudices as being of the time.

I must say here that as much as one's times may make some historical person's attitude understandable, I will not accept it as a legitimate excuse. Washington and Jefferson, for example, made very different choices as to freeing their slaves. As soon as there was a legal mechanism available, Washington not only freed the slaves he inherited from his wife's family, but bequeathed money to Jefferson for the sole purpose of freeing his – which he did not.

But looking more closely at Pike's life reveals another lesson. People can change. El-Hajj Malik el-Shabazz (Malcolm X), after the experience of haj, embraced kinship with non-Black people. Likewise, Pike's attitude toward the Negro seems to have evolved. In 1875, he wrote,

> Prince Hall Lodge was as regular a Lodge as any Lodge created by competent authority. It had a perfect right to establish other Lodges and make itself a Mother Lodge. I am not inclined to meddle in the matter. I took my obligations from white men, not from negroes. When I have to accept negroes as brothers or leave masonry, I shall leave it.

And yet years later he was close friends with the head of the Prince Hall Scottish Rite, who took on the use of his ritual. All this aside, he is more known for his book "Morals and Dogma" but the racist aspect of his legacy continues to lead many African-Americans to believe Freemasonry in its totality is racist.

I'm personally very conflicted over taking strong moral stances while being also being a Masonic author. The overlap of personal conscience and political view seems more blurry than ever. Why must civil rights be so controversial? I know, it's never that simple. Taking a stand means, in other people's minds at least, you but must be against an "opposing" position. It's damn-near impossible to sidestep such polarization. The result is that people are asking Freemasons if they really are for or against this or that whenever we post something. To be part of the solution, I've reduced the visibility of my Masonic membership publicly to minimize such associations and assumptions when I express myself on social media. Even in something like this, people fall easily to stereotypes, and there are enough of those already. (If doing that crossed your mind, please don't be that guy.)

The most dangerous Masonic conspiracy is political – the belief that Freemasonry is part of a Jewish plot for world domination. This association with Zionism is why Freemasonry is banned in many nations that are predominantly Muslim. But where does this come from? Similar anti-Semitic sentiments can be found through the 19th Century, but all global-scale conspiracies trace back to a single written work: *The Protocols of the Elders of Zion*.

The Protocols detail the mechanisms and goals of a global cabal of Jews to take over the world, with legions of knowing and unknowing footsoldier groups, including Masonic Lodges. Some say it was a parody of the Russian Zionist Congress in 1902; much of it was borrowed from other written works of the time. It was most likely written by Russian propagandists (or even intelligence operatives) to stoke anti-Semitism at home and in other countries, notably France. In America, it was published by no less than Henry Ford (ironically a Freemason), and like others of the time connected it in his mind with the rise of Communism, the first Red Scare.

Hitler shared this belief. It became an impetus not just to expunge Jews from the realm, but also Communists and Freemasons, both of which were designated as political prisoners. (It is painful but necessary to note here that another of Hitler's inspirations for Nazi genocide and German Lebensraum was America's history of dealing with Native Americans.)

We've heard bits and pieces of this conspiratorial mould our whole lives – we just don't realize it. The second Red Scare after World War II fits the earlier pattern. Perhaps it's no coincidence that Hollywood was the target of McCarthyism, with parallel talk of "the Jews" controlling the motion picture industry. And when you roll in modern Illuminati theories, usually tied to central and global banking (the Rothschilds), our minds make the same shape from the random static based on previous images.

Today, it's QAnon. All the elements are there. Instead of the Rothschilds, it's George Soros. Instead of Soviet Communism, it's "Marxist" BLM and Anarchist "Antifa". And the #SaveTheChildren cover movement for QAnon accuses Liberals and Hollywood elites of pedophilia sex trafficking, a new iteration of Blood Libel. It never ends.

I don't have a solution for that, but let's go back to Freemasonry as a model for what can be done to make the Fraternity and the world a better place.

First, we can stop tolerating intolerance. One of the Masons in New York I admire the most is Richard Friedman, a psychologist from Rochester. A highly respected leader in the fraternity, he won't hesitate to ask someone to take off their jacket and step outside if they have a problem with another person's race or creed. He's a man after my own heart. And this must be done. Like America, and ourselves individually, our actions don't always reflect our ideals. And yet integrity demands it. That's why silence is a sin.

At the very least, we can learn from each other. There is a cultural, symbolic difference between the two sets of Lodges. Whereas Masonic legend involves Solomon's Temple and the Shrine is generally Arabic in theme, in Prince Hall circles, there is also a specific focus on Egypt, undoubtedly a facet of Afrocentric historical identity. This was most obvious in the man-cave of a Prince Hall Brother I consider a mentor, adorned with all sorts of Masonic-Egyptian art and artifacts. Historically, Prince Hall Lodges have more accurately preserved original practices and rituals, if for no other reason than to deny any excuse they aren't "real" Freemasons. The fact is we share stories of visiting other states and countries and revel in the diversity of Masonic expression, yet we don't explore the Lodges of Brothers who are practically in our own backyards. This is like one friend I know who has traveled to nearly every country in the world but probably has never been to an event on the East Side of Buffalo, a mere two miles from his house.

To become a member of a Masonic Lodge, you must be of good report. In many places, a felony disqualifies membership. The slogan is to "make good men better", and they only want good men to begin with. It was explained to me that Prince Hall Lodges come from a different angle, where becoming a Mason may keep at-risk or troubled youths out of trouble. There are "White" Lodges in some cities that could probably see this opportunity as well.

Prince Hall Lodges tend to have more active involvement in the community, whereas mainstream Lodges have become more regional rather than belonging to a particular village or town. Part of this is due to a decrease in membership in recent decades. But it also has to do with deurbanization, which leans heavily toward non-minorities moving outward. In Buffalo, there are no longer any mainstream Lodges within city limits. All Prince Hall Lodges are, more specifically where the population is predominantly African-American, which is understandable. Visitation between Lodges would foster respect that would bleed into racial dynamics; combining efforts on community projects would give us interactions with the public in neighborhoods we may not otherwise visit.

Easier said than done. This geographic segregation presents the same issues as any other social or economic activity. There's a pushback against driving into the city, especially among older people. They are worried about their cars, though I have never had a problem. To be honest, my Prince Hall Brothers usually escort me to my car, which I find odd. Buffalo is hardly "the big city" and I've never felt unsafe in any neighborhood, even areas with the worst reputations. I'm not a woman, and I have a few kung fu tricks up my sleeve, so maybe it's just me. But the farther out someone lives, the larger the "forbidden zone" seems to be. Someone three townships out might not go anywhere near the city line, even though some city neighborhoods are virtually indistinguishable from the suburbs. Further dynamics of this are discussed elsewhere in the book, but suffice it to say it's an impediment we can either ignore or address.

We're really still at the infant stages of this. Yes, there are Lodges of both types that share buildings in some places. But the average Mason from one has never visited a Lodge of the other. And we have to establish trust each time. Is the Brother visiting as a Masonic tourist of sorts, or genuinely want to build a bridge and make new friends?

In any situation where one racial or ethnic identity is dominant, the presence of someone different will raise eyebrows. There may be mixed reactions. Freemasons have an obligation of acceptance and Brotherly Love, but I would hope this virtue could be applied in any circumstance, be it a VFW Post or a barbershop. Those who are uncomfortable (or even object) will at least try to bury that and be polite. We might go overboard and expect reciprocal trust without fully understanding the baggage left by those who went before us.

But Freemasonry, and any organizations that share a common culture or interest, may turn out to be one of the most profitable paths in breaking down social segregation.

22. Thanks, Obama

I don't have any strong opinions on Barack Obama, and I hope we can talk about this in a context larger than partisan politics. The fact is he was our president for eight years. Shortly after he was elected, we went from "It's Bush's fault!" to "Thanks, Obama!" Before, during, and after that time, the elephant (donkey?) in the room was racism – accused, real, and imagined.

It doesn't matter or not if I voted for him in the general election (I didn't), but I will say that I was a Democrat that year specifically so I could at least vote in a meaningful primary, and I supported him over the other candidate. I even formally canvassed for him. The night of the primary, I was in a church hall on the East Side. Prominent figures in the Black community were present, but it was a somewhat mixed crowd. It was a completely separate (segregated?) function from the rest of the local DNC, which was very much *not* for this particular candidate.

When they called in one of the Rocky Mountain states in his favor, I turned to the African-American woman next to me and wryly said, "You know they only voted for him because he's Black." After the smallest pause, she and I burst out laughing. I retold that story to a fellow farmhand months later (I used to spend time weekly on a Community Supported Agriculture project), and although White, she was not convinced it was humorous. But she did agree it will be a wonderful age down the road where people won't get the joke at all.

To be honest, part of the reason I liked Obama was because he was different from the usual old, White, male persona the rest of the world was convinced was all we had. I firmly believe that no one leadership stereotype should define us to the world, and going back and forth between carrying a big stick and an olive branch keeps the doors open when negotiating on the global scene. And I was hoping his international upbringing would give him an advantage in building bridges with other nations instead of just bombing them.

But it worked against him. He and his family's multiculturalism were too easy to create conspiracies – about where he was born, his religion, and by extension, his allegiance. As if being dark-skinned "with a funny name" (his own words) wasn't enough, these all crept into people's tribal definition of "other" rather than what the majority thought of as "real American". Looking only at his early socialization and ideology we might begrudge the view he was not quite "American", regardless of *bona fide* citizenship.

But the attacks on his identity seemed more visceral than logical. I would even say many people clung to the Birther conspiracy, not because it was compelling via facts and reasoning (it wasn't), but because it gave a tangible form to our gut feeling he wasn't American in any sense White America could identify with. A non-White president subconsciously just didn't make sense. To much of America, Chuck Heston was their president for two terms. The rest of us White folks had to either laud him as a novelty or craft some cognitive dissonance to deny his legitimacy. People took it even further. It wasn't enough to not be American because of his color. He had to be rejected as belonging to America as the Christian Nation. Putting aside the ironic accusations of being radicalized by his Christain pastor, he must be a secret Muslim. The very fact so many people thought being a Muslim was scandalous speaks to the prevalence of Christian supremacy and nationalism. This indictment was coupled with the highly debatable, if not offensive notion you can't be faithful to both Islam and the Constitution.

America's reception of him was polarized along political lines, of course, but overlaps of politics and race have always been a bit blurred. In recent years, Democrats have successfully branded themselves as the party for minorities, and the Republicans being branded racist in spite of their taking the lead in civil rights between the Civil War and the Moon Landing. Look it up − it's surprising and complicated. The parties, and our perceptions of them, have changed a lot over the years. I'm not sure what shifted so much since then, but I suspect it has something to do with White Evangelicals becoming such a strong force in the GOP. (That discussion is for another time.)

But even if none of my above political interpretations ring true for you, there's something we can't deny − political parties count on people voting for people like them. If you run a woman candidate, you can expect most women to vote for them. If they are Black or Hispanic, you expect the votes of minorities. And you will get them, more or less, every time.

It's human nature. Don't believe me? Consider this: If we vote for someone NOT like ourselves, we always *consciously* find reasons to do so. When you ask someone why they are voting for someone like them in ethnicity or gender, they very often can't even give a good reason when pressed. And it is even possible to have a politician people will vote for against all sense and decency simply because they are the sort of person they can see themselves joking with in the locker room, or says what we're thinking even if they shouldn't. Tell me I'm wrong.

And it's not always a bad thing to vote (or hire) based on ethnicity or gender. Maybe we need different voices than we had before. Maybe we want people who, because of their place in society, may better understand certain challenges and offer different ways of thinking. And back to the subject, many of us White folks voted for Obama because he was Black.

Well, he wasn't blatantly Black, but of mixed descent. He was just Black enough to rally minority voters, but not *too* Black as to elicit excessive White discomfort. His accent was "White" enough and his skin light enough to not seem in oppositional contrast to the other end of America's racial spectrum. The Reverend Jesse Jackson could have never garnered that much support, and perhaps a man like him still cannot. His unique ambivalence – usually a curse for biracial individuals who can't find full acceptance from either side – was seen as an advantage. Some argued that electing him would assuage "White guilt" and prove America was over racism. Playing on this political "superpower", radio talk show star Rush Limbaugh regularly aired these sentiments during the 2008 election in the form of a parody song, "Barack the Magic Negro". It's based on a *Los Angeles Times* editorial by David Ehrenstein and supposedly mimics the voice of Al Sharpton. It's not pretty.

Acceptance had to do with pride as well. If you were African-American, he was one of yours, even if he was not descended from slaves and his upbringing was virtually devoid of the African-American experience. Then again if you are Asian-American, you may call Tiger Woods one of yours. It's very much a matter of subconscious choice to associate or not associate with others via race, even if it's not based in facts. And some People of Color assume different identities based on social situations. I say it's all okay. I don't have any desire to judge. Let's just be honest about it.

And sentiments about politicians, especially those cast into the hero mold, are rarely rational. It's what they represent that has power. Before he had even won the Nobel Peace Prize – something that made even him shake his head considering he just got elected – he was being proffered up as the greatest President since Lincoln by African-Americans. This was how people felt. Many Americans waited a lifetime for someone their color to lead the nation, or never thought it would ever happen. (There was even a fleeting belief in prisons that if he were elected, the doors would swing open by edict of a new Moses.) This idolization is perhaps why it was so hard for those of all colors who wished for a post-racial America to process the Freddie Gray Baltimore protests in 2015. The promised land seemed a mirage.

But what of White America? Is it reasonable to say overall they hated him (and still do)? Well, at least allegiant Republicans did – it's their job to do so as much as it's expected loyal Democrats preserve his image as a political messiah. I don't think he was particularly good or bad as a president, but I know some saw him as an existential threat. Was it because he was a Democrat or "Lefty"? I'm not convinced that was all. There was a constant undertone of personal distaste, even though he was the least scandalous President of our time.

People mocked the "style" and fashion of him and his family, memes contrasting them with the Kennedys, them being some American, apple-pie ideal. That's not surprising, given our society judges people of color in how well they measure up to a White standard of language, dress, music, hairstyle, everything.

But people didn't talk about race as much as expected. They only used it as an arguing point. I once dared criticize an aspect of one of Obama's policies and it was automatically assumed I was racist. Others expressed hatred of him and tacked on thin rationalizations after the fact to not sound too racist. The race card being played and not being accepted became a barbed wire fence between any of us and common ground.

And we did it to ourselves. President Obama did little if anything to stoke racial tensions. He had no noticeable focus on dealing with racial issues. So where does all the blame come from? He's still being blamed for a racially divided America that existed before his election and only rose to fever pitch after he retired from the Oval Office. The answer is simple: A person of color was in our face. His very existence was a challenge to America's longstanding identity.

It's no wonder so many turned to the least "ethnic", sleeps-in-a-suit candidate – Archie Bunkeresque to boot – and let out a four-year sigh of relief America can just "be itself" again. And from that perspective, there was only one silver lining to those eight years – a Black man in the Presidency could be used as proof America didn't have a racism problem and we could stop talking about it. "They" had their turn and now things were "normal" again. A Minnesota Senator said recently, "But to sit here and lie to people and say we are in a horrible racist situation in this country, I'd have to ask, how did Obama get to be where he is? How did these professional sports stars get to be where they are?" Saying we went "backwards" during the Obama administration has been about partisan blame as much as a commentary on the actual state of affairs.

Obama and his successor brought race to the forefront in very different ways, and wasn't even truly about either one of them. Obama's identity caused a cultural uneasiness in much of White America, consciously or not. It expressed itself in theories about him not even being American via the Birther conspiracy. Even without the rhetoric in the aftermath, it felt like a chance to take back an America that was more familiar to us. We went from feeling our apple pie was stolen to shoving it down the throats of whoever we think stole it. At the extreme end of this, we saw White Supremacy groups simmering and stewing with Obama (and stockpiling guns under the usual fear of Democrats taking them), but now openly roam the streets looking for a fight.

Things may calm down for a while when the baton is passed again in 2021. But it may not. Kamala Harris is the first veep I've heard actively included in the usual anti-president vitriol by an opposing party. One of the lawyers of the current president is even trying to start a new birther movement centered around her. Regardless of traction on that, we are still left with a gulf between two Americas. One says there is work to do. The other considers it an unfair allegation against a Great Nation. To the extent we can all sit at the table will determine how difficult or peaceful our immediate and long-term future will be.

But minority voices cannot be ignored politically. Even Obama didn't receive a majority of White votes, but African-American voters pushed him over. The margins of elections in 2016 and 2020 were smaller than the number of African-American voters, and minorities now make up 40% of the population. And that proportion is growing. The myth of a White, Christian nation servers fewer and fewer people. Diversity and integration is inevitable. We may as well embrace them as the American values our Founding Fathers promised but we failed to deliver.

23. A Dream Deferred

I wasn't around during the Civil Rights movement of the 1960s. I've asked many older people how similar or different it was, and they say it was nothing alike. There was far more death and destruction back then. And there were other issues – Vietnam, deep, widespread poverty in an otherwise unprecedently prosperous economy, and far more blatant voter suppression. But the more I dug into it, the more I saw the same patterns of rhetoric and response. And the more I see we are fighting some of the same battles beneath it all. I have to wonder if people's memories have been as whitewashed as our textbooks, or superficial differences are deceiving us. Will an honest look at the past give us a more honest perspective of the present? Let's jump in our time machine and find out.

The biggest debate America never had openly is if African-Americans as a whole deserve their plight. That is because it has always been assumed by so many that they do. No one seriously asks why they as a demographic are where they are, economically and socially. Well, someone did ask – Lyndon B. Johnson. Mind you, he was a code-switcher, and definitely a typical racist for his time. And Dr. King criticized him for not going far enough in the end. But he was also somewhat of a reverse example of many Americans' contradiction between attitudes and actions.

Johnson set up The National Advisory Commission on Civil Disorders ("Kerner Commission") to investigate the riots of the time, and in 1968 they released a report blaming "pervasive societal inequalities" in American ghettos. The cause was determined to be structural Black disadvantages previously unaddressed. It concluded that we were "moving toward two societies, one black, one white – separate and unequal".

That was also the year of "Resurrection City", a community of about 3,000 citizens from around the country that occupied the capital for 42 days in hundreds of wooden tents and other structures. It was part of Rev. Dr. Martin Luther King, Jr.'s "Poor People's Campaign" but he didn't live to see it. With his death and that of Bobby Kennedy still fresh in everyone's minds, they engaged representatives from various federal agencies, such as the Department of Agriculture, Housing and Urban Development, and the Department of Labor. In short, they were pushing for an economic bill of rights. Earlier that year, King held a planning symposium in Atlanta called the "Minority Conference

Group". The purpose was to meet with prominent Mexican-Americans, Puerto Ricans, American Indians, and even poor White activists. These and others such as Quakers, Appalachian Whites, farmworkers, and labor leaders, were exactly who showed up at Resurrection City.

In 1964, more than half of African-Americans lived in poverty. Civil rights demands and presses for economic justice went hand-in-hand, especially in the North. Johnson's War on Poverty initiated various social programs, but the debate about their impact on minorities mimics sentiments today. Those times were influenced by previous ones as well. Before the Civil War was even over, Union generals suggested Negroes will need to be taught how to work for a living, rather than be dependent on government as they had been previously dependent on plantation owners. Ironically, it was the end of slavery and an influx of available workers that shocked the economy. Animosity over this drastic economic change sowed seeds for hate, and was a major impetus for the establishment and growth of groups like the original Ku Klux Klan. And yet this belief in predisposition to government dependency persists, unabated by facts and contrary Black voices.

Whitney Young, president of the National Urban League, made his position clear that he would "rather get one black woman a job as an airline stewardess than to get twenty black women on welfare". King, at the 1964 Democratic convention, says the Black man "does not want to languish on welfare rolls" and would "rather have a job". They wanted unemployment opportunities, not handouts. But it was more than that. Particularly offensive was the notion that Black culture needed to be "fixed" by White people.

To these ends were proposed the Freedom Budget, and the establishment of some sort of Economic Bill of Rights. These were seen as Marxist, and to some extent, they were, at least in terms of anti-Capitalist criticisms. Perhaps that is why Dr. King was considered by the FBI to be "the most dangerous Negro of the future in this nation from the standpoint of Communism, the Negro and national security." But it doesn't matter at this point – broader measures to address poverty instead of band-aiding it never materialized.

Johnson's approach never satisfied King. In fact, he was dismayed that Blacks were accepting absorption into the Democratic Party. He maintained that protest was necessary over participatory politics and that solutions "will not magically materialize from the use of the ballot". He observed that "the Federal Government, and most especially Congress, never moves meaningfully against social ills until the nation is confronted directly and massively." King still believed aggressive, yet non-violent demonstrations were key.

His "I Have a Dream" speech touched me when I had finally come across it late in my teen years. In college, I chose him as a hero to research and write about. But I feel that all my research at that time was from a point of privilege. I did not – and still do not – appreciate all the nuances of his message and interaction with other views and forces of the time. This was when Black Nationalism was born, and figures like Malcolm X are contrasted with King. But now I am seeing why some People of Color take offense to my citing King or making assumptions about what he would and would not say today. While Malcolm X discovered a love for broader humanity from his *haj* experience that pulled back his disdain for the White man, King became more radical, perhaps in despondency, as time went on. I *want* to place him on the pedestal of post-racial thinking while *kumbaya* plays in the background, but that's not who he was.

With various voting acts and programs passed, the signal was sent that racism is no longer the status quo of America – at least on the outside. Euphemisms replaced epithets and blatantly racist political positions, and the resistance of segregation merely took new forms. Was the call to abolish slums answered? Did affirmative action solve more problems than it created? Did we ever fund education and other social support mechanisms to improve quality of life, or make tougher laws and build more prisons to remove the problem from sight? In 2020, we can say all boats have been lifted by a tide of prosperity, but there's still an economic, legal, and educational divide. (We can add a digital divide to the list, but in recent years that's more of an urban versus rural issue.)

In today's civil unrest, incidents of police misconduct and a broken justice system are front and center. But it throws wide open the conversation about race in all its aspects. Is it a conversation we're willing to have? Just as certain laws were passed in the 1960s, the issue was racism was declared as a mission accomplished. When Obama was elected, even more hailed the triumph. Could racism as a blemish on America and White people just be put to rest? Many of us desperately want that to be true, and groan at the thought we're not over it yet after so many years of relative peace.

What if we were wrong? What happens to a dream deferred?

PART III
BLACK AND BLUE

24. Intersections and Bandwagons

While putting this book together, I've come to realize the intersections of race, poverty, and crime are not vague notions. They are practically the whole enchilada. Those who only pray in the church of individual self-determination think it heresy to suggest society is at fault. And yet we either must accept social conditions as a major factor, or be left with the belief large groups of people – identifiable by their skin – have some inherent lesser industriousness or moral fortitude. The debate seems to be over which is the cause and which is the effect. We want to say any one person can rise above their circumstances, but we know most people in certain circumstances do not. Hopefully, this book makes a solid case that poverty and crime and yes, race, influence each other greatly. To judge one without addressing the others is why we are where we are today.

I have to be honest about why I chose now to write this book. The current movement spoke to me. I have always advocated against racism, but I also always believed issues of accountability of authority need to be resolved, such as political corruption and abuses of law enforcement. I've seen and experienced good and bad interactions with police, and have struggled not to harbor prejudices based on individual actions and a system that enables it. Seeing cops in a bad light (and reacting negatively with fear or mistrust) are similar to racial prejudices. The difference is we're not dealing with masses of relatively unrelated people and groups, but very particular institutions that can and should have high standards and formally answer to society.

Saying police brutality or injustice in the justice system is or isn't a race issue is a half-truth. As a White person, I know it affects all of us, and can affect me personally given the right (wrong) circumstances. And plenty of officers who are People of Color may be involved in these issues, however you want to perceive or explain that. But the other half of the truth is that People of Color experience injustices far more than others. Like other challenges in society, it is a more pressing issue for them, even if we may experience it as well.

The unrest of the 1960s didn't focus on police killings, but "No Justice, No Peace" is still a message that resonates today. And you can find photographs of people holding signs that say "Stop Killing Us" as far back as a hundred years ago. We can disagree about particular incidents as examples of justified or unjustified deaths, but the facts are not in our favor to deny the problem.

Twice as many people who are Black are killed than those who are White, nearly all male, and over half between the ages of 20 and 40 years old. Unarmed Black men are six times more likely to be killed than White unarmed men. (Only one recent study contradicts this, and the researcher admits a huge capacity for error given the lack of consistent police tracking in the limited areas he surveyed.) And when it comes to excuses and cover-ups, one in five medical examiners report being pressured to change cause-of-death determinations by a politician or the police.

We fail to understand the protests weren't about a single incident in a single city. The George Floyd video was only a spark that re-ignited a longstanding heap of embers that was already there. Every American city has its own list of those believed to be victims of police in recent years. You could fill the back of a T-Shirt with names just from the little ol' City of Buffalo.

The protests referred to colloquially as "Black Lives Matter" in America is a global phenomenon. Why would people in France join in? Because they have their own "George Floyd" in recent memory, Adama Traore. Why is BLM in Canada? There are similar incidents. National Canadian law enforcement officials admit systemic racism in what Americans think of as a much less racist society. And much like New York City's stop-and-frisk practices, Black citizens in Toronto are three times more likely to get "carded". A record of such police interactions can then be used to flag a person for further harassment and used against them in criminal cases. And it's not just people with dark skin. Indigenous peoples are also disproportionately killed.

Other countries have other racial or ethnic groups as their focus. Native peoples of New Zeeland have done war chants in solidarity with BLM. In Australia, there is a huge Aboriginal incarceration rate and many deaths in custody. (This hits home due to my own county's holding center having more suicides and deaths than any other facility in the state, including ones in New York City.)

While Brazil is known globally for its own forms of pervasive racism, one politician's response (to an incident and protests sparked the very day I'm writing this) decries that "there are those that want to destroy [Brazilian unity] and put in its place conflict, resentment, hate, and racial division". Vice President Hamilton Mourão chimes in that "there's no racism in Brazil" while President Jair Bolsonaro is called out for his racially-provocative rhetoric, lack of addressing the issue, and use of law enforcement to make the situation worse. This should not be unfamiliar. Even if the naysayers were somehow right and "there's nothing to see here", Brazil's battle over the "mythology of racial democracy" will not go ignored without efforts at resolution.

This is even broader than racism altogether, as the issue of police brutality and injustice are things by themselves. In Nigeria, the #EndSARS movement stands in solidarity with BLM – a video of officers of the Special Anti-Robbery Squad killing someone at a traffic stop was the spark. Nigerians are demanding reforms across all their law enforcement agencies, including their often revered anti-terrorism unit.

But in America, patterns of People of Color killed by law enforcement traces back generations. And like today, extrajudicial actions against citizens and prisoners, no matter how blatant, may result in acquittal, if there is an arrest at all. And there have often been riots over it.

The universality of this breaks down the dangerous myth this is some political conspiracy to destroy America. A sociology student at Dillard University laments, "[T]hese pressure groups – those racists, superpatriots, whatever you want to call them – tag every move toward racial justice as communist-inspired, Zionist-inspired, Illuminati-inspired, Satan-inspired... part of some secret conspiracy to overthrow the Christian civilization." I'd say this was in reference to QAnon propaganda and does describe with some accuracy some people's beliefs, but that would be dishonest. It was said in the 1950s, quoted by John Howard Griffin.

However, economic agendas have always been somewhere in the mix. Before I researched the earlier movements, I thought anti-capitalism was just jumping on the bandwagon, the same way the Ayn Randians jumped on the TEA Party in its early days. To be clear on my own bias, I agree with President Obama that "the world is more prosperous than ever before ... [C]apitalism has been the greatest driver of prosperity and opportunity the world has ever seen." Let's look at the problem another way. Whatever we want to label the current economic paradigm, it represents a status quo of defended inequity. I don't think Socialism – however people want to define it any given day – is an answer so much as a response to endemic faults in an *unequally*-free market. However much you agree or disagree with that, we can at least accept that political and economic power are highly correlated to each other. Particularly in Black America, lack of political and economic power has pushed the social starting line far behind the rest of America since forever. Only recently have entire communities of Color even have bootstraps to pull themselves up by.

There are other areas of intersectionality in race-based civil rights. Abolition and women's suffrage are an intertwined journey. African-Americans became more and more involved in suffrage, starting with Sojourner Truth. At a suffrage parade in Washington, D.C., Ida B. Wells-Barnett refused to march at the back of the parade, as was expected of Black women. Buffalo, New York suffrage reporter and activist Mary Talbert was vice president of the National Association of Colored Women, and founded the Niagara Movement that later became the NAACP. The role of African-American women in suffrage could fill a chapter on its own.

In fact, nearly all the issues in this book have a gender aspect worthy of mention. (If I were to include sex and gender issues in this book, I'd need another lifetime to give justice to it and the book would twice as thick.) Drag queen Marsha P. Johnson was central to the Stonewall uprising, a watershed moment of Gay Rights as omitted from the average classroom as Black Wall Street. The Movement for Black Lives says "Black cis and trans women and femmes have always been at the forefront of our movements." Most of the violence against transgender or gender non-conforming people are African-American and Latinx transgender women. Forty have been reported killed already in 2020, and there is no telling how many others went unreported or misreported.

The 2020 protests have also caused a fervor to combat all things racist, both unresolved and accused. Call me an opportunist (actually, please don't), but I will be honest and admit any major popularity of this book will be because of this wave of sentiment. The conversation has been opened wide, or at least I hope it has, and I want to be a part of it. We've seen statues toppled and calls to rename military bases and other places. There's no more Aunt Jemima or Uncle Ben in my pantry. We've named a bunch of streets "Black Lives Matter Way", Mississippi changed their flag, and the Dixie Chicks are now just the "Chicks". I don't even know why that last one had to happen. From this White man's perspective, all this cancel culture feels like a witch hunt. I'm just showing my cards here, so please forgive me. I know a lot of these things are important to other people and it's easy to scratch my head because it doesn't have to do with me personally. But even People of Color are wondering how all this is going to fix the big issues. Heck, it might even be a pacifying substitute for real change.

There's no clear boundary to what the movement is about, even if systemic racism and police brutality are front and center. At Buffalo protests, you will find signs relating to CPS (Child Protective Services) and the foster care system. There are other individuals I have met that have their own particular issue they want to be addressed. On a larger scale, we find lists of Progressive "truths" on signs and t-shirts and memes that combine issues of racism with LGBTect, immigration, and abortion. There have been protests focusing solely on ICE detentions. Mention of Palestinian rights and other geopolitical oppressions appear now and then as well. Like life itself, it's all a bit messy. As if very different notions of police reform weren't enough, the protests are shouting out different messages on all frequencies. And not everyone sees eye to eye on every issue. The movement is very amorphous, which is why I get annoyed when people try to peg-hole protestors as being this or that. There is no "they".

25. Minority Report

Since 2011, Pasco County in Central Florida has had a surge of fines and arrests. Using "predictive policing" algorithms, police target households and individuals they deem likely to commit crimes, and then with no just cause, interrogate or visit them, even in the middle of the night. In the process, citations are given for everything from missing mailbox numbers to heavy fines if they see a teenager smoking in the house. These infractions then get fed back into the system for further consideration. The sheriff defends it. Run by former federal and military agents, the program "was designed to reduce bias in policing by using objective data" – except much of the data is put into the system based on officers' judgments. A former deputy says the directive's purpose is to "make their lives miserable until they move or sue". Some have moved. And violent crime has actually increased. Confrontations with police are growing, and in turn, people can be cited with "contempt of cop" charges.

Reminiscent of the movie "Minority Report", predictive policing software, such as *Palantir*, is being used around the country, often unbeknownst to citizens and even municipal leadership. Critics have shown it does not work on significant crimes, and algorithms reinforce systemic biases. Poorer residents end up in arrears on excessive fines, resulting in further charges or arrest warrants, all starting with petty citations. With no actual change in a population's criminal behavior, townsfolk can be criminalized as much as computing and manpower allow.

Most of us cannot imagine living in such a dystopia. Here's the shocker: many in urban communities have lived this their whole lives. Long before computer algorithms, the "broken windows theory" of criminology changed the process of policing. The theory, introduced in 1982, is that general "lawlessness" creates an environment of crime. The practice is to be strict about vandals, fare evaders, or even people who loiter or jaywalk, in the hopes it will curb larger crimes. Some researchers believe it to have that effect when applied carefully in the context of community policing along with leniency of judgments. However, a zealous "zero tolerance" approach is sometimes applied, and minority neighborhoods are targeted in a way described as "criminalization of communities of color".

It is both a fact and human nature that there will be more crime in areas that are economically depressed and buildings neglected. There is truth that a broken window unfixed will turn into a bunch of broken windows. And this has been demonstrated by sociologists to be true regardless of a community's color. But African-American neighborhoods have been economically marginalized or excluded from development for so long, such an environment is associated with them.

If you look for crimes – especially from the litany of vague offenses on the books – you will find them in any community, and keep finding them where you keep looking. It's a self-fulfilling prophecy. When applied to African-American neighborhoods, it reinforces a belief of irredeemability, triggering sentiments from an earlier time, such as, "You can take a man out of the jungle, but you can't take the jungle out of a man." It's ignorant, but not even conscious. We complain about a "revolving door" policy of arrests, releases, and being arrested again, not realizing the cycle is the system's fault and ... well ... stupid.

When you go after petty offenses you assume will be in minority neighborhoods, they – often minors – are more likely to be targeted. Crimes that my White daughter, represented by a hired lawyer, wouldn't get a slap on the wrist for would easily result in jail time for a poor Person of Color. Disparity in sentencing is a statistical fact, excessively researched. While people lament that crime a revolving-door, you are TWENTY TIMES more likely to receive a life sentence for a non-violent crime if you are not White. We even know there's truth to "the lighter the skin, the lighter the sentence", not unlike in the time of slavery where those with lighter skin tended to be given lighter work.

Public defenders have a predilection toward insisting on plea bargaining, even if there's no case, and people take it. Conviction rates are higher among People of Color as well, and the total equation of disproportionate incarceration leads people to conclude that African-Americans and Hispanics are naturally more criminal.

But are African-Americans really targeted? If you are Black, chances are you've had "the talk" and may have given it to your children. White people may not even know what that is. It varies from person to person and family to family and can actually refer to two things. One talk is when, at a certain age, a child will realize they are treated differently for being Black and have to be told why. This isn't some perpetuation of victimhood as some suggest, but absolutely necessary given how prevalent prejudice is, even today. The second talk is how to act when confronted by police. If in a car, you are instructed in detail where to have your hands, where to look, not to make sudden moves, and answer "yes, sir" even if you feel wronged. As a White person, I may have been given similar advice in a general way, but not as such a matter of survival as it's impressed upon some People of Color. For some families, it's almost a rite of passage.

I talked with one of my old high school classmates the other day, who had adopted an African-American child. He lives in a diverse community where color isn't a pressing issue, but knows someday he'll have to deal with it. His son is still a bit young, but there isn't a day it doesn't cross his mind with a touch of dread. At the same time, he doesn't want a big part of his parental relationship to be about race. Some children who are raised in White neighborhoods by White parents find themselves surprised and unprepared the first (and second, and third) time they are pulled over or questioned – or worse.

"Driving While Black" (DWB) is a real thing. It is the undeniable experience of countless People of Color who get pulled over repeatedly in certain neighborhoods and municipalities, especially if they have a car that is assumed to be "above their means". It's a leftover from "sundown towns" where it was illegal for Blacks to be out after dark. A nearby town actually had a bell or horn of some sort to give warning to those working in town to head home. Residents tell me it was in place until the late 1990s. A sign referring to that policy – mistaken by many to be an ordinary neighborhood watch sign – was taken down this year. The movie "Green Book" brought attention to this. (I keep a 1954 reproduction of the "The Negro Motorist Green Book" in my glovebox.) Back in the day, the first thing Chubby Checkers did when he moved to Beverly Hills was visit the police station to make clear who he was (and what car he drove) so they would not constantly follow and question him.

One of my brothers works the night shift at a local Wal-Mart in another suburb notorious for this. Officers on their scanners regularly used the term "NPH" – "N* Past Harlem" – in reference to People of Color crossing Harlem Road, which is near and parallel to the city line. In some places, the attitude of the police is to keep "those people" in "their" neighborhoods. This is another reason it is concerning when officers are hired who live outside the place they would serve. In Buffalo, opening up employment outside the city is being considered. Then again, according to a contact of mine at city hall, none of the leadership of the Buffalo PBA (police union) lives within city limits as it is.

My brother's workplace is very diverse, reflective of the community who shops there, but not who lives there. It's the nearest big box store to Buffalo's East Side, predominantly African-American, while the store's neighborhood is almost exclusively White. It's unaffectionately called by some "ghetto mart" due to its clientele. There are few cars on the roads at night, and many times he's had patrol cars go out of their way to pull up next to him, look at him, then drive off. His associates who are People of Color get pulled over all the time, sometimes in the parking lot to play 20 questions while the other staff have to corroborate they are fellow employees. One White worker, giving a ride to two co-workers who were African-American, was pulled over, ordered to step out and away from the car, and asked if they were forcing him to drive them. These sorts of interactions happen thousands of times, every night, across the country. We may still have a need for a Green Book.

There may be arguments for profiling in particular circumstances, but to deny it isn't a conscious or unconscious part of policing is to deny statistical evidence. Unconstitutionality aside, statistics on "stop-and-frisk" practices punctuate this reality. The Office of the United Nations High Commissioner for Human Rights (OHCHR) states that "discrimination in the administration of justice is a common phenomenon in virtually all countries". But how much more or less in America? The United States justice system incarcerates more citizens per capita than any country in the world, even those of oppressive regimes such as Orwellian China. How is it conceivable that we have so much more criminality among us?

Of course, that is conceivable, given the bookcases of laws regulating every breath we take. You can't step out of bed without having broken some code or ordinance at some level of government. We can't possibly know all these laws – ignorance is one hell of an ethical excuse contrary to legal precedence – and the best one can hope for is that law enforcement doesn't know of the law either. And they usually don't, which is a double-edged sword, meaning a sword is illegal only if the cop wants to give it to his son for Christmas. I would say this is in jest, except that as a former owner of a martial arts supply and cutlery business, I've heard too many stories.

A corrections officer (in the process of defending the shooting of a dark-skinned child in the back because they "shouldn't have been running away") once asked me if I thought all inmates were innocent. My answer was no – but almost NONE have been found guilty of the crime they were charged with. Roughly a quarter of those incarcerated, mostly in local jails, are awaiting trial at any given time. The median bail amount is $10,000 for a felony, roughly two-thirds of the yearly income of a typical person detained. Of the three-quarters of inmates actually convicted, between 94-97% of those accepted plea-bargains. Of those, countless people declare they took or were coerced to take a plea only to avoid a harsher sentence under fear of a longer sentence with a high (almost guaranteed) conviction rate.

Let's look at this from the other end. The number of full exonerations – even for the most serious crimes – is limited only by the available efforts of lawyers and organizations (such as the Innocence Project). In the last 30 years, over 2400 individuals have been exonerated, having already served collectively over 21,000 years in prison. ONE IN NINE death row inmates is found to be innocent. Many exonerations are due to progress in forensics such as DNA matching, but the majority of cases were due to misconduct of prosecutors and law enforcement. And given that many officers who give false testimony or plant evidence continue to serve even after being caught, there is no telling how many other convictions are false, or at least suspect. Thousands upon thousands of cases are being reviewed on these grounds as we speak.

Texas has some of the toughest laws on crime and leads the nation in exonerations. Maybe there's an obvious connection? Instigated by a blatant false conviction that could have been avoided, Texas passed the "Michael Morton Act" in 2013, forcing prosecutors to disclose all evidence, including proof of innocence. The case in question was the first time a district attorney actually served time (10 days) for knowingly sending someone innocent to prison (for 25 years). What people do not realize is that it's not law enforcement's job to find the truth, but to substantiate arrests. It's not the prosecutor's job to find the truth, but to get a conviction. This is why lawyers advise people to never talk to police when arrested – they can only use what you say against you, not in your defense.

Murder is the number one crime exonerated. Is it because they are higher profile for attorneys to pursue, or because there is greater pressure on police to "find their man"? When a murder solve rate nears 100% in some places while in nearly all others it's half that or less, you find credible claims certain neighborhoods are trolled for People of Color to take the fall. And when it's a cop that is killed, it's a whole new level. If it goes unpunished, one can argue it may not deter other law enforcement from being murdered. But when "cop-killers" are exonerated and people realize the pressure to find and convict drives police decision-making, it logically *increases* the chances of someone getting away with it. They just have to lay low long enough for someone else to be grabbed and railroaded. That's a scary thought for everyone.

A lawyer friend of mine is currently working on one such case. Jailhouse informants seek benefits from their testimonies all the time, but this went further. The police had allegedly arranged parole of a woman's boyfriend in exchange for her testimony to identify the accused as being at the scene of a cop's murder. She was the only eyewitness and there was no other evidence to tie him to the crime.

There are also officers who get awards for disproportionate amounts of arrests, only to be found planting evidence or using questionable just cause to arrest drugged or drunk drives with clean breath and blood tests. There is even formal training on visually identifying impairment such that some judges place subjective observation above available science. At such points, conviction depends on the quality (and expense) of one's lawyer at best, once again intersecting race and poverty.

Over 30 states have higher incarceration rates than the next-highest country, El Salvador. Less than 10 countries have rates higher than the rest of our states. If all other things are equal, we can say that at least half – over a million American citizens – would not be in jail if they lived nearly anywhere else in the world.

Mass incarceration grew to its current weight-class (by a factor of four) in the 1980s and 1990s thanks to the War on Drugs. Drugs have been a political as well as social issue since at least 1910, when cannabis was demonized surrounding a wave of Mexicans crossing the border to flee revolution. It was exacerbated by fearmongering talk about "them" coming here to rape "our" women. (History rhymes again with recent xenophobic rhetoric.) It became the drug of minorities and poor Whites. "Reefer Madness" was a scare tactic targeted at White people, but it's telling that even today we refer to the drug by its Spanish name, marijuana. President after president claimed to wage a "war on drugs" but I find it ironic that the most recent "War on Drugs" was instituted by President George W. Bush, former head of the CIA, which has been accused time and again of self-funding via global drug trafficking.

National statistics are easily available online, but here's a current glimpse of the local slice of the War on Drugs in relation to overall crime: In 2019, the Buffalo Police Department had 8,424 arrests. Most were for non-felonies, and low-level drug arrests made up 29% of all such arrests. One charge alone, "Criminal possession of a controlled substance in the 7th degree", the lowest-level drug charge in NYS, made up 15% of all arrests. On a side note, 71% of people arrested for "obstructing government administration" were African-American, as were 62% of people arrested for "resisting arrest".

Drugs are most associated with minorities, and yet their addiction rates are similar to Whites. White people are more commonly drug dealers than African-Americans. Heck, I remember a huge drug bust in the local Amish community a few years back – talk about stereotypes not being the whole truth!

And then there is the prison-industrial complex, with the privatization of facilities expanding greatly in the last 20 years. Just like Wild West judges used to get paid per hanging, inmates are profit, and some judges are investors – or let's just say campaign contributions talk. Two judges in Pennsylvania were notorious for railroading children for the slightest altercation on a school bus – the "Kids for Cash" scandal. These robed criminals got a taste of their own poison with their own incarcerations. I would suggest this is not a rare occurrence, only a rare turn of justice.

I have heard "slavery is in the past" more times than I can count. No one alive today remembers it – unless you count human trafficking, coerced servitude of undocumented immigrants, and so forth. But at least we officially outlawed it by a referendum in Nevada in 2020. We forget that the 13th Amendment had a loophole, where slavery and forced servitude were illegal "except as a punishment for crime whereof the party shall have been duly convicted". After the Civil War, many of those freed were arrested and convicted for all sorts of alleged infractions and contracted out as labor to the very plantations they were freed from! On top of this, African-Americans have been excluded from juries even up to recent years, regardless of many court decisions that declare such a practice unlawful.

It has been argued that our justice system has replaced slavery, and given massively disproportionate incarceration, it's not a crazy perspective. In some states, those who committed a felony cannot vote, the assumption being that those with such heinous crimes (which may include stealing cable for an extra TV in your home) are just plain bad people and cannot be trusted to exercise their political rights. Michele Alexander, author of "The New Jim Crow," wrote in a Huffington Post editorial that "More African American men were disenfranchised due to felony convictions in 2004 than in 1870". (That was the year the Fifteenth Amendment was ratified prohibiting laws denying the right to vote on the basis of race.)

Frederick Douglass knew Abolition wasn't done when he wrote, "Slavery has been fruitful in giving itself names ... and you and I and all of us had better wait and see what new form this old monster will assume, in what new skin this old snake will come forth next." Modern "abolitionist" agendas talk about a divest/invest strategy, where sentencing focuses on programs of rehabilitation rather than punishment and isolation. And less incarceration means less recidivism. Prisons are often places where inmates pick up criminal skills rather than self-improvement strategies, and having a record can preclude a person from most lawful employment.

The thing is that fixing this system is good for everyone. Minorities aren't the only ones in need of exoneration or real rehabilitation. Less incarceration and better reintegration improve communities, especially those who do not have access to quality legal counsel or are more targeted by law enforcement. Solving this could move American society as a whole forward, or at least make it commensurate with other free nations.

26. Whose Lives Matter?

As final statements were being made on the Martin-Zimmerman case, my daughter was preparing to lead a literature group in the discussion of *To Kill a Mockingbird*. My waking moments of that day involved a local talk-show host ranting the sentiments of White America, providing fodder to be parroted as his listeners' opinions at the water cooler and on Facebook.

Some were asking why this case was so important, saying it is the news media who decided to make it noteworthy, to make it a race issue. We can never know for sure if Trayvon Martin's fate would have been different if he had lighter skin, but our own reactions as a nation after the fact suggest it is probably true. Not just allegedly over-sensitive African-Americans or allegedly racist White people – we *all* made it about race. No one suggested the murders in the OJ trial were race-motivated, and yet the lines of satisfaction or dissatisfaction of its outcome were emphatically drawn along racial lines. It wasn't rational.

Zimmerman sometimes identifying as Hispanic made things more problematic for people in his case. He couldn't be racist, right? But even racism isn't really about race at its base level. This was someone believing they were protecting their privileged neighborhood from someone who didn't belong there. The police told him to back off and he didn't. Confrontation and tragedy was the result.

Honestly, I don't think most people cared what the facts were. How many of us who argued over it even bothered to follow the details of the trial? Instead, the debates were about broader things. Were our institutions sanctioning an open season on shooting African-Americans? Or were they willing to convict someone based on assumed racism and public outrage? It was taken for granted by everyone the trial would not be judged on facts, but reflect a judgment upon who has racial privilege. We all looked for ways to be outraged, not trying to understand – or choosing not to understand – each other's point of view. White people feared it may mean jail any time they defend themselves or their property against a Person of Color, and already believe that minorities are given such special rights or considerations. African-Americans are afraid of returning to a time (or are still in a time) of lynchings and hate crimes going unpunished. Like the accused in Harper Lee's classic book, they must wonder if the weight of one man's word is heavier than that of another based on the color of their skin.

The racial implications, no matter who "wins", showed us how little progress we have made. The Black Panthers threatened premeditated riots specifically in White communities. How did White people respond? The talk show host wasn't the only one to make snide comments about the ridiculousness of "white riots" if Zimmerman was convicted. Such a statement may be superficially true, but it's an underhanded way of judging African-Americans in a most un-novel way, making White people out to be less "savage".

We could say both sides are being racists, but they are not equal. American history isn't filled with black-on-white crime going unpunished, while the opposite cannot be so easily asserted. There were few White riots because people as a rule aren't oppressed for being White. But they did exist. It was a century ago this year that white mobs in Ocoee, Florida killed dozens, torched houses, and nearly all of the African-Americans in Ocoee were driven out of town – all because a man insisted on his right to vote. There are many other instances we could describe as White riots, but those involve mob retaliation for (usually falsely accused) crimes by individuals who would no doubt be punished if they weren't lynched first. The bottom line is there's just no comparison.

It escapes many White people that the real outrage wasn't about Trayvon Martin's death, but George Zimmerman's acquittal. The same holds true for nearly all other incidents we've heard about where there doesn't seem to be accountability when African-Americans are killed, and keep being killed. It's not about the particulars of the incidents themselves, or why they happened and who was to blame, but the way it appears to be assumed by White America such deaths aren't an injustice. It's like ... well ... their lives don't matter.

That's why a recent meme about a White toddler being killed by an African-American man was utterly offensive to many of us. The point people pretended to make was outrage that the news was burying the story of this sweet little angel's death (they didn't) while giving so much attention to the death of a Black man. It was signaling absolution from caring about people like Floyd because of a supposed reverse-racially-biased media agenda. I wonder if it is a problem with the head or heart that would cause anyone to play one terrible loss of life against another. The people who make such memes in my opinion are evil; those who were duped into sharing them were unthinking at best. In stirring up left-handed racist attitudes, it ignored the most important distinction: one was a random tragedy with justice being swiftly served; the other was seen as part of a larger problem of justice deferred.

This is not merely an outward race issue, but something deeper. I saw everyday people tightening their springs in anticipation of throwing tantrums if they didn't get their way in the case. Yes, *their* way, as if it was personal. It's like we were all rooting for "Team White" or "Team Black" and some of us were willing to take it out on the next fan wearing the wrong color skin.

Today is no different. There have been terrible acts all around in this year's unrest. Every incident emotionally speaks to us, regardless of the facts. We identify with the victims or the police officers or the protesters or business owners whose stores were burned because in our minds, they could be you or me. We mentally act out these plays, seeing ourselves as one side or the other and our empathy ends there.

And we do this on a national scale. Both Kyle Rittenhouse and Michael Reinoehl shot and killed protesters and counter-protesters, respectively. Either or both may have been in self-defense. One had to turn themselves in (twice) and will receive the full protection of due process; the other was hundred down and killed by police by a barrage of 30 rounds in broad daylight around women and children, and a question as to whether or not an arrest was even attempted. But the reality that imposes itself most is that churches and celebrities stepped in to support and raise money for one, while the other's name was quickly forgotten after the president praised his death as "retribution". I think this tells us that sometimes "Law and Order" is little more than a cover for cultural machismo and control.

The "Black Lives Matter" (BLM) concept started in response to Zimmerman's acquittal but didn't become a household-recognized phrase until 2020, after many more protests over innumerable police-involved tragedies. There is an organization "Black Lives Matter Network" central to its origination, but it has no power or authority over BLM as a trademark. The "founders" and their ideological statements (allegedly Marxist) have been the target of criticism to delegitimize the movement, but few among literal millions who wear the label could even name who they are. In reality, it's a decentralized and amorphous collection of groups and people. Much like the umbrella term for the leaderless Anonymous non-organization, activist DeRay McKesson says BLM "encompasses all who publicly declare that Black lives matter and devote their time and energy accordingly."

But the phrase has become a trigger for many White people. They just can't wrap their head around it for some reason. The rough message the press delivered was pointed, as could be expected. Some of the rhetoric was arguably reverse-prejudice. The simple message that BLM is a response to a society seen where "Black lives *don't* matter" is lost in the noise. Radio show host and TV personality Steve Harvey says it well – if you don't understand that it means African-Americans just want their lives to matter as much as everyone else's, "YOU AREN'T LISTENING."

A common response is a sort of rebuttal that "all lives matter." These three words, seen everywhere as an alternative to BLM, represent two very different agendas and perspectives – one racist and one well-intended.

The first agenda uses "All Lives Matter" as an accusation that "Black Lives Matter" means "Black Lives Matter More Than Yours" or "Only Black Lives Matter." I personally have never heard anyone, ever, say or mean this. (The rare, more militant slogan that "All lives don't matter until black lives matter" seems to confuse people even more instead of solving the problem.) I have to believe this use of ALM is an intentional misinterpretation by those who wish to dismiss the legitimacy of the movement. At worst, they are racist pots calling the kettle black. They ignore or deny the rational context of it meaning "Black lives matter, too".

The other perspective where people may say "all lives matter" is well-meaning but problematic. There are two fundamental ways that people (People of Color and those who aren't) approach the race concept. One is to acknowledge race as a powerful, persisting social reality. Activism derived from this view focus on addressing particular injustices against the social group and individuals identifying themselves within it. It starts from a place of the past, a world (or rather two worlds) in which we inherit a baseline of privilege determined by the skin we are born into.

Some of us don't want to see it that way, either because we can't handle it, or because we are idealistic or naive. We say we don't see color at all and the sooner we all subscribe to that sentiment, the sooner we can "move on" or even let go of the injustices of the past. We insist on living in a post-racial mindset, dragging us toward that future by sheer will. Some of us assert that focusing on race at all is a hindrance, and either through ignorance or an unwillingness (discomfort?) cannot face the reality that we have a long way to go.

If we go this route, it is found to be far easier said than done, and it potentially disrespects any celebration of diversity that many of us believe can be done without division. This is also based on more conservative American social beliefs that racism is personal and we can just opt out, absolving institutions and social forces from their role in the destiny of any person of any color. In fact, we find this even among conservative African-Americans, such as author Shelby Steele. He recently wrote an opinion piece for the Wall Street Journal, titled, "The Inauthenticity Behind Black Lives Matter: Insisting on the prevalence of 'systemic racism' is a way of defending a victim-focused racial identity." Any truths in that aside, this rhetoric denies there is an imbalance of justice more worth addressing than not. (It's also ironic given that victim-blaming is the chief *modus operandi* in the public's dismissal of police-involved tragedies.)

But we can back off on theory and see there is common ground from this perspective. "All Lives Matter" is a positive sentiment that means the exact same thing as "Black Lives Matter". Those sign-holders are not being jerks, but trying to say African-American lives do matter as much as everyone else's (in principle) and we all can choose to stand for that together. It is on the surface more inclusive.

The point is that "All Lives Matter" is not always from a place of ignorance or minimizing the issues. Even "Blue Lives Matter" does not have to be an opposing ideological force. For some, that phrase represents a real concern that the safety of our brothers and sisters in law enforcement is being forgotten, and not necessarily a denial of injustices perpetrated by members and institutional faults surrounding that group.

However, this misunderstanding of ALM ignores or detracts from the unique statistical and typical injustices against African-Americans. BLM is meant to address a very specific plight. Sure, every day should be a day we address all injustices and challenges faced by everyone. Ideally, we should make it about equality rather than race-specific justice. I really feel that way in my own heart. But I know in my brain you don't treat every tumor the same and give treatment to every part of the body equally under the notion "All Organs Matter".

So where do we go with all of this? What have we learned? These differences in perspective cannot be deciphered by reading a sign. They are a shorthand used by different people that can be easily misjudged. Three words are inadequate space to say what's in your heart or mind regarding a complex issue with a troubled and convoluted back-story. There are ever-changing social norms as to what sign you should hold and when, and you can't control what other people think.

But we can be sure of ourselves and gentle with each other. Such slogans can spark hostility because we let it. Any of these can be a slap in the face to others. There's no perfect choice here except to be as good and understanding of each other as we can – to listen before we judge and let love step in before anger. I don't know what sign you choose to hold, or why. I'm not even sure what perspective I think is best in dealing with the race issue today, and even most People of Color I've spoken with are honest enough to know they don't know either.

Being supportive of a cause addressing injustices against one group does not mean you are giving special treatment over any others. This isn't a contest. "Black Lives Matter" is an affirmation you make when and how your conscience dictates. It is everyone's rightful choice to be specific, as none of us can fight all causes at the same time, all the time. And it doesn't have to be your cause. But you do live and participate in a world where this is part of its reality. Even if you are White – perhaps especially so – what you do or say or consent to by silence or inaction may have far-reaching and long-lasting effects on people who not only take to the streets, but whose lives matter as much as yours.

We don't have to agree on solutions, or approaches, or even the scope of the problem. Maybe we don't need just one answer. Maybe accepting each other's answers will fill in a larger puzzle where we can work things out without having to see things the same way. That was what America was supposed to be. This is what will make us better as a nation, and better human beings.

27. Is Blue a Color?

Some of us teach our children those with a badge deserve respect and are there if you need help. Some of us teach our children cops are to be avoided and obeyed out of fear, even if you did nothing wrong. Both these sentiments are true, but neither is the whole truth. The root cause of our problems with law enforcement is that we see them as heroes or villains, not human beings.

When people shout or wave a sign saying "Blue Lives Matter", some argue there is no such thing as a "Blue life". You can take off your uniform; you can't take off your skin. But police are still perceived as a social group and treated in certain ways because of their uniform. And just like a White or Black person may "represent" the baggage of stereotypes in the eyes of others, law enforcement represents things aligned with values and charged with emotions. And these assumptions are very different depending on who you are. But behind each badge is a human being, and we need to not only acknowledge that, but try to understand the shoes they are asked to fill.

Let's be clear – I'm not giving anyone a free pass here. If you cannot accept that cops doing bad things may not be isolated incidents, or if you cannot accept that there are honorable people on the force, you will be better off to skip this chapter.

When talking about large numbers of individuals, we still must start with some generalities. Members of law enforcement could be said to have a common culture of training and experience. Departments may be run differently, but there are basic legal and tactical considerations that influence what they do across the board. So let's first talk about the role of police in the community, and understand it has an important backstory. And the way policing works was never written in stone. It evolved and can continue to evolve.

The concept of police is a modern construct. Previously there were night watchmen (often volunteers), private security (often criminals), and slave hunters. Early departments (and similar private forces such as Pinkerton) were mostly used to control urban immigrant populations, and quell worker riots against powerful city merchants, which then morphed into union-busting. But let's start at the right time to deep dive here.

Public, professional forces became commonplace in America by the 1850s, but the model for policing was created in England, by Sir Robert Peel (where they get the term "Bobbies"). Peelian Principles are based on the idea "the police are the public and the public are the police," and saw police as an alternative to military presence and harsh punishment as crime deterrents, dishing out "justice" on the spot. It promotes things like impartiality, congeniality, not using more force than necessary, and legitimacy of authority based on public approval. His final point hits home hardest, "To recognize always that the test of police efficiency is the absence of crime and disorder, and not the visible evidence of police action in dealing with them." This means low crime statistics is the goal, not high numbers of citations and arrests.

Perhaps the most important notion of his philosophy is the most abstract. As a block club organizer in South Buffalo, I preached what I had learned working with CPOs, namely, that we are the eyes and ears of the police. They can't be everywhere and do everything themselves. Peel's view was even broader. It is not the "job" of the police to solely provide law and order. Law enforcement is a *concentration* of the community's overall efforts, not an outsourcing of citizen responsibility. Perhaps we should all give our last thoughts of the day to this and sleep on it.

American policing seems to have followed much of these principles, but there was a lot of corruption due to politics and organized crime. Things got more professional and organized in the early 20th Century. August Vollmer, who is considered America's "father of modern law enforcement," created a model of policing that included sociology, psychology, and social work. This sounds a little like what some are calling for when they say "defund the police" by diverting some of the budget to mental health care professionals and social worker partnerships. He also calls for officers to patrol, on foot, the neighborhoods they lived. This is a sharp contrast to police often used as watchdogs to keep "those people" in their own neighborhoods, where suburbanites or those in "good" parts of town join departments as a means of racial interdiction.

Vollmer also expected policemen to go to college, another requirement some today would like to see. Ahead of his time, he encouraged the hiring of African-Americans and women as police officers (1919 and 1925, respectively). Unfortunately, the curricula he developed that became the basis for Criminal Justice courses reiterated beliefs that heredity, racial types, and "racial degeneration" contributed to criminality. I doubt that is taught today – police are taught to be colorblind, if such a thing is possible. But teaching colorblindness may not even be desirable, given that People of Color will have different attitudes and experiences in dealing with law enforcement that profoundly affect interactions.

Some of us (who are almost assuredly White) have a nostalgic, idealistic view of police. In that Leave-it-to-Beaver world, you'll never have to worry about anything if you don't do anything wrong. (Remember, this was a time disrespecting any authority was a grave sin, and we reminisce of the days when a teacher would give you a whooping and then get one at home for good measure.) The *Thin Blue Line* places every policeman as the last safeguard against lawlessness and chaos. I'd censure myself for exaggerating the point if a local Sherriff didn't say that exact thing earlier this year.

The point is, we look up to first responders. And we should. The probability of not coming home is nowhere near what some imagine, but it's still regularly putting their life on the line. And along with those serving in the military, there was a surge of support around them after 9-11. Police became symbols of patriotism.

But let's see this another way. There were a number of heroes in blue that fateful day in Manhattan when the towers were hit. We will always be grateful for them and their sacrifices. And there were a large number of other emergency workers – entire fire departments were wiped out. But most impressively, many private citizens ran to help instead of run in the opposite direction. In a way, it made less sense for the police to be there than fire, etc.. There was no one to arrest and no peace to keep by virtue of their badge and gun, which technically is their core function. I would suggest they went above their duty as human beings that day, not because of their job.

I tend to believe this from personal experience. As a college student, I helped evacuate a nursing home from a bomb threat on the West Side of Buffalo, circa 1989. It shared a parking lot with my dormitory and I remember hearing the alarm go off as I was talking with a friend. The police refused to enter the building, and the fire department wasn't there yet. We grabbed whoever we could to help go floor by floor and escort people in walkers down stairwells for over an hour. But I'm not berating the police here. I'm just saying they aren't paid to be knights in shining armor and we shouldn't expect them to be.

We also shouldn't give them the power, immunity, and exemption from oversight based on a false idolization. It corrupts otherwise good people, not just those who join the force to be paid bullies (as confided to me by friends in law enforcement, not my words). Their perceived role has grown out of hand, and many of them would agree. They don't want to be the answer to every solution. They don't want to be seen as heroes.

In fact, putting them on a pedestal makes it harder for them to ask for and receive help. We praise them for doing an incredibly stressful job and dealing with difficult people day after day. We excuse acts of improper force by chalking it up to these pressures, or call them bad apples and mentally dissociate them as not really cops. We don't do anything to help *them* in a job that very much has a lot to do with why bad things happen.

Two studies in the 1990s showed that law enforcement families were 2-4 times more likely to experience domestic violence than others. Since then, there have been many news reports of spouses and even children killed with service weapons, often ending in the officer shooting themselves. Hundreds of reports and arrests from incidents occur across hundreds of departments every year. Over half of all officers convicted kept their jobs. Counseling is sometimes offered but is it a substitute for punishment or answering a cry for help?

From talking with officers I know and vets I work with, I think there are some similarities between these two groups. They are held up to society's expectation of "strong" while any emotional need for help is perceived as "weakness" that may prevent them from doing their duty or continuing their profession. Experiences of trauma, constant heightened vigilance, readiness to use violence – these are not character traits but conditions that cannot go improperly tended or treated. So when a department or union wields their power to keep someone in a job at all costs, well … that cost is sometimes too high, and paid by the officer, their families, and the community.

Every officer's actions affect trust between law enforcement and the community. When things deteriorate past a certain point, as has happened in Baltimore in recent years, longtime informants won't even talk. In some neighborhoods of Minneapolis and other cities, police aren't allowed in by citizens, as crazy as that sounds.

So much of the public's frustration and even hate isn't directed at offending officers but all police by extension. And this has been a thing around the world for as far back as you look. The term "ACAB" ("All Cops Are Bastards") is offensive to my ears, as is any vilification of all people in any group. It is even considered hate speech and punishable in some countries, such as Austria. Such words are not fair, but understandable, given mistakes and outright violations of trust go regularly unaddressed. And given that interactions are dictated by the level of trust over fear, all officers (and citizens) are at heightened readiness, and therefore more likely to result in tragic incidents. We can't just write off this sentiment.

Many unarmed people, and on occasion officers, have been shot because of this. But let's not oversimplify and eagerly take sides. Many of these incidents involve altercations where the officer's life may have been in danger – their gun being grabbed, etc. – but also instigated by the victim's belief they were going to be brutalized or killed. When fear of law enforcement reaches a certain point, justified or not, we can expect a certain number of suspects to not comply or resist and may even fight.

We also need to acknowledge that, like in the military, racism does exist. White supremacists have infiltrated law enforcement agencies across the country according to the FBI. In Los Angeles, we even find cop gangs – the Lynwood Vikings, Reapers, Regulators, Little Devils, Cowboys, 2000 Boys, 3000 Boys, Jump Out Boys, Banditos, and the Executioners. This has been going on for decades. Even though law enforcement training puts the words in every officer's mouth, "we don't see color," there are undeniable disparities and statistics that suggest principle and practice are not the same.

Questions of systemic racism aside, we can either strive for better training and support for those in law enforcement, or we can reenact these tragedies over and over. Transparency and accountability benefit everyone, and yet these have been eroded over time, in spite of technology like body cams. That simple precaution protects officers and citizens alike, and yet has been resisted or not consistently implemented even where available. Instead, we have a YouTube generation capturing every perceived misstep. The equivalent of equipment used to film Rodney King being beaten is now in every person's pocket, and can bypass the media straight to the masses online.

The difficult-to-explain thing is why clear violations of person still take place, knowing cameras are rolling. I'm not talking about incidents where it's difficult to know the context and easy to say "you had to be there to understand." I'm talking about people hog-tied face down being kicked while being screamed at to "stop resisting". I don't think it's right to be told you have no right to question or criticize such things because you never wore the uniform yourself. And yet that is exactly the message from the ultra-pro-police public. I don't think officers (or victims) should be tried by the court of public opinion, but public opinion cuts both ways nonetheless. It makes the work environment more hostile, and on the other extreme makes it socially acceptable to excuse even the most egregious injustices. Some people compile or share canned lists of reasons victims deserved to die, from having a previous record, or a previous medical condition, or all sorts of things that basically invoke a "comply or die" rule.

We as citizens have to take responsibility for this. In our zeal to address injustice, do we vilify law enforcement in general, amplifying mistrust? Do we believe those in blue are beyond reproach and chastise those who criticize or condemn what a reasonable person would consider unacceptable? The actions of bad cops, amplified by our taking sides either way, put all cops deeper in harm's way.

Other than external citizen-based accountability boards and the like, I don't think it should be the public's place to judge every action caught on video. However, if we demanded the same scrutiny of law enforcement as we do doctors or teachers, we wouldn't be where we are either. It took legal battles to confirm the right of citizens to photograph or record public police activity. Now some want to impede these rights with specially crafted laws and increased fines related to distance and obstruction. On the other hand, catching police in the act can stray from legitimate citizen safeguards to fishing for wrongdoing that results in even good officers (and their families) being harassed.

I was talking to a leader of one of the New York Police Department fraternities the other day, and he shared with me the difficulties presented by this. Officers are being told to not even touch or bump into suspects or other citizens by mistake. They don't want another Eric Garner. Various restraint techniques have been outlawed because of such incidents, but even the perception of risk of harm can cause bad PR. And the news doesn't tend to differentiate or judge what is or isn't just – only what is sensational.

Police departments are impacted by these challenges and lack of support in many cities. In places like Seattle, Minneapolis, and New York City, there has been a boost in attrition rates, the first two losing 20% or more of their entire force since the protests started. Early retirements and outright quitting is common, but hundreds of disability claims have come in. This appears to have made a bad situation worse in terms of crime, but we cannot ignore the toll on the officers themselves. The dominant disability claim is PTSD.

A friend of mine whose father was a cop wrote a heartfelt mini-story about an officer who got cornered by protesters and never came home. I do not believe there has been any actual incident like that, and it sounded a bit cliche at the time. But I have since read claims that some officers in the midst of riots have expressed they "did not feel that they were going to come home", with talk of goodbye texts to loved ones. Some allegedly planned to commit suicide (their last bullet) if they believed they would be beaten to death by the mob. However, these claims might be legal posturing on the part of the union and lawyers fighting for disability benefits. It's conceivable they are true, but you can't blame a hesitancy to accept them due to the fact that these teams of law enforcement have extreme asymmetrical advantages in terms of equipment and authority. Even a small number of trained officers can change the tone and outcome of a situation. In fact, that's the point. Actualized threats of life have been extremely rare, thankfully. But this is all armchair quarterbacking on our part. I think we should be open-minded and evaluate each situation on its own merits. These considerations are just that – considerations, not overarching assumptions to be made.

Let me be clear here. I'm not making these points about the injustices or the anger surrounding it. It isn't about ideological arguments when the stuff hits the fan. I'm just trying to help people realize that every person on either side of the line in even the worst situations is a human being. We cannot see every officer sent out to keep the peace or protect property as complicit in the situation(s) that caused this. I would believe that some LEOs skip out because they are looking to avoid the accountability they are used to not having. Now that records of complaints and determined wrongdoings are being made public, habitually bad cops must see the writing on the wall. But I can try to appreciate how difficult this time must be even for the noblest in their profession. Like White people don't purposely perpetuate a biased system just by living in it, police as individuals don't set out every shift to make justice unjust.

On the other hand, we have to understand the point of view of those who only see it from the outside. If police departments don't clean house when bad things happen, or are resistant to reform, it feels like playing the victim by crying foul when torches and pitchforks show up. At some point, citizens see the only choice other than be at the mercy of laws and policies embodied by law enforcement is to fight back. Law enforcement needs to be aware of their blue privilege, whether they abuse it or not. Having the ability to hide behind that wall of solidarity, even in public perception, puts all police in a difficult-to-trust position. And trust is necessary for the job. See the problem?

Police strikes (large numbers of officers calling in with the "blue flu") are problematic. After officers in Atlanta were charged for the death of Rayshard Brooks, some areas had no 911 coverage for days. The guilt or innocence of the charged officers is beside the point. Any lack of due process would continue the impression of the badge as a license to kill. The police taking sides instead of reserving an opinion until investigation adds insult to fatal injury. Striking can be seen as a dereliction of a sworn duty, putting themselves over the needs of the community. If the intent was to make the public "miss" them when needed, that would make their actions something between punishment and extortion. If they truly felt they were in danger by doing their job – a legitimate argument – it should have been plainly announced without gameplaying. But that is just my opinion, and perhaps I'm missing something.

Solutions to reform or improve the role and practices of law enforcement must still allow police to do their job, and make their lives better, not just benefitting the general public. That is why we absolutely need them at the table in this discussion. But calls to "Defund the Police" have created severe adversarialism between the BLM movement and the whole law enforcement establishment. Even people in African-American communities, particularly those of older generations, value or see the necessity of police presence and have voiced that they do not support the BLM agenda because of exactly this. Defund the Police is perhaps the worst branding misnomer of our time. What it means to proponents is as varied as what opponents think it means.

At one extreme, some want to outright "abolish the police". But even that can mean different things. Some municipalities have shut down their police departments – a total reboot – to rehire with performance record reviews and stricter guidelines, reform policies and procedures, and establish a new union contract that doesn't hinder reforms that made the complete overhaul necessary. Abolishing can also mean reordering society itself away from incarceration and punishment-based justice structures that in the eyes of some (using a critical race theory model) are supremacist institutions. When abolish literally means eliminate police, it's unclear there is an alternate pragmatic solution, but there's still a call to look for one. Christian Davenport, a political scientist at the University of Michigan, poses the challenge "for us to discuss what is being protected as well as who is being served" and looking at the underlying place of coercion and force in keeping order. Georgetown law professor Christy Lopez talks about the "need to reset public safety ... to eliminate our overreliance on law enforcement."

To more prevalent and moderate voices "defund the police" actually means reducing or rightsizing the footprint of law enforcement, primarily by giving them work they are best trained to do and makes sense, not play babysitter or social worker or grievance mediator. It's about reallocating resources to things that actually reduce instead of fight crime – education, mental health counseling, affordable housing etc.. We must realize many of the tragedies we've seen with police-involved deaths this year were answering mental health crisis calls. Police don't need to be put in those positions. But defunding also means backing off on military-grade vehicle and weapon purchases. Such gear is incompatible with the sort of police culture many of us deem necessary or acceptable.

There's s much more to say on this topic, but what is pertinent is the difficult issues of policing is intimately tied to recent protests. There is no escaping the fact that law enforcement is the premier interface between whatever racism exists and a justice system whose scales are grossly imbalanced.

Honest members of law enforcement know the system isn't perfect, and can help us help them be better. It's too much for others. Some are eager to retire and even second- or third-generation cops wouldn't recommend it to their children. It was so much easier (at least for police) when there was so much less scrutiny. Many in law enforcement lost trust in politicians on the grounds they are taking sides rather than striving for harmony. There are too many fears of lawsuits and even criminal charges for just doing their jobs. (We have to admit, though, this is ironic given the common sentiment that if you don't do anything wrong, you won't be arrested. Oversimplifying is a double-edged sword.)

Right now, we're building more prisons and dodging lawsuits and riots as we go along. It's not sustainable.

More than police and police unions, the idolizers of those in uniform can't accept their friends and relatives in blue being criticized, even if the criticisms are aimed at the institution. An accusation or challenge to any of it is personal and those making it are on the side of criminals and anarchists in their minds.

"Back the Blue" rallies aren't helping. Waving the "thin blue line" flag isn't new, but like the proliferation of the Stars and Stripes after 9-11, this overpouring of support is a reaction to Black Lives Matter and especially fears the police will be defunded and stop taking calls. Like patriotism, there's nothing ignoble about rallying for first responders. Heck, I think they all deserve a combined holiday. But glorifying authority that is being protested for abuses of authority is throwing fuel on a fire to hope it goes out. And people notice that such rallies are most common in communities known for racism. The exceptions are when they are used to directly counter-protest BLM marches. Locally at least, some rallies have connections to QAnon conspiracists, and most of them include banners in support of the "law and order" president. There's a lot going on here that has little to do with actually supporting the police for its own sake.

This has become a political war that all but forgets the human beings in uniform and those they serve. New York City painted "Black Lives Matter" onto a city block in front of one of the president's properties, to become a regular spot for protests and counter-protests (as well as repeated vandalism against the mural). On several occasions, huge flags were marched over those words combining the American Flag, the Thin Blue Line, and the name of the president in bold letters covering a third of it, underscored by the message "Kepp America Safe". At least two NYPD unions endorsed the incumbent for this year's election, which is not traditionally something that is done. Fortunately, statements have been made recognizing their members have a spectrum of differing opinions, and that impartiality in their duties be maintained.

However, the overall response of law enforcement to protests in America exposes a clear bias. Data shows force has been disproportionately used while intervening in BLM-associated demonstrations compared other types of demonstrations – three to five times more. And there is more use of quasi-lethal force (rubber bullets. chemical weapons, etc.). Many incidents are being determined by courts to involve disproportional or unwarranted force. The response from much of White America? They shouldn't have been out after curfew or blocking traffic or didn't have a permit.

We have to seriously ask if the most protected profession in America (besides politicians perhaps) really needs lipservice support that badly. The thin blue line is actually a thick, opaque wall. It protects the good and the bad. When I hear "no one hates a bad cop more than a good cop" I have to wonder how they can tolerate earning the same pension and having equal promotability (when seniority is a dominating factor) as another officer who may have a stack of complaints against him thicker than the phone book. If we truly "back the blue", we would support the well-being of officers, and do things that reward good ones, even heroes. And we would work to tackle head on conditions in which their trust and respect in the community is diminished.

Or we can just keep blaming the way "kids today" are being brought up. But these kids aren't kids anymore. They protest, they vote, and some of them are joining the ranks of law enforcement. But our problems have come to roost. We can deny it or reframe the issues to where it's "those people's fault" or say it's just baseless complaining, but those voices aren't going to be silenced by more of the same "law and order". Whatever policing becomes, it has to be something we can all believe in. How well we start seeing the police as human beings in human institutions, capable and worthy of reform and support, the sooner we can all maintain the peace.

The simplest solution may even be the best – bring back beat cops with a vengeance. Make a patrolman presence (proactive) the focus instead of being responders (reactive), even if it means refunding the police. New York City starting getting back to this in 2019. Buffalo has CPOs (Community Police Officers) that work directly with neighborhood organizations, but those are two per precinct. And more block club type activities are being done online these days with apps such as NextDoor. Fortunately, police departments have been utilizing social media, but direct presence may be the key.

Peel was right. Vollmer was right. Police should not be overseers but an integrated part of the community. They should spend more time listening to citizens and less time responding to dispatch. Working with us, they have the power to prevent crime through relationships rather than fight crime after-the-fact, racking up arrests and fines as measures of success rather than failure.

And it is these direct interactions not dependent upon incidents or reports that will ensure that citizens and officers see each other as human beings, no matter what color or age or social standing. The watershed issue in racism today could become the greatest solution.

28. Civil Rights, Continued

Many people just don't understand the protests this year. They don't see the police incidents as a race issue, or that these aren't the acts of a few bad apples – if it is ever the officer's fault at all. From this perspective, we must wonder what is the whole point? What do African-Americans really have to complain about? What good are they doing by all this noise and violence and destruction? These questions are symptoms, revealing more about us than "them". When pressed, people who hold these views (or blind spots) are found to be downright furious about BLM and everything surrounding it. Even without the politics and QAnon insanity in the equation, these reactions speak of everything we've talked to up to this point.

All our demons, pushed into the basement time and again, are resurfacing. Looking back at an article I wrote in 2015, I warned my readers, "if you're still betting on the State to fix itself in some higher road of enlightened gentility, listen to the ticks and tocks of people in the streets. Time is running out." Too many incidents followed after each other, year after year. Time ran out.

The Freddie Gray incident happened two years after Trayvon Martin's death. We had the usual finger-pointing and comments that it was yet another excuse for riots and looting, but something unexpected happened. The ever-rival Crips and Bloods issued a joint statement, publicly condemning the violence. They even took measures to protect citizens and businesses in their communities. On the other hand, Ben Carson opted for a message that could be interpreted as just staying home.

> As a former resident of the city of Baltimore, it is very sad and unfortunate to see the destruction taking place by irresponsible individuals ... It is vital to remember that the best way to create positive change is through peaceful conversation and policy ideas that display a commitment to resolution.

Not quite the sentiments of Malcolm X, or even Dr. King, who both as a baseline violated and obstructed the law to affect change they did not believe would occur simply by letter-writing and voting. They didn't stay home. The whole point was to be visible, to clog restaurants and bridges so they could not be ignored. Civil rights leader and Senator John Lewis (who passed away this year) was arrested over 40 times and suffered beatings and injuries in the process, all for making what he called "good trouble".

Nearly all of us can agree riots and looting are *not* a part of protest in a lawful or moral sense. Such things aren't usually even rational. But some can appreciate Dr. King's explanation that

> [T]the cry of "black power" is, at bottom, a reaction to the reluctance of white power to make the kind of changes necessary to make justice a reality for the Negro. I think that we've got to see that a riot is the language of the unheard.

This quote, rarely expanded to include the whole context, is a bit harder to hear than the bite-sized, whitewashed version of King I remember. I'm not going to wax philosophically (here at least) over the nuances of understanding yet condemning violence and destruction. Heaven forbid we recognize it as a pragmatic solution in spite of being what the media chooses to give power to. But I have heard time and again people say, "It's no longer protest once it becomes violent, then it's criminal". When they run out of clearly violent examples to condemn, they expand the definition to include *any* form of protest that inconveniences anyone for any reason. In other words, protest is acceptable as long as they don't have to see it or hear about it.

The reality is that institutions rarely change on their own, if at all, from purely internal machinations. Nearly every struggle in American history, be it labor, or suffrage, or voting rights, proves that. But the encouragement of politicians on the Left is also strangely absent this time around. Princeton Assistant Professor Keeanga-Yamahtta Taylor has been quoted as saying, "the response of Black elected officials has been cautious and uninspired". It's almost as if this were an election year and taking a stand would cost votes in a highly polarized political environment. And frankly, the Right gained control of the narrative first, successfully framing everything in terms of law and order rather than civil rights.

Over this last year, I have wondered and worked toward understanding the differences and similarities between the Civil Rights movement of the 1960s and today's George Floyd / BLM protests. And I suspect current times will be subject to the same endless interpretations, and sadly, the usual whitewashing to make it palatable to America's conscience. But I do know that the movement today is much larger – over 20 million people, making it the largest protest movement in American history. And yet there has been much less violence with only a handful of deaths in contrast to hundreds of deaths between 1964-1971. There is also much more White involvement, though public support in general has tapered off, similar to sentiments back then.

So many people talk about rioters and looters as synonymous with protesters. It infuriates me that so many people only use the word "peaceful" in quotes when talking about protests, the same way Islamophones mockingly refer to "The Religion of Peace" when talking about terrorists.

What I researched (and personally experienced) regarding the 2020 protests was nothing like what people thought they saw (or rather didn't see) in the news. Unusually strong opinions outpaced knowledge from the start. It is hard enough to get the whole story by scouring many conflicting sources for any given incident. Few bother to do more than listen to their pet network and fall into the blanketing assumption that all protests, by all protesters, in all cities, are the same. Nothing could be further from the truth.

In August, the Washington Post reported on research from the University of Washington, indicating the disparity between perception and reality is based on political orientation and biased media framing, including disproportionate coverage of violence. The Anti-Defamation League and other groups documented organized disinformation campaigns. The aim was to spread "deliberate mischaracterization of groups or movements [involved in the protests], such as portraying activists who support Black Lives Matter as violent extremists or claiming that antifa is a terrorist organization coordinated or manipulated by nebulous external forces".

However, on-the-ground accounts, independent research, and even official law enforcement reports provide a more comprehensive, objective perspective. I will try to present here the most important details to untangle this, but be warned – this may not line up with what you've been told by your favorite talking head.

First, cities weren't burning. The "Urban Rebellion" of the 1960s came close to such a description perhaps. But actual large-scale fires and destruction this year happened in very few cities, contained to two or three city blocks at most. People I know in Portland, for example, had no idea what the rest of the country was talking about from inflated news reports. The most chaotic situation was perhaps the CHAZ "autonomous zone" in Seattle, and I don't claim to understand what all that was about. It seemed more like a continuation of the Occupy Movement a few years ago with very different players and agendas than typical BLM crowds. But how prevalent was violence?

ACLED (Armed Conflict Location & Event Data Project) usually does aggregated data collection, analysis, and crisis mapping in other parts of the world, but decided to tackle our domestic situation. What they found was the peaceful protests were reported in over 2,400 distinct locations around the country. Violent demonstrations were limited to fewer than 10% of these places. Only a few places like Portland saw sustained unrest since Floyd's killing, and violent demonstrations were confined to specific blocks.

FiveThirtyEight reported on polls showing that 42% of respondents believe "most protesters [associated with the BLM movement] are trying to incite violence or destroy property" when ACLED's data shows that only 7% of incidents had any violence or destruction.

Responses by law enforcement varied from admirable restraint or disengagement to what would be war crimes if they had been done on foreign soil. In the thousand-plus incidents of journalists injured or attacked, over half were by police, not protesters. Medics were often targeted, even in the midst of administering aid, and medical supplies destroyed. (The presence of trained, assigned medics and medical and physical countermeasures to tear gas and other weapons were lessons borrowed from the Hong Kong democracy protests.) Legal Observers (LOs), with their distinctive bright green hats universally recognized by law enforcement as non-participants, were not always spared and sometimes targeted as well.

For full disclosure, I have taken Legal Observer training and am a member of the National Lawyer's Guild, which had proved itself to be one among many useful inside sources for me to accurately state things in this book. I would encourage anyone who may not wish to protest yet protect freedom of speech and assembly to consider taking such training.

In some cities, authorities expressed support. Some joined in marches and have been receptive to attending open community meetings on reform. Unlike die-hard police fans, many agencies issued statements condemning the actions regarding Floyd and other incidents. On the other hand, there are times where officers have kneeled in solidarity during prayer or moments of silence while cameras rolled, then initiated crowd-clearing by force. In fact, over half of the 7% of incidents with violence started by police use of force.

Law enforcement investigations also tell a different story. It was discovered that in those very first days in May 2020, organized groups traveled to cities specifically to incite violence and then performed organized looting (or more accurately, burglary). From "Umbrella Man" to the firebombers of one or more police precincts, agent provocateurs turned out to be White supremacists looking to blame BLM. But readers of news rarely catch page six retractions months later. And many protesters and BLM-related groups, even victims' families, spoke out against the violence, asking people to stop. Again, sixth-page news.

Politicians politicized the hell out of the protests, using the "defund the police" rhetoric as an accusation against various candidates running for office. Though few if any Democrats participated in protests, Republican Mitt Romney did, who in turn was ridiculed by the president. Many see the riots, looting, and peaceful protests as part of a unified conspiracy. Rhyming with the past, the protests are seen as a plot by communists, anarchists, and those under the vague label "antifa" (anti-fascists) to bring down America. The "Long, Hot Summer" of 1967 involved 159 race riots across the nation. Local to me, it is said that certain underground walkways between buildings at Buffalo State College are closed because of bombings from that time. It was also that year a Miami police chief coined the slogan, "When the looting starts, the shooting starts." Roughly half of those surveyed equated rioters and looters directly with the Civil Rights movement; 65% said they thought it was coordinated. Over half of Whites said it was not brought on by racial inequalities. We see the same perceptions today.

The counter-reactions have proven more dangerous than any riot. "Patriot" militias have been mobilized, overlapping hate groups. A number of actual lynchings have occurred across the nation, some being called suicide without an investigation. "Strange Fruit" still grows. In no small measure influenced by poison seeping into the mainstream from the QAnon pillbox, people are muttering about being ready for a race war. Such people don't get it. They are the ones confused or rationalizing why so many White people are in the BLM movement. What many fail to see is that everything going on here is *not* over race. It's over *racism*. And you don't have to be a certain color to take a stand against that.

Much of what you read here may be news to you. You may have expressed loud opinions without having a forest-for-the-trees perspective. If you've mocked the movement and seethed at it for its violence, you may blame the media. But ask yourself, how many violent videos have *you* personally shared to point a finger and say "look at them!" How many peaceful ones have *you* praised, or even bothered to look for, adding power to the positive? Do our memes show we care more about a knee during the National Anthem than a knee on someone's neck? I hope you see the point. We are all partly responsible for people thinking a mountain is a molehill and a molehill is a mountain. And downplaying the positive takes away its power. If we do nothing else, we should stop doing that.

29. Niagara Square

All eyes were on Buffalo, New York on June 4th, 2020. It was the "head crack" heard around the world when 75-year-old Martin Gugino was pushed and fell to the ground, unconscious and bleeding. Footage of the incident went viral within hours, reaching 70 million views around the world. The riots and looting had happened the weekend before, followed by several days of peaceful protest, but this unexpected event put Buffalo in the spotlight. In a way, it was a distraction from all the particular local incidents protesters were trying to bring to the public's attention. But that is what the press was looking to cover.

Footage showed the world an old, unarmed, White man being hurt by police. Overnight, and in many other cities, the way police handled crowds seemed to change from strongarm tactics to passively keeping the peace. City administrators pleaded that even their presence could compound tensions given the protests are about police actions to begin with. (You'd think it would have been obvious.)

However, the incident itself wasn't particularly confrontational. The protest had been entirely peaceful. Around the time of 8pm curfew, orders were given to clear Niagara Square, starting from the front of city hall. The Buffalo Police Department's Emergency Response Team, made up of volunteers from the ranks, used practiced formations and tactics for crowd control with body armor and batons. Gugino didn't immediately clear and tried to engage in conversation with one or two officers, and after a moment of hesitation, they pushed him back.

I talked personally with a number of witnesses. Their telling of the incident was more of outrage than detail, focusing in particular on him being left unattended on the ground. An officer who instinctively stooped to check on him was told to continue formation while a medic was called. A friend of mine who had worked with police for many years as an ambulance medic said the person telling the officer not to help was in the wrong; those who train in crowd control tactics say the priority is to expand and hold the line so that in such cases medics can safely attend. The question is more if they should have been running riot drills on a peaceful crowd.

Being a martial artist who studied kinesiology and has taught self-defense over the years, I reviewed the video over and over and realized what had happened at that moment. I shared my unique perspective in an email to the department and city hall. Here is an excerpt.

> It is my opinion as such the following seemingly contradictory statements: his fall was a result of contact by the officers; they had no intention of harm. One officer pushed Martin on the right side of his upper torso from nearly arm's length distance without bracing his lower body. This limited the force to a very gentle shove that could not have knocked down anyone by itself. The other officer shoved the other side of his upper torso at nearly the same time with the side of his baton. It did not appear to have been with any considerable force and, by itself, is very unlikely to have caused someone to fall.
>
> The problem is the timing. Applying even gentle pressure to both sides of the midline of one's upper torso – especially a taller man with a higher center of gravity – would prevent the usual rotational autonomic nervous system response to rebalance. The fact this was done by two people who may not even be aware of such a technique, and the haphazard timing, makes it unreasonable to believe it was coordinated or, therefore, intentional. To most observers it would seem like a gross overreaction or that he tripped over his own feet. The official statement that he "tripped and fell" was a reasonable, honest observation, even if it was incorrect.

I made it clear I was not judging their actions from a legal perspective. I wasn't making a moral judgment. Appropriate or not for the situation, they didn't handle themselves in a way I considered unprofessional, or at least not overly belligerent. Well, except for one detail no one talked about: just as this physical contact was taking place, a third officer was rushing up to the line toward him. As unfair as speculation can be, if he had not fallen, it is conceivable blatant brutality may have occurred.

Out of left field – or alt-right field rather – the conspiracy-laden and fact-sparse One America News Network suggested he was using an alleged "antifa tactic" to scan or disrupt police equipment with his cell phone. The President tweeted their claim, because ... well ... of course he did. The community knows Gugino. He's been a lifelong peace activist for things like climate change and closing Guantanamo. Not some rogue SJW, he is associated with the Catholic Worker Movement and works with the Western New York Peace Center. It was just another attempt to tie civil rights protesting to an antifa boogeyman that even our own intelligence agencies refuse to consider a "terrorist threat".

Like many ambiguous incidents, I don't see the need to take sides on this as much as examine the reaction and result. The two officers were suspended without pay and later charged with second-degree assault. Right or not, this kept things from escalating and assured a day in court. All 57 officers quit from the Emergency Response Team. However, it's unclear if it was a voluntary move to protest the arrests or the fact the Police Benevolent Association (PBA), Buffalo's police union, said they would no longer cover legal fees for police actions at protests.

There was also a missed opportunity. Any time tragic police interactions occur, a department can at least try to express concern and compassion for the individuals harmed. There doesn't have to be an admission of guilt, at least not at that point, since lawsuits could quickly unfold that complicate public statements. The nearby sheriff of Niagara Country took a hardline "Law and Order" tack. His solution to protests and tragedies was "comply or die" blame-throwing, and proposed what I call a "Badge Bully's Bill of Rights". The opposite of reform and accountability, it was a wish list of heavy or heavier penalties for those who resist arrest or fight back during brutality or protest, and criminalize bystanders close enough to video police interactions. Such a proposal becoming law would chill freedoms of speech and assembly, and amplify "resisting arrest" into a heavier means of abuse and deprivation of suffrage.

Months later, Martin has now mostly recovered but does not remember the incident. Showing no personal animosity toward police, he was interviewed as saying "I come from the suburbs, and there's no problem with police in a white neighborhood ... I'm not scared of the policemen, but the system is screwed up." While the County District Attorney, Governor, Senator Schumer, the ACLU, and others blamed and condemned the actions of the police, Gugino simply said, "There are plenty of other things to think about besides me."

And some protesters agree. His situation wasn't directly tied to what was being protested. The rallies and marches were for all the victims previous to that time, and some felt the spotlight was hijacked. Why did this incident stand out for the public, public officials, and the news?

What may have been not much more than an accident is decried with strong language, but is nothing compared to other incidents we've seen (or not seen) across the nation. What turned the tide of public sentiment in the 1960s was seeing firehoses and dogs unleashed on women and children. This event seems to have had the same effect, at least for a short while. But it was followed by horrific attacks on peaceful protesters in some cities while the mainstream media chose to air footage of vandalism and water bottles thrown at heavily armored police. You had to go to YouTube to see incidents like crowds cornered against fences being teargassed with no way to disperse or escape (a technique called "kettling").

But immediately after Gugino's fall, heavy police presence at protests disappeared. And so did the sporadic clashes with them. Some other cities chose this path, though the motive is unapparent. Were police trying to "prove a lesson" by backing off to let the chips fall where they may? If that was the intent, it failed. Backing off on riot-gear-clad police deescalated tensions across the board.

Nowhere was this more obvious than in Portland. They were one of the few cities hit regularly with riots and not merely protests. But before we go deeper into this, one thing needs to be clear – even police reports across the nation establish that typically incidents of violence and vandalism happen later at night, after most or all peaceful protesters leave. They are rarely the same people. So when agents of various federal agencies arrived and started snatching and interrogating peaceful people without just cause or any charges being made, Portlanders were livid. Purported to be there to protect the federal courthouse, they instead actively attacked and swept crowds down streets. These agents were not trained for crowd control, or how to use the "non-lethal" weapons in a way that is more likely to be ... well ... *non-lethal.* Yet they were acting in a law enforcement role without the city or department's request or permission. In retrospect, it seems obvious now it was more a political stunt by the White House to look tough for White America and spank "Democrat cities". And it backfired.

Everyday citizens not previously involved in the movement stepped in to protest this Federal presence. Lawyers and teachers marched. There was a "Wall of Moms" and grandpas with leaf blowers to keep away tear gas. After a Navy veteran was maced and has his hand broken with a baton for merely standing there and asking a question, veterans groups showed up. (You may have recalled a somewhat notable photograph from this time – an older woman being dragged away by a man in military tactical gear. She was the mother of one of my online friends.) After many nights of unnecessary battles, the feds retreated, and the violence subsided. Unfortunately, the nation was more focused on the violent few than the countless unarmed citizens injured for nothing more than civil disobedience. The people of Portland saw what we remembered from the 1960s and were outraged. The rest of the country remained divided in their views.

After the Gugino incident, Buffalo's Niagara Square became the scene of press conferences and rallies of various community organizations, particularly from the African-American community. They were in solidarity with, but not the same group as, the mostly younger crowd protesting regularly. But that doesn't mean the demographics of protesters fits the living-in-their-parents'-

basement stereotype. They are actually quite diverse. A few were business owners. Others still had taken off from work to occupy the Square full-time. Some were military veterans. while some, like Gugino, were veterans of protests for other causes and times. And one or two were instigators the rest tried to avoid or keep in check, known to the police from previous public gatherings over the years.

Niagara Square is basically a circular greenspace traffic circle in front of Buffalo City Hall with the McKinley Monument, a 96-foot tall obelisk with lions and pools, at its center. For many weeks, it was occupied around the clock, with vigils, speaking events, music events, street art, and sleeping bag campouts.

At all protests and marches, unlike those unrelated to BLM, social distancing and masks were the norm due to the COVID-19 pandemic. There was even a DIY, foot-activated sanitizer dispenser at the Square. I find it weird how many people think it unfair, or even seem jealous, that protesters can get away with being in crowds when they can't go to a sporting event. Nevermind that entertainment isn't on par with the right to assemble and free speech. Research has shown the there have been no significant spreads or contact tracing back to any protest.

Police really didn't intrude, except once to stop a candlelight vigil on the ground of it being a fire hazard. The crowd was self-organized to some extent. There were people acting as security, and the few situations that occurred, even ones involving weapons, were de-escalated without harm. People did wellness checks. One of the protesters who ran a sort of free concession stand was a trained mental health counselor. Many agitated people were guided to organizations and services for them to get help.

It wasn't long before homeless people discovered they could get some moderate sustenance at the Square, but also something more precious – a good night's sleep. Many said they'd been woken by police in the middle of the night with a gun barrel in their face. This sanctuary became the only place in the city they felt they would be utterly safe.

Just before midnight on June 23rd, police cleared the area, arresting thirteen people who refused to leave. Looking back, it was like a miniature version of Washington, D.C.'s Resurrection City. In 1968, 1,000 police officers cleared the camp, arresting 288 people, including Ralph Abernathy, a civil rights leader and minister of the time.

The reason given was litter, graffiti, and hygiene (people bathing in the fountain pools, which no one will deny or confirm). The litter issue I can tell you was false. I was there many times, and my own daughter coordinated a team of people to keep the Square free of garbage. That's the way I raised her. You're welcome. The graffiti, as were messages written on the walls of city hall from time to time (varying degrees of appropriate and inappropriate language), was chalk. The exception was a local student mistakenly using permanent markers or paints at an art event, at which time the protesters raised $500 toward cleaning supplies for the city, which insisted on handling the cleanup.

Nearly everything there was loaded into trucks to be picked up by their respective owners at the precinct. One person's phone went "missing", even though GPS tracked it to police headquarters. After a week of being told it was either in another location or they had no record, it was recovered. While in police custody, it was used to threaten bodily harm toward one of the head protesters. A lot of the possessions were abandoned to not have protesters identify themselves. Supplies donated from people and businesses throughout the city were lost.

Protest activity shifted to marches in other parts of the city and suburbs. Even in neighborhoods known historically for racist attitudes, few epithets were hurled and many residents showed solidarity or at least tolerance. One march that was planned by African-American clergy had a lot of older people come out, mostly White. Police presence was mostly to ensure traffic and pedestrian safety, and protest groups often informed police departments of activities so there would be no surprises. Police acted with restraint in all cases I was aware of, even though protesters didn't always comply with not blocking a lane or so of traffic. At least locally, protesters were courteous to drivers and always let people through. Blocking traffic was not a common local tactic.

What transpired these months in Buffalo could fill a book when you dig into the details, but a few incidents should be recalled here. Near the end of a march in South Buffalo, a pickup truck pulled up to the protest. A man wearing a bright green shirt that read "Hospitalize Your Local Antifa Scumbag" came out with a baseball bat, repeatedly making false swinging motions at a young woman medic as other protesters tried defending her. He was later identified as an Erie County corrections officer who had gone earlier that day to the "Back the Blue" rally in the nearly Cazenovia Park. He had bragged in a Facebook video that he was eager and ready for trouble, even though the rally and protest were a few hours apart. Once reported, he was placed on administrative leave "pending the conclusion of the investigation".

In addition to Legal Observers, there was a corp of medics at events and marches, trained by a network of professionals that prefers to be anonymous.

At least one of them wears a helmet-cam and body armor. Early on, they were prepared for medical countermeasures to teargas and other tactical traumas. Even having buckets of milk (to treat eyes) at protests was seen by some as "looking for a fight", but citizens from Hong Kong to Washington, D.C. learned that being unarmed and peaceful will not protect you if law enforcement decides to use force. As time went on, the supplies medics carried shifted toward treating general violence-related injuries, as attacks became more often a threat from roque anti-protesters.

One night, a driver hit a woman on a bicycle in the crosswalk in front of city hall. It was unclear if it was intentional. Many attacks with vehicles have occurred at protests over these last months. Heck, a Boston cop was just caught on camera bragging and laughing about running down protesters. But each incident should be evaluated on its own merit. She may have been careless in her eagerness to get around a car stopped in front of her. It is possible that she panicked, having heard of people dragged from their cars in a few cases during riots, and all protests are being equated with riots in many people's minds. Like many failed interactions with police, I would suspect tragedies during protests often stem from issues of fear and mistrust rather than malice. Regardless, the police who were present allegedly ignored pleas to pursue her until protesters stopped her vehicle a block or so away.

There was very little direct counter-protesting at events and marches, but there were counter-activities. There was a summer day where pickups drove up and down main city streets flying blue line flags, presidential election banners, and signs about "saving the children" – a sure sign of their relationship with QAnon conspiracies. Almost a day after a march in East Aurora that went off without a hitch, photos of "BLM" spraypainted on signs and walls in the village hit the Internet. A witness I trust said they were the last one to leave the area and the graffiti wasn't there. More telling was that the corner of some of the taggings had the number "88" – the signature of neo-Nazis. Other incidents attributed to protesters unraveled upon even simple questioning or investigation.

Several groups formed among the protesters, working together at times and trying not to compete or overrepresent themselves as leading or speaking for the protests in general. Black Love Resists in the Rust (BLRR, pronounced "blur") seems to be the group most clearly defined with Black Lives Matter, with entirely African-American leadership. Perhaps the largest cohesive group was the Western New York Liberation Collective. Most of the people at the Square associated themselves with that name, and it was inclusive and diverse.

It held or supported various events to bring attention to all the law-related tragedies and injustices in the Buffalo area, including the conditions and high death rate at the Erie County holding center, a baseball throw from Niagara Square.

A special consideration was always in play. White protesters did not want to take the spotlight from People of Color, but some felt even White presence (sometimes bordering on a majority) was an intrusion. White protesters were nonetheless passionate about doing their part, whatever that meant. As seen in other cities, when police confronted a group, such as when they marched on the mayor's residence, there would be a shout of "White people in front" – and they step up.

As well as support among employees in city hall, a few police officers privately told protesters they appreciated what they were doing. And there are very different opinions and attitudes toward the police by protesters. Some literally want them abolished – and their rhetoric can be extreme – but most just want meaningful reform. Some of the protesters are family members of local LEOs. This array of messages, from "f* the police" to work with them to fix the system for everyone, makes it difficult for the public to understand the nature and relationship of BLM with law enforcement.

Some have bridged the gap. My daughter, Christina Stock, has been active with local protests from the start. She set up a group called Hope in Action Buffalo, which focuses on promoting civic involvement. One of the first projects was to collect school supplies for needy children at protest sites and have them distributed by one of the local police precincts. She's built relationships with a number of people in law enforcement and had candid (albeit off-the-record) talks about some incidents.

This attitude is not unique. My friend Oswaldo Mestre, head of Citizens Services for the city, expressed to me how impressed he was that this young generation is educating themselves on civic processes to work within the system for change. They aren't just making noise. They are attending municipal meetings. They are writing legislators. And on a national scale, BLM has worked to register large amounts of new voters that may very well have determined more than a few electoral votes this year.

Personally, this gives me hope for the future. What I have seen is a passion for justice, and a willingness to learn and work toward it. And I feel a deep regret that we didn't fix these things before they had to live with it. My generation didn't finish the job. We felt things were good enough and not our problem. We thought prejudice would go away if we just didn't participate in it.

We were wrong. New generations, far more than ours, won't tolerate personal racism. And they won't ignore the racism that covers institutions established under a White supremacy culture we have been socialized into and can't see.

We can't tell them to get off our lawn, nor should we. But they might set us out to pasture if we don't help guide them, or at least get out of the way.

30. The Reckoning

There was a time when I thought waving signs around was a waste of time – a substitute for real action. I was wrong. Personal experience and history irrevocably changed my mind. People want to believe the protests didn't have a point, and therefore no goal or result other than expressing rage. Well, you may have to change *your* mind, because substantial progress has been made. The protests have exposed the underbelly of supremacy in America. Progress regarding racism as a social phenomenon may be hard to quantify, but the details of police conduct and accountability aren't.

At the time of this writing, 24 states and innumerable municipalities have passed police reform legislation. Transparency of complaints and charges against police, body-cam requirements, measures against racial profiling. and stands against unnecessary lethal force and deadly techniques are policies spreading across the nation. Breonna's Law, banning no-knock warrants, just was signed into law in Virginia. In spite of restrictive regulations on the state level and public sector unions, municipalities are making progress on the local level.

Buffalo's mayor Byron Brown says purging racism within the BPD requires addressing management, training, and citizen participation in the process. Stop-gap measures include issuing citations instead of arrests for low-level offenses. The City has also reached out to people in barbershops. No, this isn't a joke. Barbershops act as a sort of informal community gathering place of males within African-American communities.

Perhaps the most meaningful reform is Cariol's Law, possibly the first of its kind, that *requires* officers to step in and report breaches of conduct. It was named for officer Cariol Horne, who intervened when another officer was choking a handcuffed black suspect. She was dismissed just short of retirement, while the other officer suffered no repercussions. Since that time he was jailed for excessive force on handcuffed black teenagers, but was only forced to retire – keeping his pension – after assaulting other officers, twice. Horne is fighting to have her pension reinstated.

I have a theory why "defund the police" became the battle cry of BLM. Past protests were about justice for specific cases, be it lack of punishment of cops or those who killed People of Color, or disproportionately harsher sentences for African-Americans, such as for the Jena Six. Money. It sometimes seems the only way to get the attention of police departments and unions is through their budget.

Change must be about policy, which includes money, and ultimately power. That's why citizen oversight is essential. That's why legislation can't always wait for privileged sentiment to give a damn. Kendi suggests that activism must be about policy, not attitudes. Moral persuasion may not ever be enough, pointing out that acceptance often comes generations after laws are passed. And that's the beauty (at least the intentions) of our system – it serves and protects minority interests. Maybe we need to witch-hunt policies and those that institute them rather than brands of syrup and rice.

We also need to get over or replace the "defund the police" slogan. Nearly everyone agrees it does not make sense when taken literally, nor accurately represent the reforms being demanded. At worst, we find cities agreeing that a police department may have to be completely dismantled, but it always means a replacement, not an elimination, of the police force.

In a nutshell, it's a reimagining of how more community issues can be handled outside the policing paradigm. But it is not police-less. The Law Enforcement Assisted Diversion (LEAD) Program, for example, reduced recidivism by 22% across the nation wherever it was implemented. It's described thusly:

> [P]olice officers exercise discretionary authority at point of contact to divert individuals to a community-based, harm-reduction intervention for law violations driven by unmet behavioral health needs. In lieu of the normal criminal justice system cycle – booking, detention, prosecution, conviction, incarceration – individuals are instead referred into a trauma-informed intensive case-management program where the individual receives a wide range of support services, often including transitional and permanent housing and/or drug treatment.

There are also citizen groups participating in policing, such as the Buffalo Peacemakers where I live. They are simply people who walk the streets to gather information regarding potential violence. They work with the police, who say such efforts at community engagement are responsible for a 24% drop in shootings from 2018-2019. Part of their secret is to confront youths at risk within their own neighborhoods.

Replacing or modifying the current community policing schema aside, training is becoming more common for dealing with de-escalation and racial bias. Actually, any regular training would probably help, given you need more training hours in some states for hairdressing and interior decorating than law enforcement. The only consistent barrier or resistance to training and changing structure and policies seem to be police unions. Their protections are untenable if we are to have accountability, and I would suggest is the cause of so many abuses. In fact, there are unions that defy municipal policies by encouraging or even providing for combat training that is contrary to acceptable guidelines.

We can't be at war with the police. The police shouldn't ever have the mentality they are at war with us, even if it's just "those people" in another neighborhood. We must work toward ending blue privilege, even if it did not intersect with White privilege. We must recognize that merely having People of Color on the force does not reduce instances of brutality, as they have often the same prejudices against "their own people" as White officers do. Diversity in law enforcement since the 1960s has not yielded sufficient results. We must keep our eyes on the real goal that *all* must be equal under the law, from responding to a complaint to appearing before a judge.

And we must address police idolization, but for a reason I haven't heard people talk about. Whether it's Rittenhouse's professed dream of being a cop or Zimmerman's rejection from joining the force that led him to play vigilante, there's a hero complex worse than mine at play here. Law enforcement is attracting the wrong people, and sometimes they get in. I don't claim to know the dynamics, but there is a prevalence of military training or being in law enforcement families with nearly all recent mass shooters. I'm not going to blame guns here, and certainly not the military or law enforcement. What if the real issue is the glorification of this sort of power? And what if this power amplifies personal and systemic prejudices? One of the COs I mentioned earlier wants to become a police officer. Is it for the right reasons? Can they overcome their prejudicial thought processes before being entrusted with that power?

Regardless, crime isn't all about the police and will still exist even with reforms. Society *racializing* crime is the problem. We need to stop throwing our hands up that there's nothing we can do – "those people" are just like that and will never change. The delusion "they" have done it to themselves. No wonder police act like zookeepers in "bad" neighborhoods at times. It's where we get the racist term "Black on Black crime". Why is that even a statistic? Are there numbers for "White on White crime"? In a largely still-segregated world, wouldn't most people be victims of people of their own color?

The bottom line is that justice should not be based on the perceived conduct of a people. Ibram X. Kendi, in *Stamped from the Beginning*, writes about "the idea that White people could be persuaded away from their racist ideas if they saw Black people improving their behavior" as a futile approach. Some white abolitionists promoted this strategy, and many African-Americans internalize it to this day, blaming "their people" for the perception of them by White society.

But statistics don't lie if we let them tell the whole truth. Crime rates correlate to poverty, especially long-term employment opportunities, regardless of color. There are very different crime rates in different African-American neighborhoods, just as in White ones. There is less delinquency where there are more African-American-owned businesses. Then there's population density. During some random reading of sociology journals at my daughter's college a few years ago, I came across some research about types of crimes. Violent crimes are more prevalent in cities, while theft is more common in suburbs. The missing piece here is that African-American and Latinx poverty is concentrated, whereas White poverty is distributed more evenly across urban areas.

Property ownership is a whole other story. I used to think African-Americans didn't value land ownership and instead pimped out their cars as a status symbol. I really thought that was a cultural trait. Now I know that historically, banks will lend money to African-Americans for cars but not so much for mortgages or, heaven forbid, business loans. Like the stereotype of trailers on Native reservations, it's founded in institutional circumstances. There are lending laws to fix this, but apparently not everyone got the memo. Perhaps like the microloan industry in India transformed poverty into mass micropreneurship, we need new institutions focused on urban renewal rather than band-aid programs and laws.

Until we more successfully tackle issues of justice and economy, will protests continue? Do they need to? I think the ball is in our court. We shouldn't wait until the next big tragedy. Rodney King pleaded for people not to take their frustration out on everyone because of what a few cops did; Reginald Denny, who barely survived an assault by rioters shortly after offered the profound words, "Nobody ever gets even with anybody". But these messages cannot be heard nor heeded by emotionally-frustrated masses. To further racialize and dehumanize people targeted for economic and legal injustice is adding insult to injury in the extreme. If we think America doesn't deserve riots, but the part of America rising up doesn't deserve consideration of grievances, then we are the absolutely, one-hundred-percent, the problem.

But I am hopeful. I want to believe we're not just at another juncture, or even a crossroads, but an endgame. I would like to see the revitalization of White supremacy as its death throes. Supremacists have caused more deaths than Islamist terrorism, and far more than all far-Left groups combined. "Patriot" militias are mobilizing for the wrong reasons, which only exposes the duplicity of their claims to support Liberty. They are defending a White Christian America that never existed except in the exercise of majority powers not granted them by the Constitution. We now have a clearer idea of who the closet racists are in our social media friends list, versus those who are merely socialized into ignorance like the rest of us.

And just as we discovered that Russian bots have subverted our elections in 2016 through false news and inflated volumes of opinions, we now know their big game plan. Bad actors from Russia and other countries actively set up social media groups to promote identity politics, then slowly turn the heat up on hate and fear-based rhetoric. They don't just do this as softcore White supremacists but as lightly-radicalized People of Color. But they can't exploit what isn't already there. A lot of Americans are eating it up like candy, eager to justify their worst natures.

If there is a "race war", it will not be between People of Color and Whites, but between bigots and anti-racists. Mohamad Safa's words lay clear that line is drawn. "Our world is not divided by race, color, gender, or religion. Our world is divided into wise people and fools. And fools divide themselves by race, color, gender, or religion."

PART IV

WHERE DO WE GO FROM HERE?

31. Our Beloved Supremacies

Here's a big question: can we remove prejudice and bigotry from our society without fundamentally changing it? If I had to guess, the answer is ... drum roll, please ... no.

And that's going to be hard on some people. Racism in all its forms traces back to power, and it means giving up some power and control. And this isn't just power over minorities, but power over all of us in that any group is self-policing. White people are expected to be and act a certain way by the consciously and unconsciously enforced norms of White people. Most of us don't even realize this. I know I didn't until all the reading I did for this book. Don't believe me? Consider that Italians and some other groups were not considered White at one time. What changed? Their skin tone? They learned English and integrated over time into the economy, "becoming" White. We could say we allow *some* diversity within Whiteness once assimilated, but it does not extend outside of it.

What if I told you some African-Americans crossed this threshold and are White in this sense? You may still have to play 20 questions with the police after a neighbor doesn't recognize you taking a walk. But in professional and formal community circles, going to a "good" school and being "articulate" and dressing out of today's equivalent of the JC Penny catalog will buy your way in. This is where "selling out to the man" or accusations of being an "Uncle Tom" comes in, but I'll stay in my lane over the nuances of that. But this is where we find the battle over what it means, or should mean, to be African-American. It is no surprise that some highly successful and politically powerful African-Americans have views that mimic the attitudes of White privilege and White fragility. Insomuch as they internalize racial supremacy, some People of Color have even become members of the Proud Boys.

Socialized prejudice and racism, on a personal level, is about getting caught up in fear and hate. Supremacy isn't about that. Supremacy is an ideology. It is radicalized prejudice for the purpose of power. It is fear of what "they" represent − other people not conforming to their brand of power, and being threatened by such people having power. When this model is employed, you *may* be accepted if you leave your culture at the door, or you will be told to go back where you came from. If you don't leave, you will be segregated or incarcerated or killed. Integration and assimilation in this sense are just other words for racism.

This power isn't just political, but cultural. White supremacy is not an excisable tumor, as if it has clearly defined boundaries. It is integrated into society itself, and is only one facet of a larger paradigm. Kendi describes racism as an addiction, along with its behaviors of denial. And we doth protest too much. But like political correctness looks for targets of malignant cells to cure, we miss the pattern – the blueprint of supremacy itself. And I don't mean supremacy in the sense of the majority naturally having more power, but not giving space for minority interests to have equal power. It's the enforcing of this majority rule, which requires the use of its power to prevent its loss or sharing with others.

How do we share power equitably? The whole reason we have a Senate and not just a House of Representatives – a proven bicameral model in both modern and ancient times – is so that smaller stakeholders won't be overruled all the time. Pure democracy, after all, is three wolves and a lamb deciding what's for dinner. It's also why we have the Electoral College, as controversial as that is these days. But this isn't just about less-populated places having more advantage in one way to make up for disadvantage in another. It's not just about vote counts.

People and communities with unique needs shouldn't be underserved in any way, especially in an otherwise prosperous nation. It means the voices of the few should not be drowned out by the voices of the many. It means you can bring your menora to the office and not just stare at the Christmas tree. It means you don't get shamed for speaking in Spanish or not joining in prayer. It means reasonable and thoughtful accommodation without having it turn into a battle over political correctness or asserting one's identity to have control over others. (These situations can get sticky if we don't better ourselves in terms of tolerance and patience.)

Supremacy has many faces. White supremacy is the child of European economic and political supremacy. Western Chauvinism (similar to the WASP concept) is its uncle, enforcing notions of culture and patriarchy. Its heavily-armed half-brother is Exceptionalism, or national supremacy. This last one is NOT patriotism, a love of one's country, but an insistence of superiority and compulsory allegiance. This is why it concerns me when people suggest we should all be forced to serve in the military because people aren't "patriotic enough". Being one of the only nations in the world to have a pledge of allegiance isn't enough. Being one of the only nations to sing its anthem at sporting events isn't enough. American supremacy demands opposition to other ways of life (and economic models). It looks guardedly at anything that does not fit our idea of American values, including other languages and religions that aren't "American" enough.

From a supremacist viewpoint, people who aren't supremacists "hate America", and the accused rightfully shy away from even healthy patriotism because of its association with the country's ambient fanaticism. The flag has been flown prominently by those of all three supremacies, leaving patriotic people like myself feeling it's been stained and no longer represents liberty, tolerance, and a cultural *e pluribus unum*. Them wanting their country back, and me wanting us to just live up to what it professes, are incompatible positions.

We stopped talking about America as a White, Christian nation back in the 1950s, but we still talk about America as a Christian nation. We feel we can defend that under the cover of religious freedom. Inclusive words like "Happy Holidays" offends us, as does having to push "1" for English. We don't even know why it bothers us. We just intrinsically assume righteousness is ours on these points and ... well ... f* your feelings. It is an existential moral imperative that America be and stay what only some of us think it is. Separation of Church and State be damned, we lift up the Constitution in one hand with the Bible in the other. (Both are scriptures to us, and I question if some people have read or understood either.) "God and Country" is taken beyond a worthy zeal to radicalized fanaticism. Like the 1942 hymn says, "Praise the Lord and pass the ammunition!"

We don't know why we're defending these things. Yet without question, we accept any suggestion English-speaking White Christians are under attack, and therefore America is under attack. In God we trust, and Jesus is as American as apple pie and Country music. God blesses America, and other countries are gentiles in need of mission work and democracy (even though so many have better democratic systems than ours). Immigrants, minorities of all colors, and even Native Americans aren't "real Americans" by this standard.

But the legitimacy of supremacy was never true, except by the force of law and social sanctions. We were never exclusively a Christian, blue-laws-following, English-speaking, White-society-conforming country. The question is why should White America care about what other Americans do? I think there is only one answer – power. In a way, all racism stems from power. Power decides what everyone should do, not just within a group, but within any collection of groups. It's bigger than color, as power concentrates itself irrespective of such things. Many White people, particularly the poor, have little power, but are not as easily excluded as those who are newcomers, or newly freed.

How do we know our supremacy? When we feel our way of life is threatened, even though people like us dominate positions of power in government and the economy, that's supremacy. When we say we are "not allowed" to be ourselves, as if people asking you to be inclusive is an imposition, is supremacy. Stereotyping any group as not deserving a place at the table is supremacy. Worrying about "other" people taking jobs from "real Americans" is supremacy. Worrying about the influences of other cultures on our own society and laws is supremacy. (I'm looking right now at people who have no idea what Sharia law is but are sure it's out to get us.)

Like White supremacy and privilege comes with White fragility – all the ways we can't handle dealing with race or our place in the machine – Exceptionalism comes with American fragility. We can't handle legitimate criticisms of our country. We imagine it an insult to all those who died defending the Flag. The horrible facts of history cannot be reconciled, and therefore cannot be discussed, only underplayed and pushed "in the past" while tales of glory during these same times maintain their luster and relevancy. The fact that only White people (and not even women or poor ones) had the full benefit of our ideals makes White Supremacy equivalent to American Supremacy. And when you consider the dominance of political Evangelicalism in much of the country, it's no wonder the three of these supremacies intersect, forming a massive demographic of predominantly White theocratic nationalists. Imagine if a political figure could tap into all three of these ...

But why should getting rid of supremacy matter to White people? The nature of its power keeps down poor White people, not just People of Color. Secondly, because diversity is resilience. That's not a small part of America's success. It brings more value in terms of skills and knowledge and ingenuity than anyone realizes. It is also proven that migrants of all colors – regardless of legal status – do not subtract from our economic bottom line, but add to it. And, contrary to memes by supremacists, a comprehensive review of world history will show you the rise of cosmopolitan nations and the decline of isolationist ones as the norm, not the other way around.

As a nation, our exceptionalism causes us to bury our faults instead of addressing them, and it shows. China has been given plenty of ammunition to (hypocritically) call us to task on human rights. Even close allies that respect us are concerned these days. Lech Wałęsa once said America's number one import is human rights, and yet we've slipped down the scale quite a bit since the Cold War. Our Freedom Index measurement challenges our exceptionalism as well. But then this really isn't new. It was reported under President Johnson that our civil rights unrest was a hindrance to foreign policy.

We should be very wary that power to maintain power is codified into the system. It naturally would transfer to whatever group becomes a majority down the road. We see this play out in South Africa after Apartheid, to mixed results. They are still trying to figure out who owns farms taken from Black Africans but kept for generations by White owners. If we're really worried about Sharia being enforced as law someday, then we need to strengthen the wall between Church and State, not further shore up current majority religious mandates and infiltrate power with dogmatic issues.

It always amazes me that both major political parties want to expand the authority of the presidency when they are in power, as if they will always be in power. We want to expand the surveillance state to make us feel safe, not thinking about what kind of government will have access to our texts in 20 years. (Anne Frank's family was known to be Jewish in Nazi records because their family divulged their religion on paperwork eight years earlier.) We have a country based on centuries of skewed racial and cultural power, and whatever "retaliation" a Black or Brown America imposes would understandably be due to the precedent of White America. So can we dismantle and rebuild our structures to create equity not based on groups, or wait until the wheel of history spins again?

Culturally, how do we give space for all who dwell in a country that no one culture should own? How about we forget about the melting pot and make it a salad bowl? Better yet, how about an all-you-can-eat world-encompassing buffet!

32. The Promised Land

Where do we go from here? It depends on what kind of world we want to live in. Do we want to play a game of conflict and balance, or try to live in the spirit of teamwork and equity? Can we psychologically stop making Black be the opposite of White, or worse yet, a deficient version of it? Can those of us in the majority think in terms of liberating rather than civilizing others? Can we stop letting the terms of victim and oppressor dictate our relationships without denying there is some truth in them? Dr. King said it well: "We are caught in an inescapable network of mutuality, tied in a single garment of destiny ... Whatever affects one directly, affects all indirectly." Even choosing to be more conscious of this is a start.

The Emmett Till Interpretive Center's slogan, if taken to heart, can change our world: "Racial reconciliation begins by telling the truth." We must own our past. All of it. We can't stick it onto particular states or ancestors but must wear it as Americans and human beings.

The alternative is to stay where we are. El-Hajj Malik el-Shabazz describes our society overcoming slavery as only pulling the knife out halfway. Maybe these civil rights movements have pulled it out further. But it's too easy to walk away if the knife or wound isn't in our own back. Maybe it isn't that simple; maybe there isn't one knife, but a hundred smaller ones, and new ones, or the same ones we thought we pulled out are pushed back in again by somebody else. As much as we focus on individual injustices and inequalities, it's like playing a game of whack-a-mole. We need to address the underlying attitudes that keep up the whole construct.

The kind of world I want to live in already exists here and there – the Kingdom of Heaven is at hand! I once ate a falafel from an Egyptian street vendor in Korea Town in Manhattan, surrounded by people speaking French. I ate "Liberty sushi" while looking up at the Statue of Liberty. I went to school with people from other nations, have Masonic Brothers of all colors and backgrounds, and neighbors who speak Arabic, Chinese, Spanish, and English. I can dance to polkas at the Buffalo Central Terminal on Dyngus Day, get my retsina (admittedly an acquired taste) at the Greek Festival, and take my wife to Buffalo's historic Colored Musicians Club for an evening out. I can hear the call to prayer from a distant minaret while entering Our Lady of Victory Basilica. I can go to Shabat after a session of meditation at a Buddhist center on the

East Side or a Yoga institute on the West. Isn't this expression of Freedom far more liberating than trying to corral everyone into one set of customs and traditions?

I am not saying we should force diversity, but almost all accusations of that have been crying wolf. We need to at least try to stop being threatened with advances in inclusion, diversity, equity, and all those other trigger words of White fragility. I know some say it isn't enough to be "not racist" but even getting out of the way is far better than fighting every little social change. Our opinions matter. And thanks to social media being a sort of Human Language 3.0, people's sentiments are expressed, passed around, and paid attention to by policymakers like never before. And it affects most media, which, thanks to algorithms and Nelson ratings, conforms to what we want to hear and how we want to hear it. All this has a huge impact on progress, for good or for ill.

Perhaps the greatest thing we can do is to unracialize social phenomena. We must start seeing drugs as a health problem and crime as a poverty problem. Making it about race has borne us no progress. However, it can work the other way around. Fixing these issues that bear down heavier on People of Color improves health. It's not just to avoid repeating historical evils such as the Tuskegee Syphilis Experiment and mass sterilizations of minority women (and allegedly women at the border today). Inequalities in the baseline of health persist. "Racial stress" has been statistically demonstrated in the prevalence of hypertension and other physiological measurements. And that is a symptom of all racism's constituent aspects.

Kendi says, "Individual behaviors can shape the success of individuals. But policies determine the success of groups." These could be corporate policies, church policies, municipal policies, or state and federal policies. I'm not saying we all have a moral obligation to be activists, but any amount of awareness can add our voice to the conversation. It only takes a moment to sign a petition or add your name to a mass emailing to your representatives through various websites. Voting doesn't hurt. Supporting community organizations that level the playing field economically or in terms of power helps. But clinging to "racial neutrality" adds your brick to the wall of the status quo.

If you have economic power, as a consumer or producer, you can choose where to spend and invest. My father, for example, made a point of putting his plastics recycling warehouse in a depressed area of the city and employed people from that community. The business didn't survive the oil price crash in the mid-1990s, but he was proud to have at least given work to many people over those few years. Shopping in, instead of avoiding, economically disadvantaged neighborhoods can make a huge impact for everyone.

If you're a person in power, invite and include representatives of stakeholder populations in decision-making. Make the conscious effort to do this consistently and the world will change. And by a person in power, I mean you could be a block club president, or a pastor, or an advisory committee for the municipality or local law enforcement agency. The Woodson Center lays out a workable philosophy that isn't dictated by bureaucracy but by the community.:

> Low-income individuals and neighborhood-based organizations should play a central role in the design and implementation of programs to address the problems of their communities ... Value-generating {market economy principles} and faith-based initiatives are uniquely qualified to address problems of poverty that are related to behavior and life choices.

And better communities economically benefit everyone. The success of People of Color is America's success. It could add untold billions to the GDP, while alleviating the conditions that underpin violence and crime. Wherever you think we are in this process, take another look and find out what still needs to be done. Even if we think the Promised Land is an unreachable ideal, there are better places ahead that we *can* reach.

Even if we do achieve a higher level of racial and ethnic harmony, and gain appreciation rather than mere tolerance, the job is never done. We must be on guard against our human nature as new "others" arrive at our shores. And they may import their own prejudices. I had a medical doctor actually tell me Himalayan salt is pinkish or brownish because "those people" are "dirty". You would correctly guess they are from the People's Republic of China, where Tibetans are systematically marginalized. That is why students from mainland China regularly protested the appearance of the Dalai Lama on campuses. It's geopolitical baggage we don't need but have to deal with.

I honestly don't have much other specific insight to offer on the subject of what a future looks like or how we will get there on the macro scale. But writing this book got me thinking and asking the right questions, and I hope you can join me in that. What I will say is that the Promised Land cannot wait. Having yet another generation expect their children to be treated unfairly is, in the words of John Howard Griffin, "the least obvious but most heinous of all race crimes, for it kills the spirit and the will to live".

My hope is that we can become educated, and then make the moral choice to act on it as best and honestly as we can. At the very least, we must see that "we have met the enemy and he is us." There is no one else here. Dexter Gelfand, a friend who is a Therapeutic Spiritual Counseling Specialist, gives us a higher perspective on this:

> Coexistence is not a choice, it is the only existence.
> Awareness and acceptance of coexistence is a choice.

It's time we choose wisely.

33. Race Trek

Hope and fear. Those are the two ways we perceive and therefore build our future. I have a penchant for post-apocalyptic fiction (which my wife abhors) so I can attest there is plenty of casting our fears into the future by the storytellers of our time. But there is also fiction that posits potential bright futures. Perhaps the mythos that most reveals our social consciousness is Gene Rodenberry's *Star Trek*. The original series had a crew with diversity unimaginable at the time, working together in a universe with a post-poverty Earth. It extolled a zeal for exploration and confederation rather than conquest.

Nichelle Nichols, in the role of Lt. Uhura, was an inspiration for many NASA astronauts, particularly the first African-American woman in space, Mae Jemison. But turnabout is fair play – Jemison played a member of the bridge crew in an episode of *Star Trek: The Next Generation*.

We cast our prejudices into space as well. We merely shifted undesirable aspects of human nature to alien species. Our fearful fictions bring to earth conquerors, exploiters of our resources, even exterminators. Why? Because that is clearly within the realm of human activities. We may as well outsource such unpleasantries to space bugs or robots. It is not unlike the fictions of history, where we paint perpetrators of terror, horror, and holocaust as demons, monsters, or animals, but never, ever honest examples of our own flawed human nature.

In all science fiction, aliens also tend to be monocultural, with one creed, one style of fashion, architecture, etc.. And they are deeply stereotyped. All members of a race display one dominant personality trait or behavior, one driving motivation. For example, the Ferengi are a caricature of Capitalists in the extreme. They pursue wealth above all else, even family, and with *Rules of Acquisition* that make an ethicist like me shudder. Until the series *Deep Space Nine*, they were little more than randomly-encountered, savage opportunists, even slavers. But then individuals of the species were introduced as regular characters, with names and distinct personalities. The nuances of their individualism made their cultural peculiarities tolerable.

I myself developed a strange prejudice against them. You see, I used to play a BBS game called Trade Wars. (For those who don't know what a BBS is, think a hobbyist's version of the Internet in 16 colors before the World Wide

Web existed.) In this game, you would build up a ship by buying and selling resources, and you were constantly attacked by Ferengi pirates trying to steal your cargo. I know, it's just a game, but remember, racism isn't rational. Only after getting to know the characters Quark, Rom, and Nog as distinct individuals, was my reactive cringe response blunted. I might even do business with them ... watching my back, of course.

As for a less fictional prejudice I must admit to, the only knowledge I had of Somalia for many years were news reports about Somali pirates. My friend Jim Shanor removed that slant from my mind. An American citizen with an African family in Nairobi, he openly shared his Somaliphile experiences. There's a small Somali population in Buffalo (about 90 people last I heard), and if I run into them. at least I won't be apt to treat them like Ferengi.

There's another prejudice revealed in science fiction, and that is a vast bias toward human nature and culture as a species. Not only do we assume aliens will have territorialism, strong self-interest, subterfuge, and other familiar traits, but storylines tend to give extraterrestrial cultures value based on how close they are to ours. And there's always a character that wants to be human – transformed, evolved, or redeemed to be like us. Spock. Data. Odo. Seven of Nine. It's the old game of "civilizing" some "other", the same way indigenous people and minorities are expected to "rise" to a default, White ideal of humanness. It's like we expanded White supremacy into human supremacy. Dear aliens, you will be assimilated, or else.

On the other end of the race-in-space spectrum from showing an inclusive, diverse future, we have Anne McCaffrey's *Dragonriders of Pern*. Conceived around the same time as Star Trek, it takes place {spoiler alert!} on a planet of distant descendants from Earth. The original colonists had been from all over our world and eventually become racially convergent and indistinct, though any given individual may have particularly dark or light skin. Will we as a species maintain our diversity of culture and appearance? We will likely become vastly more culturally diverse as we colonize new worlds, reworking old mores and traditions into new forms. Different calendar systems will surely give us new holidays. Circumstances may dictate drastic divergences in biology for any given set of gravity and other planetary conditions, such that *homo sapiens* may become alien in appearance to one another. Will we establish a new hierarchy, and therefore a conflict of space races, as found in James S. A. Corey's *The Expanse*? Let us hope we can fundamentally improve human nature by that time.

Or perhaps a fundamental shift will take place once we discover conclusively we are not alone. Even though many saw the moon landing as an American achievement, people around the world recognized it as a human one. Astronauts tell of the transformative experience of viewing the whole earth at once – the ultimate affirmation of our unified fate as a species. How much more can we see ourselves as one when we are faced with an extraterrestrial "other"? I would hope our unification does not come from the necessity of survival, but even then we may have doubts given the threat of climate change and nuclear annihilation has not knocked us to our senses. No wonder we aren't invited to the interstellar block club ... yet.

In researching for this book, I came across many things I had never been aware of before, including "Afrofuturism". It's an art form onto itself, not merely a sub-genre of science fiction. This global African aesthetic can even be found in the music fashion of Parliament-Funkadelic. The most recognizable example would be Marvel's Black Panther. The fictional kingdom of Wakanda in a way serves the same purpose as Tolkien's Middle Earth – to provide a mythological framework for a culture that needs help to fill in archetypes and legends. Creation or reclamation of identity, after all, is part of the journey of African-Americans. Slavery had previously severed connections with the culture of those enslaved, suppressed its development, and now in White America are left with little more than options of assimilation or segregation.

The response to Chadwick Boseman's death in 2020, not just by African-Americans but many White people, shows that even comic books and movies can bring cultural acceptance and value in a unique way. Erin Poulson tells us a story, a shoutout to the actor ...

> In May 2018, I was newly Queen of Newcastle, at the Georgia Renaissance Festival ... I had a young black girl and her dad come and visit the Royal Court. I introduced myself as Queen of England and the girl said, 'I'm a princess!!' And then she got shy.
> I wanted her to keep talking, so I said, 'Oh! Are you a Princess of England?' She shook her head. 'Are you a Princess of France?' Another head shake. I don't know why, I'd never done it before, but I thought I'd take a chance. 'Are you a Princess of Wakanda?'
> Her eyes grew so big. Her father jumped with excitement. And she nodded regally.
> I crossed my arms over my chest. 'Wakanda Forever, my princess. We are so honored to have you in our Kingdom!' Now she stood a hundred feet tall, and her dad nearly trembled behind her. I touched my colleague Joshua Miller's shoulder, who'd been carrying on a very different conversation as King Henry, and said, 'My dear Henry, we have a visiting guest from Wakanda!'
> Without missing a beat, his arms crossed over his chest. 'Wakanda forever, dear princess!! And welcome to England!!'
> That shy girl walked out of pavilion with her head held high like an

empress. And I remember her dad just dancing next to her, whispering, 'Wakanda, baby!! They know you're from Wakanda!! You're royalty too!!'

Mr. Boseman, I've worked Renaissance festivals for almost twenty years now. Since that point, I have seen dozens of black boys and girls accept themselves as royalty in a way that I'm not sure they would have before. The doors you opened echo throughout time like Arthur pulling the sword from the stone.

Anachronistic fantasy can be more potent than any dusty history. And maybe we can learn lessons from the worlds we want to believe in and make ours more like them where it matters.

There is also a question how to handle artificial intelligence (AI). Should robots have ethnicity and gender? In America, a female in broadcast English seems to be the default. We may already have our GPS speak to us as Morgan Freeman or Samuel Jackson, but that's in jest. Just like many of us want role models that reflect our unique ethnicity, maybe it's time for Alexa, Siri, and Cortana to move over. Gender and dialect (more than just "American English" versus "UK English") should be an extension of language options as accessible as your time zone. One might also suspect that White female voices are chosen under the socialized premise they are the least threatening, and a positive-use spectrum of voices could unwire some of that for everyone.

Then again, my cousin, Dr. Frank Pasquale III, author of *New Laws of Robotics: Defending Human Expertise in the Age of AI*, argues that artificial intelligence shouldn't imitate or try to replace many otherwise human tasks or interactions. The book just came out (it's on my reading list) so I won't speak to that, but this brings questions of prejudices against machines. It started with the Luddites during the Industrial Revolution, and automation has replaced more jobs than China in the American workforce. But it's broader than that. This theme is not unknown in science fiction, and fears of conquest by our own inventions is a real concern for some futurists, such as Elon Musk.

Whatever the future holds, we're already in the process of making it. Science fiction and related artforms give us arm's-length metaphors to reexamine our social premises and deficiencies. This indirect approach gives us both increased objectivity and the ability to loosen our grip on current emotional tensions. It is also not merely a predictor, but a guide for future advancement. There arguably never would have been Apollo without Jules Verne, or flip phones without Rodenberry. Even if achievements and technologies may be inevitable, the form they take will in no small measure be influenced by current imaginations. What we can conceive, we can achieve. And that should go human society, not just our inventions.

34. Don't Be That Guy

When asked to define religion, I say it is the relationship we have with life, both personally and collectively. Racism is also both personal and collective. We can socially and politically work toward better policies and paradigms – and that may be the only way to undo the mechanisms of supremacy. But there is a need here and now to make our own personal worlds a better place for ourselves and those around us. What could that look like? What common lessons do we need to learn?

When things got real earlier this year and it felt like the country was being torn apart in the streets, I called one of my friends. They had their pulse on what was going on in the city, and I was actually in tears asking them what I could do to help. At some point, it hit me that I was calling him because he was Black, and his position in the community was the reason I chose this particular "Black friend". But it was worse than that. I realized I was expecting him to give me answers as if he personally represented all African-Americans. I wanted to be told how to be an ally or advocate for justice.

It's not that White people shouldn't care and listen to what People of Color want from them. And if we have a relationship of trust and respect, we can test the waters and try to have such conversations one on one. Heck, as a White person I've started asking other White people what they think it means to be White (or more specifically Italian, etc.). I think we need to become more comfortable thinking and talking about these things all around. What's the worst that could happen? We may learn something about someone personally, and maybe by extension some number of other people who may share those feelings and views.

But it's not the job of a Person of Color to explain themselves to a White person, let alone represent those who share a racial or ethnic identity. You can only ask for their opinion, and it will vary – give you one puzzle piece to help you get the big picture. There are plenty of books by Africa-American and Latinx authors that can give you some clues better than anything I can write here as White person. There are countless articles and editorials and college courses on every subject covered in this book. I've tried to represent as many opinions as possible, but you will undoubtedly find more, especially since the world is changing in small and large ways as you read this.

I have a hero complex, to be sure, but I won't try to be a "White savior". The goal isn't to fix individual people (helping them "overcome" their environment) and other cultures aren't broken any more than European cultures are perfect. To judge cultures and see them as better or worse than others sets us back mentally and morally to the days of global slavery.

Let me share something here. I love the movie, "The Blind Side". I've had a bit of a thing for Sandra Bullock since Demolition Man, but it's not that. I love the idea of someone having a chance to find happiness and people who fiercely care about each other. I love how racists are put in their place. But it's as much fiction as biographical fact, and I didn't realize the ways in which it can be seen as racist itself. "Escaping the hood" into White society is a common theme, even for people who see themselves as having done that. It's all part of a conspiracy to assimilating People of Color who are perceived worthy or willing and segregating the rest. But I never saw it that way until it was pointed out to me.

Another thing that is problematic is getting upset. When a White person expresses a sense of guilt or regret as sadness, it can be seen as pity. Or we can be in angry denial playing the victim of accusations. Either way, we risk making it about ourselves, as if we are the ones in need of comfort. I know People of Color don't need to be treated as victims, even if in very real ways they are victimized individually and as a group. Well, damn it, my empathy overcomes me sometimes and I can't help it!

But there are dangers of our reactions we aren't even aware of. In her book White Fragility, Robin DiAngelo talks about "white women's tears", where African-American men are triggered with fear when White women cry. Historically, this is associated with false, even deadly accusations against Black men. I never heard of such a thing, but then again, a few short years ago I hadn't heard of Black Wall Street, or more appropriately, Redwood. However, an African-American author weighed in on her book, saying he had never heard of it either. Who to believe?

Then the strangest coincidence occurred. My young niece showed me a prank video of a woman who got people's attention and then flipped her hair back, scaring them with a horror-movie face. In one of the scenes, she feigned crying at an ATM outside a bar. A Black man near her shrunk himself and darted away, saying, "Don't cry. I'm on parole!" I guess there is truth in it. Maybe he experienced it personally; maybe it's something passed down as a warning. But it's another example of the effect we have on people not knowing their pain points.

So what about when we see racism in a social setting? At a skating rink,

I overheard a kid call another kid "Chink". To my young daughter's embarrassment, I spoke up and said that wasn't appropriate. His father said he would be the one to scold his children, and I suggested he ought to do so then. Looking back, my daughter no longer sees what I did as embarrassing.

Miss manners put it nicely:

> Lost the art of social shunning? On the contrary; it has spun out of control. There are two new versions: Shaming and Cancel Culture. [You should refrain] from using these weapons casually. While the law can administer harsh penalties when it is flouted, disapproval is the only sanction etiquette has against rudeness, and this has often been dismissed as ridiculously weak.
>
> But for centuries, children born outside of marriage received lifetime stigmas. When bans and quotas against races or religions were legally challenged, codified bigotry persisted in private institutions, including not just clubs, but neighborhoods and schools.
>
> And the ease of going public online has encouraged rash – and sometimes unfounded – judgments against individuals and businesses, without gradations of punishment suited to the severity of the transgression.

There should be "gradations of punishment" because there are definitely graduations of prejudice and racism. A reasonable ignorance is forgivable, such as not knowing a person's preferred term, such as African-American, Black, Black American, etc.. People may use archaic words and phrasing, such as "The Blacks", which I find personally offensive but our grandparents could get away with it. You may choose to ignore or correct such things, but context matters. Intention matters. I try to educate anyone making any prejudicial statements, but don't show anger unless they are trying to be purposely derogatory. It's merely a correction of an error in logic — thought processes they never examined. Our socialization doesn't excuse our ignorance, but it doesn't make us bad people. But there are bad people out there, and they are the ones that don't care if they offend someone. They choose to remain ignorant. And some make it into an ideology, promoting hateful and hurtful actions and policies. The continuum from human prejudice to ignorant racism to virulent bigotry is a wide, wide spectrum.

As a White person, I want to show a degree of courtesy (and not condescension) that contradicts what a Person of Color may expect from me. But I understand and accept they may have prejudices toward me from their own socialization and experience. It is reasonable that people who are victims of prejudice would be prejudiced against the perceived group that shows prejudice toward them. I can choose not to be offended by this. I can only hope they give me a chance as a person.

I hope we can agree dealing with racism needs to be a two-way street. This isn't about anybody owing anyone forgiveness or consideration. It must be a choice to be responsible for our own words and actions. Not being prejudiced in my heart does not give me the right to be ignorant of things that affect others if I have opportunities to learn. I hope this book can be a part of that for you, the reader, and those whose lives you touch. Whether you are in a position of power or powerlessness, checking yourself is the only thing that can identify and keep prejudices away.

We can be open-minded about things we aren't sure of or agree with. We may not believe in reparations, for example, or at least what we think it means. What People of Color want at the very least is acknowledgment. Would you apologize as White person who had nothing to do with slavery or setting up a supremacist society? Don't you say "I'm sorry" when someone tells you a loved one dies? If you can put down the historical baggage and White fragility, acceptance of the person's cultural and economic inheritance (or lack thereof) can be liberating for all. Even if America is too nationalistically fragile to apologize, its citizens don't have to share in that hard-heartedness.

As an anti-racist of any color, consider not telling people to check their privilege. They probably don't even know what that means. Help them see it through constructive discussion. Please don't get into semantic arguments over who can and cannot be racist. Use the word "prejudiced" if you need to, but let it slide if they don't. The hardest part is not being triggered by something someone says not knowing it's a trigger. We can't control being upset, and we shouldn't have to apologize for it, but people pick up on that and out of embarrassment or a sense of confrontation may become unreachable if you do want to educate them.

People of Color have the strongest claim on defining their issues and demanding change, but White people must accept it's not "those people's" problem. Fixing systemic racism isn't a White project, either, even though we are the ones shuffling the deck. And we're in an era of at least some power-sharing. A hundred years ago, White men were the only ones who had the power to legislate the acceptance of suffrage for White women. Today, women and People of Color have a voice, economic power, political power, and so forth. The issue today is how to have equal power.

What if you are someone people consider highly prejudiced, racist, or even a bigot? Is that something you want to be honest with yourself about? Can you let others give you some self-awareness by sharing their perceptions? I'm not asking you to condemn yourself; I'm asking you to own it if that's who you are here and now. There are people out there who have the patience and compassion to help people grow, however fearful or hateful they may be. Prejudices tied to traumatic experiences can be dealt with without the need for moral judgment. The only sin is not trying.

If you're a White supremacist (even if you're not White), or a Christian supremacist, or a Nationalist, or any combination of these, I congratulate you for even reading this. Hopefully this is food for thought. Hopefully you are aware of your supremacy enough to make a conscious choice to accept that there are other legitimate beliefs. You don't have to stop believing or have pride in your identity or country. It's the fanaticism that doesn't let you sit at the table from the rest of us. Yes, it will be difficult to start the conversation if you've been socialized or radicalized into that way of thinking, and people will be offended by some of your views or statements, but that's on them if they don't show some patience and tolerance back.

Or maybe you just have hidden bias. How would you know? There are tests online, such as one on Tolerance.Org. The important thing is that our biases may be based on our place in society. It really isn't about what "those people" do, or the way "people like us" feel. The roles and labels may change, but this is a human thing. We should be able to share and appreciate that, even when it's not pretty.

If we are not overly prejudiced, should we associate with people who are? I honestly can't answer that for you. Some people say if your in a group of people and some of them are racists, you're all racists. That sounds like just another prejudicial judgment to me. Did Jesus's tax-collector and prostitute groupies make him a sinner? I think there's an ugliness we may find at a certain level of prejudice we can't tolerate to have around us. And who we associate with does have an impact on our own reputation. But I also think we can be a positive influence, or at least work together in settings where their beliefs aren't an issue.

If I hire an electrician and he hates such-and-such people, what should I do? As long as I don't have to hear about it and my wiring is safe, I'll live with that. I might even choose to be friends with them, anyway. After all, most people don't disown grandparents who are hung up on old prejudices. None of us are perfect, or ever will be. Now, if I thought they used my money to fund a hate group, the scales would shift quite a bit. I won't ever be a cancel culture aficionado, but that's a legitimate choice for someone else. These are all personal choices we don't need to be harshly judged for.

It's okay to have a racial or ethnic identity. What if I didn't tell you my name, or ethnic heritage, or skin color? Would that be fair in a conversation that is truly personal in nature? Life isn't neat and tidy. And it shouldn't be. We each bring something beautiful to the table that only we can. And it's just as important to include the harder stuff like our traumas and challenges and fears and feelings we may not be proud of. Statistics and historical facts aren't by themselves going to save us. They more often divide us. We must be first prepared in our heart – and then we can have an open mind.

But all of this isn't possible unless we desegregate ourselves. If we can't snap our fingers and do it in our society or circumstances, we can do it personally. Go to an event, or venue, or place of worship that has not necessarily diversity, but made up of another ethnic identity from yours. If you're White, chances are you aren't used to being one of the only people who look like you. Volunteer work may not give you representative exposure to another neighborhood, but it's a start and has its own spiritual benefits. If you have Islamophobia, visit a mosque. You may be surprised how welcomed you are in places you may feel apprehension about even driving to. The goal is to see the forest for the trees – individuals rather than the stereotype. Then be aware of new assumptions you may build, and be willing to reconsider them as you go.

Being psychologically present during exposure to diversity is key, but there's even more you can do. "The conversation is the work." We shouldn't only share our opinions and experiences after looking over our shoulder first. I've met many amazing people along the way who opened my eyes to things I would never have learned in school. I didn't stay in some ethnic comfort zone (if there even is such a thing anymore). I had bold conversations with good people.

We can also educate ourselves. no matter who we are. Many People of Color do not know the backstories either. I mentioned or referenced a lot of things in this book without explanation. But you can look them up. Do you know the story of Black Wall Street? Redwood? The Green Book? Have you ever heard the song "Strange Fruit" or read the poem "A Dream Deferred"? It's all out there if you look. And once you truly know something, you can't go back. Kermit Petty, a Brother Freemason dear to me, says this is the esoteric meaning of Shakespeare's "undiscovered country from whose bourn no traveler returns". It is my hope you have found, or at least glimpsed, that Promised Land.

Have you changed? Have you even shifted in your chair a little, seeing around a corner or two you were blind to previously? This book was not intended as a curiosity of journalism with hopes of large-scale sympathy and social reform as nice as that might be. I would even offend myself if I was playing the cold anthropologist, as if I were observing and reporting back on some forgotten American tribe. None of us can escape the shade of our skin. None of us are "outsiders" when we realize we share this in common.

Personally, I'd like to be seen as a deeply interested American, and equally invested human being. We have too much to learn from each other. We must become "woke" to the consequences of the attitudes and assumptions inherited from our not-so-distant ancestors – but break the cycle in little and big ways so it does not dictate our future.

And even if you do not subscribe to there being a "right side of history," one thing is inevitable – we will move into the future together or we may not make it at all. If I had to compare it to something, I would think of an experience during one of my childhood vacations in Florida. I don't know if it's the same today, but the road from Orlando to Vero Beach was so long and straight and flat, that it seemed like it went on to a point of infinity both in front of us and behind. Be it from Eden of Ordulvai Gorge, we all share a common Eve if we look out our back window. Sooner or later, we will all share the same descendants as well.

And it is up to us to rail against it with perpetual strife, or accept it in peace as a blessing.

35. What Do I Do Now?

This book is "done" but it isn't finished. I don't think it ever will be. It's coming from a place – me – that isn't finished. Author and writing coach Christine Kloser says writing an inspirational book should not just be transformational to the reader and the world, but the author themselves. I now see how true that can be. Contemplating, organizing, researching, and sharing drafts of this work has been a journey by itself. In fact, I don't feel like the person I was when I started. I'm tempted to start over, as I no longer see some of my earlier beliefs and statements in the same light as when I wrote them.

Ibram X. Mendi says "the heartbeat of racism is denial, and the heartbeat of antiracism is confession." Well, I have found new things to confess, not out of guilt, but awareness and eagerness to be better.

And I need to revisit my college hero, Dr. King, with these new eyes. I mistook him as colorblind, yearning for a racially neutral world. Now I know he approved of racial spaces and economic self-support rather than integration as a tiny part of White society. This unlocks a new perspective for me to explore. I will support and respect spaces within any ethnicity or group instead of looking upon it as "racist" in any negative exclusionary way. Communities have unique needs that they must be empowered to address within themselves. Being a Freemason, I know the value of such spaces, not to shield oneself from triggers or dissenting opinions, but to speak openly without external judgment. And maybe we can create interracial safe spaces as well. There can be a time and place for everything.

Maybe I should think of this in terms of racial puberty. Just as People of Color are forced to develop an awareness of social identity early in life, many White people have not reached it yet, at any age. Even the conscious awareness of race for Most White people isn't personal, and is easy to escape. In theory, I could just walk away. But as much as this book is a snapshot of where I am as I write this, I can't walk away. The adolescence of my racial awareness has left the building. My dear Philosophy mentor in college, Professor Bob Nielsen, taught me that if you aren't changed as a person, you did not truly learn something. I can only hope the reader has learned, and changed, as much as I have.

When I finished college, I didn't know what to do with my life. I couldn't continue school with a child on the way, and life took me over for a while instead of the other way around. Will this stanza of my life rhyme with that one? Do I become an activist? Kendi suggests that unless your actions channel policies rather than attitudes, you don't qualify to call yourself that. Do I only make myself feel better by supporting the protests? Will I continue to avoid addressing these things on my own Facebook page for fear of arguments with people who don't, or may never, get it?

Does writing this book grant me indulgences from the purgatory of my privilege? Can I fire and forget, or worse yet, judge my virtue by book sales? I don't want to be that guy. But I am conflicted. I don't want to be an anti-racist as a life-defining mission, but realize I've always been on this path. Perhaps it will come down to faith and fate. If this book touches people, if people want me to be a voice, I will accept that as work I need to continue. But even if "Some White Guy's Book" ends up in the dollar store and I never get a single speaking engagement, there's work I need to finish within.

There was a certain point in my martial arts training that I first noticed I was off-balance and my body not properly aligned. It wasn't that I was less balanced or aligned than before, but I had developed more awareness of it. As I improved, the benchmark increased. Smaller and smaller needs for improvement became apparent. This is how it is with checking my racism and privilege now. I had no idea I was doing and saying things that could hurt others or promote ideas that worked against racial equity. It didn't mean I was particularly racist before, but that I know more now. I am changed. And with that knowledge comes responsibility.

No matter where I am in this journey, I must be willing to examine myself, and have an honest desire to understand others from their own place and perspective. I must accept that I have been socialized into beliefs about how I and others exist in the world. Being White, I have to understand that I inherited a society set up by people like me, and that I may have privileges, intentional and unintentional, different from that of other people.

I know that People of Color cannot help but to see themselves through other people's eyes, and so I will take responsibility for the way I see them. I will reject assumptions and stereotypes as much as I am able, and allow them as individuals to define who they are.

If I had to craft my intentions into a pledge, this is what it would be:

> I do not identify as White, but I accept that the place my appaearance gives me in the world is real;
> I realize I have inherited a world that gives me different privelages than others;

I have the responsibility to use my power and privilege to create an equitable future created by all;

I recognize there will be times I offend others, but will react to reproach with open-mindedness

I will respond to prejudice against me, or accusations of prejudice, with Love rather than anger;

I will not be colorblind, as being impartial is not enough;

I will see people as individuals first, but recognize their choices of ethnicity and the ways they express it;

I will hold all peoples and cultures as equals, not in need of saving or fixing;

I will work to liberate, not assimilate, all who are held back for their differences;

I will personally and publicly reject and oppose any ideas and power of supremacy

What I would want to request from People of Color:

Please don't assume my intentions are racist or that I do not care;

Forgive me if I assume your racial identiy;

Forgive my unawareness of privilage and understand I may be defensive about it;

Do not assume I think I am better than you;

When appropriate, bring my prejudiced words or behavior to my attention;

Please see me as an individual, and not a member of my perceived race or ethnicity;

Undersatand I don't come from the same place of understanding about matters of race and ethnciity;

Please give me the chance to be your ally.

These may change and be added to as I grow. Your pledge and requests may be different than mine, but I encourage you to do your own, no matter who you are. Consider it a thought exercise, or a note to your future self, tucked in a pocket or sock drawer to rediscover another year.

Wherever I choose to go from here, or have destiny thrust upon me for writing this (good and bad), one thing is certain: I extend my hopes and best wishes to you, the reader. If it has brought insight into yourself and others, and the world around you, share it. If you and others don't find beliefs you can agree on, at least hear each other, and create a space for mutual respect. Be gentle with each other.

May we share descendants, and may they live in peace.

Initiatives

Zero Intolerance Initiative

One of the programs I started as an Interfaith minister is the **Zero Intolerance Initiative** ("Zii", rhymes with Wii). It has a small Facebook group for sharing educational resources and inspiring stories related to the spirit of universal tolerance, acceptance, and appreciation. This book is written in that spirit. I hope those joining the group share these sentiments:

> *We take a stand. We refuse to participate in prejudice and discrimination of ANY kind. When we see it, we don't keep silent.*

If finances allow and there is interest, I may turn Zii into a 501(c)(3) not-for-profit that highlights organizations and programs doing the heavy lifting of education and combatting hate, such as Teaching Tolerance and the Southern Poverty Law Center.

American Day of Prayer and Reflection

I would also like to establish an **American Day of Prayer and Reflection** for communities who wish to have a fully inclusive, non-political alternative to the National Day of Prayer. More information will be available at OtherFlock.Org and the Zero Intolerance Initiative Facebook group.

College Editorial

{*Published in the Catalyst student newspaper of D'Youville College in 1989*}
FOR WHITES ONLY

We "white folk" often don't see the racism in our own college community, and when we do, we don't want to admit it.

Perhaps none of us here have seen "n{*****}" spray-painted on our walls. No one has to sit in the back of the classroom or use a certain drinking fountain. But just as loud as a shouted racial or ethnic slur, our subtle actions and "polite" racial and ethnic comments ring loud in the ears of our minority students.

Consider for a moment the dream of Martin Luther King, Jr., where "little black boys and black girls will be able to join hands with little white boys and little white girls as sisters and brothers." One generation later, today, are we these children?

Can we say there is no segregation when we sit apart in the PVR {dining hall}? Can we claim there is no bigotry when an interracial couple at a mixer is met by a crowd mumbling disapproval? Can we claim to respect ALL human culture when "black music" is forgotten at an event with an otherwise "wide" music selection? We will not say aloud what we say in our actions – that we have nothing to learn from our culturally diverse brothers and sisters.

These situations are real – they happened and still do.

Here. This year.

To us in the majority, blatant racism and discrimination is seen as "socially improper" instead of what it really is — socially unacceptable in any way and to any degree. Even if D'Youville wasn't a traditionally Christian environment, such behavior would still be inconsistent with an institution devoted to bringing us forth from the darkness of ignorance. Are we prepared to lead the next generation of mankind's children as the blind leading the blind?

Perhaps, since government and law has changed nominally for the better in terms of civil rights, the greatest blindness is not seeing that we have not finished the job. The greatest ignorance is not admitting to ourselves that in some personal way, each of us still has something to learn.

-written by Ken, one of the "white folks" at D'YC

Acknowledgments

Many people contributed to the content of this book, knowingly or not. I've met so many amazing people willing to tolerate my questions and over-sharing, and most importantly share of themselves. Others, upon hearing my intention to write this book, gave recommendations to watch this or read that, and it was immeasurably helpful.

I had a plan to write something like this for years, but I may not have written it anytime soon had the circumstances of 2020 not come along. I had been an armchair anti-racist on social media, my intellectual blog considerReconsider.com, and most importantly, a role model for my daughter. I hope I inspire her half as much as she has inspired me.

Christina grew up in a not-so-tolerant neighborhood and went to a virtually segregated private school. And yet her earliest toddler friend was the son of an African-American father, her first best friend was adopted from South America; she shared an advice column, "Salt and Pepper", in the high school student paper with the daughter of one of the first African-American women on Wall Street. It's not like we didn't talk about race, but it was always in a matter-of-fact tone. But she knew I always stood on the side of Love. Like myself, she always had a natural openness and intuition about treating people as human beings with everything else being secondary, if important at all. She has a fire within her for doing the right thing – and not letting the world pass by unchallenged. After seeing her fight for social justice this year, I couldn't be prouder.

I'm starting to think much of her whole generation turned out that way. With brave allyship in the face of political propaganda, social ridicule, and outright violence, this last year proves it as far as I'm concerned. They do not share our apathy or hold the same grudges or put up with threadbare rhetoric that we were willing to swallow. And they are all an inspiration to me.

Many thanks go out to those who took the time to read the drafts of this book and give honest feedback. Special thanks to members of the Amorphous Publishing Guild, particularly fiction author Mayumi Hirtzel, who has been with us from the start. She introduced me to Kate Johnson's Team Writer Facebook group, and some of this work was done during Zoom writing sessions for their NaNoWriMo writing challenge. I also thank my longtime friend Mimi Trzcinski for reviewing this book. I will be sending copies to her book club and I hope they enjoy it.

I'd like to give a special shoutout to Tom "it's all about the money" Pecoraro, for guiding me to do research about Lyndon Johnson and that era of civil rights. His political insights offer a healthy counterpoint to my own perspectives and he exercises admirable civility in disagreement.

Last but not least, I am grateful for my mentor in publishing, Dr. Mark Donnelly, owner of Rock Paper Safety Scissors Publishing. I know I can always count on picking his brain over a cup of coffee, and his success makes me believe I can transition to a writing and publishing carer for this next act of my own life.

About the Author

Ken JP Stuczynski is a self-proclaimed "Life Artist" with lifelong interests in everything from world cultures and history to psychosocial phenomena. His degree is in Philosophy with a concentration in Ethics and a minor In Psychology. He has written articles and essays on the topics of science and religion, society and politics, business and economics, technology and futurism. Using interdisciplinary contexts, many of these focus on the ideals of intellectual honesty and tolerance.

The founder of Amorphous Publishing Guild, he still runs his longstanding web development business, Kentropolis Internet, from home where he lives with his wife and plenty of pets. In addition to various community service projects, he teaches Tai Chi to veterans at the local VA Recovery Center. As an Interfaith minister, he works with couples and families who are unchurched or have mixed faith traditions. His community project, the "Earth 2 Mouth" program, connects farms, volunteers, and soup kitchens. He also enjoys martial arts, carpentry, and keeps bees from time to time.

He's also a White guy who considers himself both an American and a citizen of the world. He believes in appreciating everyone for who they are and wants to be a part of the dialogue necessary to build bridges and overcome our human and societal challenges. Supporting the BLM movement, he has been trained as a Legal Observer and is a member of the National Lawyers Guild.

Ken is also a Freemason and member of the Grand Lodge of the State of New York. As a Masonic author and speaker, he has given presentations at meetings throughout New York State, most often regarding the role of technology in the Craft. Some of his *Empire State Mason* magazine articles have been republished around the world. His book, *Webmastering the Craft: Fraternity in a Digital World*, was published in April with a 2021 edition on the way.

Upcoming writing projects include *Everyday Justice: Setting the World Right One Good Deed at a Time*, as well as a book on Astronomy.

AmorphousPublishingGuild

Amorphous Publishing Guild is an exclusive, private publishing company that supports independent writers who want to learn and grow together as published authors. There is no limitation on genre, only quality of prose, poetry, and purpose.

Our authors have both on-remand printing and distribution availability to over 40,000 outlets, including Amazon, Barnes & Nobles, independent booksellers, universities, and libraries. A variety of back-end author services make for a professional result without the usual self-publishing limitations.

We can be contacted at **tophat@amorphous.press**. Please Note: We do not currently accept unsolicited work submissions, and requests to become a member of the "Guild" must be made through an existing member.

COMING SOON BY THE AUTHOR

Everyday Justice: Setting the World Right
One Good Deed at a Time

Pre-Order at
www.Amorphous.Press